The Rorschach Inkblot Test

The Rorschach Inkblot Test

An Interpretive Guide for Clinicians

James P. Choca

American Psychological Association • Washington, DC

Published by
American Psychological Association
750 First Street, NE
Washington, DC 20002
www.apa.org

To order
APA Order Department
P.O. Box 92984
Washington, DC 20090-2984
Tel: (800) 374-2721; Direct: (202) 336-5510
Fax: (202) 336-5502; TDD/TTY: (202) 336-6123
Online: www.apa.org/pubs/books
E-mail: order@apa.org

In the U.K., Europe, Africa, and the Middle East, copies may be ordered from
American Psychological Association
3 Henrietta Street
Covent Garden, London
WC2E 8LU England

Typeset in Meridien by Circle Graphics, Inc., Columbia, MD

Printer: Maple Press, York, PA
Cover Designer: Mercury Publishing Services, Rockville, MD

The opinions and statements published are the responsibility of the authors, and such opinions and statements do not necessarily represent the policies of the American Psychological Association.

Library of Congress Cataloging-in-Publication Data
Choca, James, 1945-
The Rorschach Inkblot Test : an interpretive guide for clinicians/James P. Choca.—1st ed.
   p. cm.
Includes bibliographical references and index.
ISBN 978-1-4338-1200-2—ISBN 1-4338-1200-2 1. Rorschach Test. I. Title.

BF698.8.R5C46 2013
155.2'842—dc23
                          2012028313

British Library Cataloguing-in-Publication Data
A CIP record is available from the British Library.

Printed in the United States of America
First Edition

DOI: 10.1037/14039-000

Contents

ACKNOWLEDGMENTS   *vii*

1. Introduction   *3*
2. Administration   *17*
3. Interpretative Basics   *27*
4. Global Scores   *35*
5. The Psychogram   *51*
6. Content   *73*
7. Form Quality and Special Scores   *87*
8. Composites, Complex Ratios, Indices, and Constellations   *107*
9. Response-Level Interpretations   *119*
10. Interpretative Process   *131*
11. Rorschach Profiles   *147*
12. Psychological Test Report   *207*

APPENDIX: PSYCHIATRIC NORMS   *237*

REFERENCES   *243*

INDEX   *269*

ABOUT THE AUTHOR   *281*

Acknowledgments

The time to search the literature and write this book was made possible by a sabbatical semester offered to me by Roosevelt University. I am very thankful for this consideration and for the support I have received, especially from Dean Lynn Weiner and Assistant Dean Lois Backas.

The support of my department at Roosevelt was also invaluable, during the time I was absent and beyond. Particularly worthy of mention has been Edward Rossini, the other clinical professor who does diagnostic work similar to mine and who offered me comments and suggestions on the manuscript.

I have learned much from my colleagues at the Society for Personality Assessment. In that group I am particularly indebted to Gene Nebel, who has been very generous with his suggestions and classical recordings of historical Rorschach figures.

This book went through several drafts and considerable improvements prior to publication. I am very grateful for the many contributions of APA Books staff, including Judy Nemes, Elizabeth Brace, and Jessica Kamish.

The Rorschach Inkblot Test

Introduction

1

When Christopher Columbus sailed to America, the speed of his ships was estimated by throwing a rope overboard and counting the knots that had been placed on the rope at specific intervals, as it was fed onto the surface of the water. A 30-second hourglass measured the period of time during which the knots were counted. Using this and other methods, Columbus estimated his speed and position well enough that his trip could be retraced with some degree of accuracy. The rope provided an ingenious way of measuring something that could not be measured in any other way, with the tools available at the time.

The Rorschach Inkblot Test, not unlike Christopher Columbus's early method for measuring nautical speed and distance, is the best measuring device we have available at the current time for some specific personality attributes.

We have come a long way since Columbus's time. Today's global positioning systems (GPS) use satellites to reveal our position, trajectory, and speed with amazing accuracy. If we ever develop a method for examining the psychological

DOI: 10.1037/14039-001
The Rorschach Inkblot Test: An Interpretive Guide for Clinicians, by J. P. Choca

makeup of an individual that approaches the accuracy of the GPS, the critics of the Rorschach will undoubtedly be right, and the Rorschach plates will be relegated to the museums. Further developments of brain imaging technology, or perhaps new technologies that do not exist today, might lead to more accurate assessment of an individual's thought processes. Until then, however, the Rorschach will have a place in our test armamentarium, even though we must limit our expectations about what this test is able to measure and use it in conjunction with data provided by other assessment tools.

Developed as a measuring device in the 1920s and subsequently refined, the Rorschach has had its critics. Yet, in the hands of capable clinicians, the Rorschach is a remarkable instrument. As I shall argue throughout this book, when properly used, the Rorschach is uniquely useful in revealing an individual's thought processes in a way that no other instrument is able to do. It allows us to see an individual in action and to explore different aspects of his or her mode of operation. Attitudes toward tasks, level of energy, degree of excitability, and control of emotions are just a few of the behaviors that may be discerned.

An analogy between psychological testing and the components of a song may be useful to clarify what the Rorschach measures. The information actively given by an examinee through an interview or through well-known questionnaires such as the Minnesota Multiphasic Personality Inventory–2 (MMPI–2; Butcher, Dahlstrom, Graham, Tellegen, & Kaemmer, 1989) and the Millon Clinical Multiaxial Inventory–III (MCMI–III; Millon, 1983) resembles the song's lyrics. The examinee's behavior that is observed by clinicians resembles the melody that runs beneath. The Rorschach is well suited to bring the melody into sharp relief.

Yet if this is the case, why is the test not more popular? As we shall see, misunderstandings about what the Rorschach can and can't do abound and have led some to criticize the Rorschach. Some have even predicted that the attacks on the Rorschach would result in its disuse (Paul, 2004). A recent survey (Musewicz, 2010) has shown that the majority of psychodiagnosticians continue to use the Rorschach and believe that the test's value goes beyond what psychometric validation can capture.

In this chapter, I review the history of the Rorschach, emphasizing the perennial tension between approaches and the controversies that have always surrounded this test. Chapter 2 focuses on ways of administering the instrument that allow the clinician to explore what is actually happening with the examinee. Chapter 3 sets the stage for an understanding of the general methodology followed in interpreting the Rorschach. Chapters 4 through 9 review the different aspects to be interpreted, including the most global variables, the determinants of the response (or psychogram), the content of the associations, the quality of the responses, the complex ratios and constellations that can be computed, and some ideas for examining the actual responses. Chapter 10 puts all of the information together in a step-by-step procedure that can be used to interpret a protocol. Chapter 11 describes common profiles that may be identified when all aspects of a particular protocol are examined as a whole. Finally, Chapter 12 describes the psychological test report, offers ideas on how to integrate Rorschach findings with other sources of information, and suggests ways to perfect the art of writing an effective report.

A Bit of History

In 1970, John Exner (1974) started a project that culminated with the publication of the Rorschach Comprehensive System. Prior to this publication, the Rorschach world was like "the Tower of Babel" (Aronow, Reznikoff, & Moreland, 1994, p. 219): Several scoring systems were in use, and the first thing one had to do when reading a study was to determine which system was used. If the system used was not the one the reader was accustomed to, he or she had to mentally replace the symbols used for the different scores in the article with familiar symbols. In some cases the score that was the focus of the particular study was not used by the reader, in which case the study was of no value to the reader. Exner managed to convince the Rorschach community to leave behind whatever scoring systems were in use and to learn his system, which was simultaneously familiar and unfamiliar.

Although Exner expressed the intention to integrate the interpretative approaches in the same manner that he had integrated the scoring systems, it is well recognized that he emphasized the quantitative features of the test at the expense of the qualitative aspects (e.g., Acklin, 1995; Aronow et al., 1994; Aronow, Reznikoff, & Moreland, 1995). Thus, the "teaching of the Rorschach and Rorschach research have come to be grouped into two camps" (J. F. Murray, 1997, p. 53). Shontz and Green (1992) noted that

> students may be gaining the impression that the Rorschach is valued mostly for its quantitative analyses and that interpretations derived from qualitative analyses are less valuable than . . . quantitative indexes. If this is the case, students may be losing much of the richness that is inherent in Rorschach records. (p. 152)

There has always been tension between the quantitative (nomothetic) and qualitative (idiographic) approaches to the Rorschach. As described by Allport (1937, 1961), the *nomothetic* approach aims to discover general laws through norms and statistics, whereas the *idiographic* pertains to the study of an individual in his or her uniqueness. To some degree, these approaches have their anchors in empiricism and rationalism, schools of thought that can be traced back to the ancient Greeks (King, Viney, & Woody, 2009). As Lerner repeatedly argued (1992, 2004, 2007), however, both approaches are necessary and complementary.

The Rorschach was introduced in the United States by Bruno Klopfer. Klopfer (1900–1971), born in Munich, Germany, in a family of Jewish ancestry, was trained as a Freudian analyst. In 1933, he fled Nazi Germany and went to Zurich. There he worked for Carl Jung and was assigned the task of administering two Rorschachs a day. The following year he accepted a job teaching anthropology at Columbia University in New York.

A charismatic man with a good sense of humor, Klopfer liked to listen to other people's ideas and enjoyed discussions and debates. He was a gifted clinician and had the uncanny ability to cut through an individual's façade and dig into the important issues. At the request of students, Klopfer held informal training sessions on the Rorschach in his home. (These seminars developed into the Rorschach Institute and a journal, *Rorschach Research Exchange,* published in 1936. The Rorschach Institute evolved into the Society for Personality Assessment, and the journal is now known as *Journal for Personality Assessment.*) Although Klopfer devised the more popular pre-Exnerian scoring system (Klopfer, Ainsworth, Klopfer, & Holt, 1954), he placed less emphasis on the scoring and interpretations dictated by norms than on the clinical insights about the patient. (For more historical data on Klopfer, see Fisher, 2006; Handler, 1994, 2008; and Skadeland, 1986.)

In the United States, the nomothetic tradition was ironically also personified by a person associated with Columbia University. Samuel Beck (1896–1980), a brilliant student who earned a scholarship at Harvard, had to abandon his education and return home after 3 years, when his father became disabled. He was in his late 20s when he was able to resume his studies, this time at Columbia. When he was searching for a dissertation topic, a European-trained psychiatrist offered him a set of Rorschach plates. Beck did his dissertation by collecting standardization data with children; he published the first of two articles on this work in 1930. Later, while doing a fellowship in Switzerland, Beck became appalled at the intuitive way in which the Europeans handled Rorschach data.

After accepting a job at Michael Reese Hospital and the University of Chicago, Beck continued his work with the Rorschach. In 1935, he wrote an abrasive critique of the Klopfer approach. When Klopfer responded in kind, a high level of antagonism was established between the two camps. For years the two groups developed in parallel fashion without collaboration. This antagonism lasted until 1965 when Beck was approached by the Society for Personality Assessment and eventually accepted the first Distinguished Contribution Award from the society that Klopfer had established (Exner, 1981, 2003). And just as Exner managed the extraordinary feat of getting clinicians to adopt his system, he accomplished the equally unlikely feat of convincing both Klopfer and Beck to collaborate on the interpretation of a patient's test results for him (2003).

Idiographic approaches to the Rorschach were established by psychoanalytic thinkers, including Roy Schafer (1948, 1954), David Rapaport, Merton Gill (Rapaport, Gill, & Schafer, 1946), and Marty Mayman (1967). Schachtel (1966) wrote about an experiential approach rooted in interpersonal theory. He argued that "the use of the test will be most fruitful if we understand fully the nature of the data . . . and if we understand furthermore, the nature of what we are doing when we score and interpret a protocol" (p. 2). This tradition, more recently exemplified by the work of Paul Lerner (2007), Sidney Blatt (Blatt & Lerner, 1983), and Marshall Silverstein (1999), now emphasizes object relations theory. Aronow and his group (Aronow et al., 1995) have used the Rorschach as a projective technique and as a way to elicit associations from the examinees.

In spite of his integrative intentions, Exner was much more of a nomothetic than an idiographic clinician. The interpretative system he created does not represent an integration of the two approaches (Acklin, 1995). In the Klopfer tradition, the clinical or idiographic approach was based on the examiner's having an intuitive sense for the important Rorschach markers—scores that are outside of the normal range for a particular person—and the meaning that such a marker may have for that individual. The Comprehensive System and Exner's books dedicate little effort in that direction while going to extremes, in my opinion, in the nomothetic camp.

Consider, for instance, Exner's Adjusted D Score, supposedly an indication of stress tolerance. This index starts with the computation of the Experience Actual (EA) as the sum of the responses with human movement and the weighted sum of the color responses. Exner then computes the Experience Stimulation (es) by adding the animal and inanimate movement to the achromatic color, and to all of the shading responses. After the es score is subtracted from the EA score, a differential score is obtained from a conversion table to produce an Adjusted es score. This Adjusted es score is subtracted from the EA score, and the value is converted into an Adjusted D score through the use of another conversion table. In my view, Exner's Adjusted D score is in the stratosphere, too removed from anything I can observe the patient doing with the inkblot that it is of no interest. Like Kleiger (1999), I believe in the usefulness of "deconstructing the various scoring categories in order to ascertain the psychological experiences that underlie the scores" (p. xiii).

I believe that many of the Rorschach markers can be interpreted in a number of different ways for different examinees, and I constantly ask myself what an elevated or low value means for the individual I am examining. Even valid markers are not valid for everyone. An excellent marker in clinical psychology may be valid 80% of the time (Baldessarini, Finklestein, & Arana, 1983). The examinee in front of me may be one of the 20% for whom a particular interpretation does not apply. B. L. Smith (1997) claimed that it was "well known" that "even the best predictors from the Structural Summary are often inaccurate in specific cases" (p. 192). I understand that Exner grouped Rorschach scores because he wanted to develop constructs (e.g., susceptibility to current stress). However, that approach implies that the scores being aggregated have only one correct interpretation, which is probably not the case.

As noted above, the Rorschach has been the subject of a great deal of criticism in the recent past. I review the criticism in the section that follows, but here I note that the other major projective technique, the Thematic Apperception Test (TAT; H. A. Murray, 1943), has been spared much of the controversy. A major difference between the Rorschach and the TAT is that although the TAT has scoring systems, practically no clinicians score this test. Perhaps the fact that the Rorschach is commonly scored has led to overselling the validity of this instrument as a scientific tool and underselling its value as a clinical assessment procedure. This realization led Weiner (1994) to refer to the Rorschach as the *Rorschach Inkblot Method,* as opposed to calling it a test. (I have no real objection to that label, but changing the name is not going to change the way the instrument is used.)

Frank Kobler, the Loyola University Chicago professor responsible for teaching the Rorschach to several generations of psychologists, wrote:

> There are wide differences between psychologists . . . that have been reflected in the use of the Rorschach. This is exemplified in the attempt of the clinical psychologist to become both a scientist and a professional with all of the attendent [sic] discomforts and difficulties . . . This implies that the clinical psychologist is not a completely objective observer of empirical data. . . . *The aim of the Rorschach interpreter is not to measure but to understand the person.* It is the failure to recognize and to be explicit about such a viewpoint and such a procedure that has led to a forty year research approach to the Rorschach resulting in substantially negative findings . . . The experienced clinician does count his data and he does measure data but he also uses experiential data that cannot be counted and measured. . . . The future of the Rorschach involves an end to the uncritical use of the score or sign approach . . . (1983, pp. 136–137; [italics added])

Views and Controversies

Kobler introduced the Rorschach Inkblot Test to me, and his views are an appropriate starting point for the views I want to present in this book. He argued (1983) that the pursuit of high scientific accuracy with the Rorschach is not only doomed to fail but is entirely the wrong goal to pursue; instead, the goal is to understand the examinee. In his writings on the history of psychology, Daniel Robinson (1995) pointed out that the more scientific aspects of psychology (e.g., cognitive and perceptual psychology) are the aspects that command the least amount of interest. In contrast, the more interesting aspects of the field (e.g., clinical psychology, what makes people tick) are the least scientific.

Scoring is useful to whatever extent it serves as a magnifying lens through which we can see something we could not see before. Emphasizing the scores at the expense of paying clinical attention to what the examinee is doing, however, is like counting nouns in a Shakespearean sonnet—it completely misses the point.

Moreover, emphasizing the scores without keeping in mind the overall limitations of our instrument is like wanting to carry six decimals on figures obtained by means of a desk ruler. Clinicians must develop expertise with the Rorschach while simultaneously retaining an awareness of the limitations of the instrument. Perhaps the limitations are most evident when norms are compared (cf. Chapters 3–8, this volume; see also e.g., J. M. Wood, Nezworski, Garb, & Lilienfeld, 2001). Different norms, supposedly collected in the same manner from the "normal" population, can show substantially different values. The Rorschach, perhaps accurately reflecting the human being, does not have a well-defined "normal" range.

Some of the issues surrounding the misuse of the instrument have their roots in its early history. The Rorschach Inkblot Test was created by Swiss psychiatrist Hermann Rorschach (1884–1922). The son of a painter, Rorschach became interested in inkblots as an artistic representation when he was in high school. This interest was pervasive enough that he was nicknamed Klex, the German word for *inkblot*. After graduating with a medical degree from the University of Zurich in 1909, Rorschach specialized in psychiatry and started experimenting with the administration of inkblots to patients, eventually publishing the 10 plates we use today (Ellenberger, 1958; Pichot, 1984). In the book he wrote about this test, *Psychodiagnostik*, Rorschach (1921) described the use of this instrument with neurological disorders such as epilepsy. Thus, part of the problem through the years has been that professionals, from Rorschach himself to our contemporaries, have tried to use the instrument to discover what they wanted to know about the patient, rather than what the test could reveal.

A notable example of this mistake in the recent past has been the attempt to diagnose borderline personality disorder with the Rorschach. The first issue is a conceptual confusion: Some people do not recognize the difference between the psychoanalytic idea of a borderline level of development (see Chapter 3, this volume) and the borderline personality disorder of the *Diagnostic and Statistical Manual of Mental Disorders* (4th ed.; *DSM–IV*; American Psychiatric Association, 1994). Despite the numerous studies examining borderline personality functioning (see Gartner, Hunt, & Gartner, 1989), Acklin (1997a) noted that "the diagnosis continues to elude the sort of definitional clarity, reliability, and validity that is ideally demanded from a diagnostic category" (p. 111). In a review of the literature, Murray (1993) characterized the effort to use the Rorschach to diagnose this personality disorder as the "Rorschach search for the borderline holy grail" (p. 342), even though he succumbed to the same malady and attempted to describe how it could be done.

Consider the task from an entirely rational perspective. According to the *DSM–5*, the most contemporary definition of borderline personality disorder makes reference to an "extremely fragile self-concept that is easily disrupted and fragmented under stress." Individuals with this condition have "rapidly changing, intense, unpredictable, and reactive emotions." The fragile self-concept, furthermore, leads the person to have difficulty "maintaining enduring intimate relationships." Relationships "are based on the fantasy of the need for others for survival, excessive dependency, and a fear of rejection and/or abandonment" (American Psychiatric Association, 2012). An examination of that definition leads to the quick realization that the Rorschach is not going to be of much help with patients with borderline personality disorder. How could the task of looking at inkblots and fantasizing about what they look like reveal much about a "fragile self-concept," about "difficulties maintaining relationships," or about a "fear of rejection and abandonment"? Ninety different symptom configurations would meet criteria for the *DSM–IV* borderline personality disorder (Widiger, Sanderson, & Warner, 1986), so it is unrealistic to expect that there would be a "borderline Rorschach" (Peterson, 1997, p. 159).

Consider another example. Much has been written about the use of the Rorschach to diagnose the psychopathic personality (e.g., C. B. Gacono & Meloy, 1992, 1994, 2009). Hare (1993) defined *psychopathy* as an aberrant personality characterized by superficial charm, grandiosity, lack of guilt, callousness, exploitativeness, irresponsibility, poor impulse control, and antisocial behaviors. In spite of all the Rorschach literature dedicated to this diagnosis, it is hard to conceptualize how a Rorschach protocol could show attributes such as superficial charm, grandiosity, lack of guilt, callousness, exploitativeness, or irresponsibility. Consequently, I was not surprised that J. M. Wood and his group (2010), in their meta-analysis of the literature, found that 32 of the 37 Rorschach variables examined were not significantly related to the Psychopathy Checklist (Hare, 1991).

I believe it is a mistake to go too far astray from what could be rationally deduced from the way an examinee performs on the Rorschach task. This is a mistake that has been made by Rorschach researchers repeatedly. There is now a Rorschach Suicide Constellation and a Depression Index to look at states of mind that are probably much better assessed through other means. Crude as it may be, just asking people whether they think of ending their life, or if they have been feeling sad, is much more likely to give us useful information than the Rorschach.

The Rorschach and Exner's Comprehensive System have had many recent critics (Aronow et al., 1994; Hunsley & Bailey, 1999, 2001; Nezworski & Wood, 1995; Paul, 2004; J. M. Wood et al., 2001, 2010; J. M. Wood, Nezworski, Lilienfeld, & Garb, 2003; J. M. Wood, Nezworski & Stejkal, 1996). The Rorschach community sometimes has responded to the criticism in a defensive manner. Exner, for instance, refused to allow an open examination of the norms he had collected, especially after mistakes in the accumulation of the norms had been revealed (J. M. Wood et al., 2003). Articles published in defense of the Rorschach did not give much credence to the criticisms (e.g., Meyer, 1999b; Meyer & Archer, 2001; Viglione, 1999; Viglione & Hilsenroth, 2001).

Part of the problem was that the critics were mostly "outsiders," people who were not known for their clinical diagnostic work. Some of the criticism the Rorschach has received is unfair. Hunsley and Bailey (1999, 2001), for instance, wanted to measure the value of the Rorschach by the extent to which the instrument improves treatment outcome or lowers recidivism. Although some Rorschach studies address such issues, that is not the purpose of the test. Anyone who criticizes elephants because they cannot fly has been watching too many Walt Disney movies. My approach will be to hold the Rorschach accountable for what it can do and not to blame it for failures that, at least in my opinion, go beyond the power of the instrument. There is probably no instrument in our entire armamentarium that would pass the test to which Hunsley and Bailey would subject the Rorschach.

Other criticisms, however, should be taken seriously. J. M. Wood and his colleagues (2003) raised three important issues:

1. The Rorschach scores are not valid, mostly because few scores are predictive of any psychopathological entity such as depression.
2. The test overpathologizes because nonpsychiatric examinees are sure to elevate some scores.
3. The norms are not available for public scrutiny.

I believe that there is something to be said for all three of these points. One goal of this book is to explore the Rorschach in the light of the criticisms and suggestions that have been aired in the literature.

Exner died in 2006. Since his death at least two Rorschach groups appear to be vying to carry his mantle. One group, represented by Anthony Sciara and Barry Ritzler, would like to remain loyal to the Comprehensive System, even while accepting that some changes may be necessary in the future. These clinicians continue to run the Rorschach Training Program that Exner established (for more information, go to http://www.rorschachtraining.com).

The other group, which includes Gregory Meyer, Donald Viglione, Joni Mihura, Philip Erdberg, and Robert Erard (Erard, 2010), has been developing a new system to replace the Comprehensive System. Their R-PAS (Meyer, Viglione, Mihura, & Erard, 2011; Meyer, Viglione, Mihura, Erard, & Erdberg, 2011) has introduced new rules for administration designed to cut down the range in the number of responses obtained. They have proposed changes in terminology, giving new variable names for some of the traditional measures; dropped some of the coding distinctions; reclassified Special Scores; and added codes and indices.

R-PAS uses norms derived from the International Norms that were published in 2007 in a supplement of the *Journal of Personality Assessment*. The authors used the R-PAS system to collect 123 nonclinical cases of their own. Then they randomly selected cases from the different countries contained in the International Norms and used their 123 cases to make statistical adjustments so that the values obtained from the International Norms samples resembled their own cases. Their *R-PAS Optimized Norms* include 640 nonclinical cases. The system uses standard scores with a mean of 100 and a standard deviation of 15. The standard score of each variable is adjusted to take into account the complexity of the protocol (Meyer, Viglione, Mihura, Erard, & Erdberg, 2011).

I have followed with interest the R-PAS development, and I am entirely sympathetic with that work. However, I have two concerns: There is a hint that we might revert to the Tower of Babel days, with different groups speaking different Rorschach languages and following parallel courses of research and development. A second concern is that the R-PAS is at best perfecting the nomothetic Rorschach tradition and makes no attempt to integrate the more idiographic clinical side. Kobler perhaps would have seen the R-PAS effort as going in the wrong direction altogether, because it represents an attempt to *measure* the person more accurately, rather than to *understand* the person. Although it is a commendable effort to improve nomothetic expertise, I prefer to draw more attention to the value of clinical observations.

Goals of This Book

Through my years of teaching, I have had difficulty finding a good textbook that focuses on interpretation. The available textbooks are either simplistic or difficult to read. Some texts portray one approach and make no attempt to integrate different points of view. This book is aimed at those interested in learning the interpretation of the Rorschach in a way that takes advantage of both the empirical and the clinical traditions. My goal is to present the material in a readable, logical, and methodical manner. This book deals only with the interpretation of the Rorschach; it does not actively address scoring, because several effective books and manuals are available to teach its complexities. It should be noted that the scoring system used in the book is Exner's Comprehensive System (Exner, 1974), which Rorschach clinicians throughout the world have been using for several decades. A new scoring system has been proposed recently (the Rorschach Performance Assessment System or R-PAS; Meyer, Viglione, Mihura, & Erard, 2011a; Meyer et al., 2011b). However, clinicians should find the book helpful irrespective of the scoring system they use.

Training people to administer the Rorschach in our present changing and uncertain environment poses several challenges. My goal was to write a text that was not tied to any particular camp, even if it uses the Comprehensive System scoring system. I hope to follow the Kobler approach by integrating, as much as I can, the idiographic and nomothetic sides of the equation.

Part of my task in writing this book was to review the literature. Throughout the book, I will be noting some of the research that is available in support of a particular Rorschach score or marker. Generally I will report all the studies found and will not attempt to judge the quality of the study. When there was a wealth of articles, I took only the articles that were published during the past 20 years. I also did not include articles that focused on scoring issues or on the interrater reliability of the Rorschach scores; these are important areas of investigation, but they go beyond the scope of an interpretative manual.

The book addresses the clinical aspects of the score first in a text format and then gives the marker information in a table. Typically the term *score* refers to the variable itself (e.g., the *score* R is the number of responses obtained). The term *marker* refers to a score that is outside the normal or average range (e.g., a low R could be a *marker* for underproductivity, low intellectual ability, or low effort being made). The tables contain the information the clinician should consider when interpreting the marker.

Some of the available studies in the literature focused on the marker, whereas others related to the score and not necessarily to the marker.

Consider again the number of responses. Using the Exner norms, fewer responses than 16 (low) or more than 28 responses (high) would be a marker. The overwhelming majority of the studies address either the score or the marker but not both. A research study may compare two groups, perhaps a target group and a control group, and report a significant difference between the groups. That is different from determining whether the score of the individuals in the target group is outside of the average range. Typically I include research that addresses the score in the text that introduces the marker table, whereas the studies that address the marker are placed in the table.

The literature on the Rorschach includes many studies with markers specially developed for particular functions. For instance, researchers have developed rating systems for aggression that are different from the usual scores or indices of the Comprehensive System (e.g., Elizur, 1949; C. B. Gacono, Bannatyne-Gacono, Meloy, & Baity, 2005; Holt, 1977). This book covers the scores of the Comprehensive System.

As I read the literature I was surprised by both its richness and its limitations. At the time I was doing my review, nearly 10,000 relevant studies were listed in the PsycINFO database. A great number of those studies did support the use of a particular score or marker. Obviously, this is not an instrument that lacks scientific attention or support. As for the limitations of the literature, I found little support for some of the Rorschach's core assumptions, a criticism that has been made by J. M. Wood and his colleagues (2003). One example may be the meaning ascribed to responses including human movement, animal movement, and the balance between those two scores. As I explain in Chapter 5, the empirical literature mostly offers only indirect support for those assumptions (i.e., the assumptions being that a good level of human movement indicates maturity, inner stability, ability to delay gratification, etc.; that a good level of animal movement suggests an acceptance of primitive impulses). Part of the problem is that those core assumptions are difficult to measure directly in any other way. In any event, the support of the core assumptions is often indirect (e.g., showing that a particular group, expected to be more mature than another group, has a higher human movement count than the less mature group). Moreover, as I explain in Chapter 2, people with similar clinical attributes may give very different Rorschach protocols.

In the interest of equanimity, I have reported all the studies found that did not support the Rorschach hypotheses. In some cases, I reported on attempts that I did not consider appropriate, such as Richard Cohan's unsuccessful 1998 attempt to use the Rorschach to differentiate pedophiles from rapists of adults. There are undoubtedly differences between those two groups of sexual predators, but distinguishing between the two was obviously beyond the power of this instrument. (The Rorschach would probably also fail to distinguish between the group of pasta eaters who prefer spaghetti and those who prefer linguini.) By contrast, the test has done reasonably well in characterizing sexual predators as a group.

To summarize, my goals for the present book were to write an interpretative manual that (a) explored the Rorschach as a method through which we are able to see the individual in action, with the Rorschach representing a source of information that is different from any of the other clinical sources; (b) integrated some of the clinical idiographic tradition to the current emphasis on scores and norms, encouraging an appreciation for what the Rorschach markers may mean for a particular person; (c) emphasized Rorschach markers and observations as opposed to other constructs, such as the pathological entities of the *DSM–IV* (American Psychiatric Association, 1994); (d) reviewed current literature; (e) presented the material in a readable and easily understood format; and (f) suggested ways of integrating Rorschach data to the data obtained from other sources.

In attempting an integration of the nomothetic and the idiographic, I am aware that I have not given the psychoanalytic tradition its proper due. I have admired the writings of Aronow's group (Aronow, 1994, 1995; Moreland & Reznikoff, 1995). Aronow's Consensus Rorschach, where couples in therapy have to agree on what response they will give to a card, represents a very interesting use of this instrument. However, my own work has involved using the Rorschach in a more traditional way, and I believe that it would be harder to integrate the Aronow approach with any approach that examines scores and norms.

The psychoanalytic tradition today includes four perspectives: drive theory, ego psychology, object relations, and self psychology (Kleiger, 1997). Drive theorists are interested in using the Rorschach, for instance, to judge if the intensity of the affect is leading to a flooding experience and overwhelming the individual (e.g., Lerner, 1991b; Rapaport, Gill, & Schafer, 1968; Schachtel, 1966; Schafer, 1954). Ego psychologists, on the other hand, speak of ego capacity and anxiety tolerance (e.g., Siegal & Rosen, 1962; Zetzel, 1949). Object relation theorists have delved into the meaning of the human movements and human content as indications of the person's ability to see other human beings as independent entities (e.g., Blatt, Brenneis, Schimek, & Glick, 1976; Mayman, 1977; Blatt & Lerner, 1983). Finally, some theorists have focused on aspects of the Rorschach that speak of the experience of the self, the person's conscious cognitive control, and the awareness of one's own affective reactions (e.g., Lerner, 1988, 1991b; Stern, 1985; Wilson, 1988; Winnicott, 1961, 1963).

The more traditional psychoanalytic legacy parts from the theory first, fitting in the Rorschach findings into the theoretical framework. B. L. Smith (1997), for instance, believed that "it is necessary to have a theoretical framework within which to fit observations and interpretations of a test battery if assessment is to be meaning-ful" (p. 191). That tradition has been with the Rorschach from the start, with well-known names like Roy Schafer, David Rapaport, Paul Lerner, and Sidney Blatt. Although I am sympathetic to that tradi-tion, this book does not subscribe to it. I believe it is perfectly rea-sonable to start at the other end, looking at the observations, and that one does not necessarily need to subscribe to a theory in order to understand an individual. Readers interested in learning more about that tradition, however, are encouraged to read *Contemporary Rorschach Interpretation* (Meloy, Acklin, Gacono, Murray, & Peterson, 1997).

My intention is to help students and professionals understand, administer, and interpret the Rorschach in a useful, practical, and scien-tific manner. Throughout the book I have attempted to recover Kobler's clinical aim of understanding the examinee, an aim that sometimes seems to be lost in the effort to provide increasingly more accurate measures, without enough empathic understanding of the person in front of us.

Administration | 2

E xner's accomplishments in developing a standard format and common language for Rorschach interpretation cannot be overstated. Nevertheless, we would not be doing the Rorschach tradition a favor if we were to accept Exner's integration as the final word on all things Rorschach. We must be willing to reconsider some of the procedures and variables that Exner either discarded or deemphasized and that may be of some value, as well as entertain well-supported changes to the Comprehensive System.

In this chapter, I discuss a few enhancements to the Comprehensive System procedures for administering the test. I assume that readers are well acquainted with and largely follow these procedures (Exner, 2003; Sciara & Ritzler, 2006). After briefly discussing the setting up of the testing encounter, I discuss the enhancements that can be made to the Free Association and Inquiry phases of the Comprehensive System administration without a significant alteration of the system procedures. I describe post-hoc inquiries that can be made to better understand the patient's responses and the flexibility

DOI: 10.1037/14039-002
The Rorschach Inkblot Test: An Interpretive Guide for Clinicians, by J. P. Choca

of his or her thinking (the testing the limits procedure). Two measures, reaction time and card rotations, can be easily obtained and occasionally reveal something valuable about the examinee.

Clinician–Examinee Relationship

Before the expansion of treatment opportunities for clinical psychologists in Veterans Administration hospitals after World War II, clinical psychology was largely defined by psychological testing (Butcher, 2009). Textbooks of that era paid considerable attention to the assessment encounter and to the inferred psychological dynamics between assessor and examinee. This was especially true for assessment techniques derived from psychoanalytic theory, as was the Rorschach of that era. Schafer's (1954) classic textbook begins with an extended discussion of the testing situation.

In contemporary practice, nearly all examinees are familiar with and reasonably comfortable with medical tests. However, psychological testing is different because it is more intimate and interactive. Before any testing is done, it is a good idea to discuss the purpose of the evaluation with the examinee and how it will be done. Emphasize the collaborative nature of the enterprise: The clinician is there to help the examinee reveal himself or herself in a joint journey of discovery. Many examinees come into the testing situation reluctantly, and it is of great benefit when clinicians can help them become invested in the task and interested in the results.

Phases of Rorschach Administration

FREE ASSOCIATION PHASE

The Free Association Phase is referred to as the Response Phase in the R-PAS system. To introduce the test, the clinician might simply state that the examinee will be shown some inkblots and should say what the inkblot reminds them of or might be. Longer instructions are available in the literature but typically make little difference in the results (Hartmann & Vanem, 2003).

If the examinee is not productive enough (i.e., the individual gives no more than the minimal number of responses), he or she should be encouraged to give additional responses. The examinee could be told that most people give two or more responses per card; the purpose is to clarify the task, not to dictate the number of responses that must be given. With examinees who are unproductive, the clinician can consider changing the prompt from *Anything else?* to *What else could this be?* Further discussion about the testing or the Rorschach may be needed with some people. The clinician should also address any apprehensions the examinee might have and encourage honest self-expression.

As Exner (2003) showed, practically everyone is capable of giving at least 14 responses to the Rorschach. Clinicians should note when they are given fewer than the 14 responses that the Comprehensive System requires, because that piece of information is important in the interpretation of the protocol. However, I do not agree with Exner's recommendation that the test must be abandoned in such cases; I tell examinees that the test cannot be scored and properly interpreted with fewer than 14 responses and that they should go through the cards again and give additional associations. The clinician should keep track of the responses given after the additional pressure was exerted, in case there is a difference between those associations and the associations that had been previously obtained. In most cases the clinician may not find any differences and can handle all of the responses as one set. One set of data in the literature included records with zero responses (Fiske & Baughman, 1953). There has to be a point at which a clinician must accept that an individual is refusing to do the test, that the clinician has not successfully encouraged the examinee, and that the clinician therefore has not been able to administer the Rorschach.

The variance in the number of responses was one of the early criticisms of the test (Cronbach, 1949; Fiske & Baughman, 1953) and continues to be seen as problematic (e.g., Meyer, 1992; Sultan & Meyer, 2009). As a result, various attempts have been made to control the number of responses. The Holtzman Inkblot Test, for instance, accepts only one response per inkblot (Holtzman, Thorpe, Swartz, & Herron, 1961). Kinder (1992) argued for statistically normalizing or partialing out the effect of the number of responses. More recently, others have recommended controlling the number of responses (Dean, Viglione, Perry, & Meyer, 2007; Exner, 2003; Sultan & Meyer, 2009). The R-PAS uses the procedure of prompting for two responses and pulling the card after four (Meyer, Viglione, Mihura, & Erard, 2011).

It is obvious that the stability of the protocol as a whole (Sultan & Meyer, 2009) and many of the scores are affected when the number of responses is out of the ordinary. Nevertheless, as a clinician I object to restricting the number of responses that an examinee gives. The beauty of the Rorschach is that it allows us to see the examinee in action. Forcing the examinee to act in a certain way diminishes the power of the instrument. I am much more sympathetic with the Kinder (1992) position of handling the problem statistically than with the idea of restricting the record. Nevertheless, since very few examinees will give more than four responses per card, the issue will not come up frequently.

INQUIRY PHASE

During the Free Association Phase of the administration, referred to as the Clarification Phase in the R-PAS system, the clinician typically has little interaction with the examinee other than to encourage the articulation of any associations that come to mind. Clinicians can introduce the Inquiry Phase by inviting examinees to clarify their responses. The beginning part of the Inquiry Phase can be handled in much the same way Exner advised, by asking the examinee in what way the inkblot suggested the response that was given. After the examinee answers, the clinician should continue to ask if there was any other way in which the inkblot suggested the response, until the person states that there was nothing else. The clinician then repeats the same procedure for every response obtained. Thus, I recommend that the first part of the Inquiry be conducted in the manner Exner described.

When clinicians are particularly interested in one Rorschach value and do not care about the rest of the Structural Summary, they may perform what may be referred to as a *focused Rorschach*. With a manic patient, for instance, the clinician may be particularly interested in discovering how many responses the individual will offer. If the examinee gives, say, 75 responses, the clinician may decide to inquire about some but not all of the responses. It may be that the large number of responses is the most important finding and that the examinee would not be able to complete a thorough inquiry of every response. Similarly, in the case of a very psychotic individual, the clinician may decide that the examinee was too dysfunctional to do more than the free associations and the determination of the location of the response.

On most occasions, however, the Rorschach should be administered in the conventional manner or not administered at all. The time saved with the focused Rorschach may not be enough to merit taking the shortcuts. Moreover, there are clearly times when shortcuts should not be taken: (a) in a forensic case, when there is a need to be thorough; (b) when a critical decision must be made and the clinician needs as much information as possible (e.g., in the case of a student who told a classmate he was going to kill other students); (c) when the crucial question is one that the Rorschach is particularly adept at answering (e.g., whether the person has a thought disorder); (d) when the person may have reason to hide some feelings or thoughts (because the Rorschach is not easily manipulated); and (e) when the case is to be used for presentations.

TESTING THE LIMITS

After finishing with the Comprehensive System administration of the Rorschach, it may be useful to go back to the responses to obtain more information. At this time the clinician can take more liberties in the interactions with the examinee and investigate the examinee's thoughts at greater depth. When an individual gives a low-quality response—or when we have a protocol with no determinants, humans, color, or movement—it is often useful to look further into what is behind the finding. In such cases the clinician may learn more about the examinee through the follow-up inquiries than had been learned up to that point.

One way in which Klopfer (Klopfer, Ainsworth, Klopfer, and Holt, 1954) accomplished the follow-up inquiries was through the method of *Testing the Limits.* He recommended the use of this method to explore the examinee's

- flexibility in the manner of approach (e.g., if an examinee gives only whole perceptions or only details, what it would take for that person to switch focus);
- ability to perceive humans in a case when no human associations were given;
- capacity to perceive a major determinant such as movement or color; or
- ability to think along conventional lines and give popular responses.

Hutt and Shor (1946) proposed the use of prompts at three different levels:

1. The first level involves suggesting the missing focus. For an examinee who did not give any whole perceptions, one could pick a card that has a very popular whole response, such as Card V, and say something like, "On this card you saw the head of an alligator on the side and the head of a rabbit on top, can you think of something that uses the whole card rather than just a part?"

2. The second level involves suggesting a response. This is more intrusive than the first and is used when an examinee is not helped with the Level 1 prompt. A Level 2 prompt for the example given above might be, "Do you think that this card could be seen as a bat, with the head being here, the wings here, and the feet at the bottom?"

3. If the examinee is not responsive to a Level 2 prompt, the clinician might explore what prevented the examinee from seeing a response that is actually a very popular response for that card (e.g., "We are all unique individuals and you don't need to see what others see. However, the bat in this card is a very popular response. What do you suppose makes it so that you don't see the bat? Or that you never use the entire inkblot for one of your perceptions?").

The manner of approach reveals whether an examinee is more inclined to develop an overall picture or to focus on the details (see Chapter 3, this volume). A balanced person would have the capacity to do both. A person who is very detail oriented and who has a great deal of trouble seeing the whole picture could be expected to have trouble functioning in an organization or even relating to other people. The testing the limits method allows the clinician to decide how fixed the manner of approach is with a particular individual and how flexible the individual may be when the situation calls for the other approach. Although the example used dealt with the manner of approach, clinicians can use this method to explore the examinee's flexibility with any of the other attributes that the Rorschach measures.

The Testing the Limits exploration can be expanded and applied to other post hoc questioning. Consider, for example, the follow-up of a poor form level response. The response, given to Card V, was "Nixon with Clinton on his back." During the Inquiry Phase the patient gave the location (Dd35), noting that there were two bulges and that he saw Nixon being the top bulge and Clinton being the second. At that point the patient could not give any more information about this association. The follow-up questioning proceeded approximately in the following way:

> *Clinician:* I want to go back to your response of Nixon and Clinton on this card. You pointed to the two bulges, but I have trouble seeing either Nixon or Clinton there.
>
> *Examinee:* Oh, well, yeah, I was just reminded of that.
>
> *Clinician:* So, can you help me understand how the inkblot reminded you of Nixon and Clinton?
>
> *Examinee:* Well, just the two bulges made me think of that, that's all.
>
> *Clinician:* But those two bulges don't look to me like either Nixon or Clinton, do they look like those two people to you?
>
> *Examinee:* Not really. You know, with the presidential elections, I just thought of someone making up a cartoon of Nixon and Clinton, and that it could look a little like that, if it was a little distorted. But it is hard to explain, I really don't know why I thought of that.

The original response did not include Special Scores or other indications of psychosis. The clinician hoped that the examinee would be able to defend the unusual response in a rational manner, but that was not the case. The follow-up accomplished one objective: It confirmed that the response was of poor quality, suggested by the occurrence of an extraneous event, the presidential election, and that the association was basically unrelated to the shape of the inkblot. However, the follow-up also uncovered positive elements. It is noteworthy, for instance, that the examinee was able to stay focused with the clinician through the questioning. Eventually he was even able to recognize that the response would not make much sense to anyone else. In his daily life, this is an individual who can be expected to derail, bringing extraneous topics into his conversation. However, he may respond well to redirection and may even be able to recognize the intrusion of extraneous thoughts from time to time.

It is useful to consider how another person may respond to the Testing of the Limits. The response involved two birds seen on Card I. During the Inquiry Phase the examinee elaborated that each of the birds occupied one half of the card divided vertically and was able to point to the wings (triangular side protrusion or Dd34), the body (rest of side D2), the head (Dd28 up on top), and a tree they were climbing (center D4). When asked if anything else reminded her of the two birds, the examinee stated, "They needs trees and the cuddle looks like fluff." When asked what she meant by that last statement, she replied "nothing" and would not elaborate. The clinician tested the limits with her by bringing her back to this response and asking her to clarify what she meant.

Examinee: Well, there is a nest, in the house, not in the card.

Clinician: In what house?

Examinee: In my house.

Clinician: You are saying that there is a bird nest in your house, but I was asking what you meant when you said "and the cuddle looks like fluff," is that what you said?

Examinee: Yeah, I said that!

Clinician: Can you explain to me what that means?

Examinee: What?

Clinician: And the cuddle looks like fluff, what did you mean by that?

Examinee: [After a brief pause] Mom screams for no reason. I need mom because I am scared.

Clinician: Are you scared now?

Examinee: Not now. [Looking at the card] I told you this was a monster.

Clinician: Yes, that was another response. But I would like you to tell me what you were thinking of when you said that the cuddle looks like fluff. What did you mean by cuddle?

Examinee: A churbee reaction in a hunting piano hole! [At this point the examinee started laughing uproariously.]

In this case, the examinee started with a fairly good response but spoiled it with the addition of a nonsense phrase. When questioned about the phrase, she derailed and started to talk about a nest in her house, a loose association to the two birds. After she was redirected, she had an ever looser association about her mother, seemed to suggest that she was "scared," and wanted to talk about another response she had given. When that maneuver was blocked, she completely fell apart, speaking nonsense once again and behaving in a bizarre manner. Unlike the examinee in the first excerpted dialogue, this patient cannot borrow resources from others to straighten out her thinking. On the contrary, it seems as if the more intrusive the other person is, the less functional this person becomes. This is the type of schizophrenic who may look better in superficial interactions than during closer relationships.

With the use of these two examples I tried to illustrate the usefulness of making an effort to understand the reason for the patient's responses. These post-hoc inquiries can be focused on the issues presented by a particular protocol and do not need to be time-consuming. Some Rorschach clinicians ask examinees to select their favorite and least favorite cards and to explain their decisions. Some clinicians pose additional projective instructions (e.g., "Select the putative mother/father/sex/death cards").

Additional Measures: Reaction Time and Card Rotation

At one time the Rorschach was administered with a stopwatch, and the reaction time was noted for each association. This information supposedly was not useful enough to merit the effort, and the procedure was abandoned. There are indications, however, that the response time may be a useful marker (e.g., Chen, 1999; Priyamvada et al., 2009), and this measure may be much easier to obtain when computers are used. Reaction time studies have shown a very nice distribution with the presence of a notable number of outliers (Choca, Van Denburg, & Mouton, 1994). As is discussed in Chapter 4, this information is expected to be useful in the interpretation of the Rorschach in those cases.

The number of associations that were given after rotating the Rorschach card sideways or upside down is another measure that was used at one time and that was abandoned by the Comprehensive System. This is another variable that may be very interpretable with a particular individual (see Chapter 4).

In addressing the test administration, this chapter resurrected two variables from the past: reaction time and card rotation. These variables are easy to collect accurately and can be very useful in certain cases. More important, this chapter further developed the approach proposed in the first chapter of this volume. I view the Rorschach as a clinical tool, an instrument that allows us to observe the examinee in action. An experienced clinician can learn a great deal about the examinee through the test administration, without ever scoring the responses (see Chapter 9 for more information). The scoring serves as sort of a magnifying lens to highlight response patterns, patterns that could otherwise go unnoticed. For the scores to be useful, the test has to be administered in approximately the manner used when the norms were collected. However, the rigid application of administration guidelines prevents the examiner from exploring what is actually going on with the examinee. I believe that the Inquiry Phase of the administration does not "exist solely to resolve coding ambiguities" (Meyer, Viglione, Mihura, Erard, & Erdberg, 2011b, p.16). Rather, the Inquiry Phase can be used to learn more about how the examinee saw the response, and the process the examinee used to arrive at the response. As Kobler (1983) noted, the purpose of the Rorschach is not to measure but to understand the examinee. Another administrative phase proposed in this chapter, the Testing of Limits, can be used in an idiographic manner after the test was administered, to discover aspects of the examinee's functioning that may not be apparent without this procedure.

Interpretative Basics 3

One advantage to using the Rorschach is that it allows clinicians to see individuals in action, problem-solving in real time. For this reason, Meyer and Kurtz (2006) recommended that the Rorschach and similar instruments be referred to as *performance-based personality tests* rather than *projective tests* (the traditional label). A similar implication is contained in the suggestion that personality tests be classified as *declarative* or *nondeclarative* (Schultheiss, 2007). These alternative labels emphasize that the essence of the Rorschach and similar instruments is in the observation of meaningful behavior, rather than as a means through which individuals communicate their perceptions. Moreover, these tests are not designed to evoke psychoanalytic projections (L. K. Frank, 1948). These tests, and the Rorschach in particular, are useful in giving clinicians an observational perspective, a perspective that is different from what individuals would say about themselves.

Standardized tests can be interpreted at three different levels: the profile level, the score level, and the individual response level. This chapter introduces readers to these levels; subsequent chapters provide a more complete discussion of each.

DOI: 10.1037/14039-003
The Rorschach Inkblot Test: An Interpretive Guide for Clinicians, by J. P. Choca

Profile Interpretation

A profile-level interpretation takes into account a set of scores, if not the entire set of scores, that an examinee obtained. Profiles are often used in interpreting self-report inventories such as the Minnesota Multiphasic Personality Inventory (MMPI-2; Butcher, Dahlstrom, Graham, Tellegen, & Kaemmer, 1989) and the Millon Clinical Multiaxial Inventory (MCMI-III; Millon, 1983). Profile interpretations are more sophisticated than single score interpretations because the meaning of one score can change when another score is taken into account.

The interpretative system used by Exner (2003) and Weiner (2003) is a profile system that parcels out the scores of the Rorschach into eight thematic groups or clusters: Affective, Stress Tolerance, Cognitive Mediation, Ideation, Information Processing, Interpersonal Perception, Self-Perception, and Situation-Related Stress. In some cases several clusters are grouped in subsets. For example, Information Processing, Cognitive Mediation, and Ideation are considered together in what is referred to as the *cognitive triad.* The scores considered in any one of the clusters is a subset of Rorschach scores. Exner (2003) then prescribed (a) an order for examining the clusters based on the data obtained through the Rorschach for that particular individual and (b) several steps for examining the data within a particular cluster.

My objections to the Exner–Weiner system (see Chapter 1, this volume) are that (a) it emphasizes diagnostic concepts (e.g., stress tolerance) rather than Rorschach findings; (b) it is cumbersome, difficult to understand, and almost impossible to teach to new students; and (c) it often relies on variables that are so complex, and so far away from what the patient is actually doing, that the examiner loses the clinical sense of the patient.

Psychoanalytic clinicians also have proposed a profile-based way of analyzing Rorschach protocols. These clinicians have spoken of a *mental structure* that is stable across time in the person's life. The mental structure is the product of developmental progressions and regressions so that the structure is linked to the stages of development (Loevinger, 1976; Werner, 1957). Associated with the mental structure is a *level of personality organization.* The different levels are, in turn, associated with the sophistication of the person's ego functions, defense mechanisms, affective response, and concepts for the self and others (Blanck & Blanck, 1975; Freud, 1965).

Kernberg (1980, 1984) distinguished between *personality organization* and *personality style.* He proposed three levels of personality organization that he labeled *neurotic, borderline,* and *psychotic.* These levels are theoretically associated with the degree of identity integration, the types of defenses the individual employs, and the capacity for reality testing. The personality style, on the other hand, speaks to the flavor or surface characteristics of the individual's personality, such as histrionic, paranoid, narcissistic, and obsessive–compulsive.

Acklin (1992, 1993, 1997b) applied Kernberg's writings to the Rorschach, indicating how the test can be used to differentially diagnose the three levels of personality organization. His system looks at 14 areas (ego development, reality testing, defenses, affect, impulsivity, anxiety tolerance, sublimatory channels, superego integration, dynamics, object relations, object constancy, self-other differentiation, identity, interpersonal relationships) to discriminate between the three levels.

Kwawer (1980) developed a scoring system for Rorschach content that focuses on identity and interpersonal issues. Concepts explored by this system include engulfment, symbiotic merging, violent symbiosis, separation, union, malignant internal processes, rebirth, metamorphosis, narcissistic mirroring, separation–individuation, and boundary disturbance.

The types of defenses habitually used by the individual have also been the focus of psychoanalytic efforts. Cooper, Perry, and Arnow (1988) proposed a scoring manual for Rorschach defense scales across the three levels. The neurotic level included denial, intellectualization, isolation, reaction formation, repression, rationalization, and Pollyannaish denial. The borderline level defenses included splitting, primitive idealization, devaluation, omnipotence, projective identification, and projection. Finally, massive denial and hypomanic denial were seen as the psychotic defenses (see also Cooper & Arnow, 1986; Cooper, Perry, & O'Connell, 1991; Kwawer, Lerner, Lerner, & Sugarman, 1980; Lerner & Lerner, 1980).

The issues one may raise with the psychoanalytic profiles are that (a) they are based on the application of psychoanalytic theory to the Rorschach and are not particularly helpful to individuals who are not psychoanalytically oriented; (b) they take into account many factors that often point to different levels of personality organization, so that the final determination often seems to be left to the clinician's discretion; and (c) like the Exner profiling, they typically rely on variables that are so complex, and so far away from what the patient is actually doing, that the examiner loses the clinical sense of the patient.

In this book, I propose profile interpretations on the basis of what I think are the most commonly appearing Rorschach score patterns. Chapter 11 describes common Rorschach profiles viewed from the vantage point of Rorschach scores, rather than the Exner diagnostic concepts or psychoanalytic theory. First, however, it is important to explore how scores are interpreted.

Score Interpretation

The nomothetic utility of standardized instruments relies on the comparison of an unknown entity (the examinee) to a known entity (how the population at large responds to the test, as represented by the test norms). To whatever extent the Rorschach protocol is a nomothetic instrument, the test has to be administered and scored properly, and the scores have to be compiled into the Structural Summary. Appropriate norms have to be consulted, and a determination has to be made regarding whether each score falls within the average range or is higher or lower than scores in that range.

Several contemporary norms are available for the Rorschach. Chapters 4 through 8 present the mean, standard deviation, and suggested cutoffs for each of the Comprehensive System scores, using three different norms. The Exner numbers are from Exner (2003). These norms are based on 600 nonpsychiatric individuals. The Exner norms have received their share of criticism (J. M. Wood, Nezworski, Garb, & Lilienfeld, 2001; J. M. Wood, Nezworski, Lilienfeld, Garb, 2003), but they have also been defended against those attacks (Exner, 2001; Meyer, 2001). The International Norms are from the last article of a 2007 supplement to the *Journal of Personality Assessment* (Meyer, Erdberg, & Schaffer, 2007). These norms are based on 21 samples from 17 countries. When the examinee is from one of the 17 countries that make up the International Norms, the reader may want to consult the supplement for the appropriate norm (e.g., de Ruiter & Smid, 2007; Dumitrascu, 2007; Ivanouw, 2007; Pires, 2000; Sultan et al., 2004).

The psychiatric norms come from my own work. Details on those norms are offered in the Appendix. These norms represent work in progress and still do not have interrater reliability values. Some scores (e.g., the scoring of the populars) were not always done following Comprehensive System rules and are, consequently, omitted.

Each of the norms compares the examinee with a different group, and the sophisticated clinician should be able to handle those different comparisons. The Exner norms are the traditional norms that have been used throughout the world for several decades. These norms presumably reveal how the examinee compares with the United States population. The International Norms have a more diverse appeal, comparing the individual with a global sample. The psychiatric norms show how the examinee performed in the context of a general psychiatric group.

In practice, the issue of the different norm comparisons is much simpler than it would appear at first sight. For many scores, the difference between the three norms is so small as to be irrelevant. Most scores for most examinees are in the normal range, no matter what norm is used. Similarly, scores outside of the normal range are so regardless of the norm used. When marginal scores are obtained for a variable where the norms do differ, clinicians have to master the skill of phrasing the finding accurately. For example, an examinee with 17 form-only responses (scored F) might be said to be more simplistic in his or her perceptions, overcontrolled, or guarded than the general population, but no more so than the typical psychiatric patient.

The scores could be compiled and the norms checked easily and accurately by means of a computer program. Several commercially available computer programs can perform these functions (e.g., Exner's Rorschach Interpretative Assistance Program [RIAP; Exner, McGuire, & Cohen, 1990]; ROR-Scan [Caracena, 2010]).

The test norms are used to determine which of the scores obtained are outside of the acceptable or expected range. Scores that are higher than the average range can then be interpreted to indicate that the individual has more of the attribute that the score measures than the rest of the population. Scores that are lower than the average range indicate less of that attribute than the rest of the population.

The usual convention with the Rorschach has been to define the average range by adding and subtracting one standard deviation to the mean. If the distributions are normal, that convention would classify 68% of the population as being in the average range, whereas 16% would be seen as high and 16% would be seen as low. Thus, using that convention statistically defines 32% as being out of the ordinary.

The cutoff level used for standardized tests is arbitrary and varies by instrument. Personality questionnaires such as the MMPI typically use 1.5 standard deviations to define the average range. That cutoff would leave 86% of the population in the acceptable range, 7% high, and 7% low. All of those figures would be true only if the scores were normally distributed. Although there are Rorschach values that are normally distributed, a substantial portion of the scores are not. Given the intrinsic limitations of the test, however, the benefit of using more sophisticated statistics is doubtful. In the chapters that follow, the suggested cutoff was calculated using 1.5 standard deviations. In my opinion, using a lower cutoff would result in too many examinees being flagged as having a problem.

With the exception of some of the ratios, the score cutoff is converted into an integer because the value the clinician would have from a protocol would be an integer. In arriving at the cutoff integer, the actual value is rounded to the next lower integer for the high cutoff value, and the next higher integer for the low cutoff value. For instance, the value for having too many whole responses (W) using the International Norms was 15.89 (the mean [9.08] plus 1.5 times the standard deviation [4.54]); the high cutoff value was then rounded down to 15. On the other hand, the cutoff value for having too few Ws was actually 2.27 and was rounded up to 3.

Many of the approximately 90 scores included in the Structural Summary are highly correlated or even directly related to one another. Consider, for instance, the manner of approach scores: A protocol with an elevated number of details and unusual details (D and Dd) must have a low whole response score because the detail responses are given at the expense of whole responses. In a similar manner, because the F score is given only when there are no other determinants, a record that has a high F% or Lambda must, by necessity, have a low movement count, a low color–shading count, or both. These types of relationships are also found across scores that are not of the same kind: A record that is low in human content (H) must also be low in the human movement determinant (M). To the neophyte, the number of scores that are taken into account may seem overwhelming, but because many scores have practically no degrees of freedom, the actual number is more manageable. The clinician also must interpret only those values that are outside of the average range, further reducing the amount of data to be interpreted.

Many Rorschach scores have a very low prevalence. Only one out of three protocols, for instance, would have a Vista (V) response, and a pure achromatic color (C′) response is practically never seen. With a good number of Rorschach scores, as a result, the clinician has to attend only to elevations, and low scores can be disregarded.

Response Interpretation

The final level of interpretation is the response level. Many of the interpretations at this level could be done without scoring the Rorschach. In discussing the response level interpretations (see Chapter 9), I explore what can be gathered from the sequence of the Rorschach responses, the particular content of a response, or the flexibility shown by the patient during the Testing the Limits procedure.

Uniqueness of the Rorschach Protocol

All Rorschach protocols tend to be different, reflecting the uniqueness of the individual. Although there are recognizable profiles (see Chapter 11), Rorschach protocols are more impressive for their uniqueness than for their similarity. How the protocol will come out with a particular individual is unpredictable, a fact that presents a problem for the science part of our world.

A few years ago my colleagues and I attempted to characterize the Rorschach patterns that could be expected with individuals with a particular personality style, as measured by the MCMI. This attempt to identify prototypical patterns has a history in clinical psychology. Schafer (1948) provided expected characteristics of Rorschach profiles for many clinical groups. In our work, in the group of people who had a histrionic personality style, many Rorschach protocols predictably appeared reactive, emotional, and dramatic. Our research was unsuccessful not because we could not find good examples of the predicted prototypes but rather because, in the same group with those dramatic and emotional Rorschachs, too many protocols did not come out as predicted. Every test has some trouble with false negatives or Type II errors, but this appears to be a big issue with the Rorschach (Chiva, 1973; Viglione, 1995). It is easier to form an opinion about an individual after seeing him or her perform on the Rorschach than to predict the Rorschach performance of an individual from other sources of data. This problem may be partly due to the response style the patient uses in completing the Rorschach (Meyer, 1999a; Meyer, Riethmiller, Brooks, Benoit, & Handler, 2000). In some ways, this unpredictability adds to the benefit of administering the Rorschach because it tends to give us information that we would not have been able to guess from other sources. For instance, Rorschach scores typically have only modest correlations with self-report inventories (Archer & Krishnamurthy, 1993; Meyer et al., 2000).

This chapter covered the fundamentals of interpretation. The book will return to the topic of interpretative strategies with more specific information in Chapter 10. Before that is possible, however, we need to review the meaning that can be extracted from the different scores (Chapters 4–8), and the interpretations at the response level (Chapter 9). Chapter 11 presents common Rorschach profiles, the topic covered at the beginning of this chapter.

Global Scores 4

n our daily lives, we often come across people who are energetic and talkative, wanting to contribute repeatedly to every project or conversation. Some of these people are gifted and their contributions are valuable; one can count on them to lead and provide the momentum behind projects. In some cases, however, the high energy seems intrusive and unproductive, a nervous chatter that we would rather do without. In contrast to the high-energy people, some individuals seem thoughtful and reserved, reluctant to be too dynamic or to be the center of attention. Some of these less dynamic people are great contributors when they do talk or interact, whereas others may be uninvolved because they actually have no interest or anything to contribute. These and other personality aspects can be readily reflected on the global scores of the Rorschach and are reviewed in this chapter.

Under the umbrella term *global scores,* I group together the most general scores of the Rorschach. Components of the global scores include the number of responses contained in the protocol, the manner of approach, the Popular responses, Reflections and Doubles, the Developmental Quality, card

DOI: 10.1037/14039-004
The Rorschach Inkblot Test: An Interpretive Guide for Clinicians, by J. P. Choca

rotations, and reaction time. For each of these scores, a general discussion is followed by a table containing the norms, the possible interpretations, and the research that was found. This chapter is followed by similar chapters discussing the psychogram or determinants, as well as the content, quality, complex ratios, and response level interpretatives.

Number of Responses

The number of responses the individual gives to the Rorschach is a most important finding. The number of responses score (i.e., R score) is a measure of the energy that the individual is putting into the task. To do justice to this variable, however, we have to develop a clinical sense of whether the amount of energy seen in the protocol is typical of that person's mode of operation or simply reflects the mind-set with which the individual is taking the test. High R protocols—protocols that have many responses—exhaust the number of whole (W) and popular (P) responses so that those scores are likely to be relatively low. Possible interpretations are given in the following items.

Norm used	High	Low	*M*	*SD*
Exner	> 28	< 16	22.32	4.40
International	> 34	< 11	22.31	7.90
Psychiatric	> 34	< 9	21.46	8.37

Possible interpretations of a high R score:
- Intelligent individual with high motivation and good resources (assuming that the quality of the responses is good and that the protocol is rich in determinants and contents)
- Compulsive need for quantity
- Expansiveness, inclination for overproduction; overeagerness in committing to the task
- Trusting, wish to be cooperative and perform a good job
- Strong achievement drive
- Manic or hypomanic state; difficulty limiting one's interventions with the world
- Research: associated with extraversion (Kopplin, 1999)

Possible interpretations of a low R score:
- Low intellectual capacity in an individual with a low level of motivation; possible intellectual impairment
- With high Lambda: Constriction of psychological functioning so that the individual is guarded and unproductive, overcontrolled

(*Continued*)

- Defensiveness, fear of disclosure, passive-aggressive approach to the testing, perhaps to life; resistance, possible intent to avoid the task, oppositional negativism
- Distrustful, suspicious, paranoid
- Depressed; difficulty becoming energized and motivated
- Research: Nonsupportive findings: Does not show the minimization of psychopathology in alleged sexual offenders (Wasyliw, Benn, Grossman, & Haywood, 1998)

Affective Ratio (Afr)

The Affective Ratio reflects emotional reactivity. It is computed by dividing the number of responses obtained on the last three cards (which are colorful) by the number of responses on the first seven cards. Because the colorful cards are also the last cards, the ratio also speaks for how productive or unproductive the person is after doing a task for a period of time.

If the number of responses to all of the cards was equal, the Afr would be .43; as the number of responses given to the last three cards increases relative to the number of other responses, the ratio increases. An Afr of 1.0 or above means that the examinee spent the same amount of energy (or more) on the last three cards as on the preceding seven. The clinician would have to decide if the additional productivity was emotionally driven or driven by the ease and comfort that came from doing the preceding cards. An examination of the sequence of responses (see Chapter 7, this volume) and the psychogram (see Chapter 5) may give some indication of what the correct interpretation may be.

Norm used	High	Low	M	SD
Exner	> .91	< .43	.67	.16
International	> .83	< .23	.53	.20
Psychiatric	> .77	< .21	.49	.19

Possible interpretations of a high Afr:
- Becomes energized when presented with emotional stimuli; may have a tendency to get caught up in emotion

(*continued*)

(*Continued*)

- With high Lambda: individual seeks emotional stimulation but does not respond to it
- Or, is likely to be constrained at the beginning of a task but becomes more productive as the person develops more comfort with what is expected
- Possibly behavioral problems, histrionic, delinquent, or manic
- Research: Color cards are likely to produce more responses than the achromatic cards (Exner, 1962; Silva, 2001); lower Afr scores have been found with neglected or depressed children (Elisens, 1998), children and adolescents with severe burns (Holaday, 1998), delinquent children (Loftis, 1997), persons with a panic disorder (de Ruiter & Cohen, 1992), worker's compensation claimants with chronic back pain or emotional distress (Lorentz, 1995), rapists (Dåderman & Jonson, 2008), and sexually abused hospitalized adolescent women (Hickey, 1995).

Possible interpretations of a low Afr:
- Not as responsive as most people
- May not know how to ventilate
- Mistrusts feelings and attempts to keep them under control
- Not enthusiastic about activities in life
- Avoids and withdraws from emotionally laden material
- Does not allow self to fully interact with world
- Likely to become tired and to stop working after some period with a task

Manner of Approach

Watch a lively debate and note the different approaches that participants take. Some individuals may argue from a holistic point of view: The emphasis will be on the merits of the whole idea, and the details receive little focus. The implication is that if the idea has merit, the details can be worked out. Others might discuss the details and develop opinions on the subject on the basis of the perceived viability of the details. Such debates often highlight two different ways of thinking: One focuses on the whole (the forest) with less attention to the details (the trees), and the other focuses on the details and barely notices the whole. Impressionist painters like Claude Monet wanted to create the overall impression of the scene, whereas realistic painters (e.g., Gustave Courbet) took pains to put in the minute details. Some people are balanced with regard to this issue, having an eye for

FIGURE 4.1

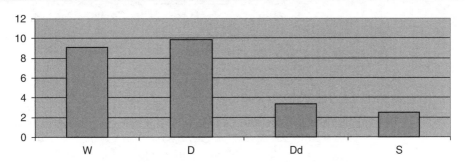

Expected distribution in the Manner of Approach. W = whole; D = detailed; Dd = unusual details; S = white space. Data from Meyer et al., 2007.

both the wide horizon and the molecular view, and there is something to be said for having both types of thinkers in an organization. The Rorschach gets to this issue with the classification of the locations used for the response.

Figure 4.1 shows the expected distribution for the different locations in the average protocol. In the ideal case there is a balance between the macro view represented (by the W score) and the more molecular view (the details, reflected in the D score). As depicted in Figure 4.1, the micro view of the small details is not very common. Also less common is the use of the white space (S) as the location for the response. As the R score increases, the W count is likely to decrease; on the other hand, the D count and the score for unusual details (Dd count) are likely to increase because the number of associations that can be seen using the whole inkblot is more limited than the number of things that can be seen taking into consideration only parts of the figure.

WHOLE RESPONSES (W)

To give a whole response, the examinee has to look at the entire inkblot and integrate all of the parts into a response. The three location scores are related so that the more whole responses (W) an examinee gives, the lower the number of detailed and unusual detail responses (D and Dd, respectively) that are given. Inkblots I, IV, and V easily generate whole responses; some effort is required to provide whole responses for inkblots II, VI, VII, and VIII; and it is difficult to give whole responses to inkblots III, IX, and X. The possible interpretations are presented in the following exhibit.

Norm used	High	Low	*M*	*SD*
Exner	> 11	< 5	8.28	2.36
International	> 15	< 3	9.08	4.54
Psychiatric	> 15	< 3	9.25	4.33

Possible interpretations of a high W score:
- Holistic thinker, strives to organize to an excessive degree
- Overly ambitious
- Makes more effort than usual to integrate world into a holistic view
- Has trouble seeing the practical, the easy answers, the actions that can be taken in an economical manner
- With a low R score: Superficial, possibly casual about tasks and unconcerned about the complexities in life

Possible interpretations of a low W score:
- Unable to see the entire picture
- Easily pulled into the practical but unable to integrate the details into an overview; unable to accept ambiguity
- Perfectionistic (rejects W perception because it is not precisely correct)

DETAIL RESPONSES (D)

Detail responses focus on a major section of the inkblot that generally stands out on its own. Consequently, it represents the easy, practical, and more manageable part of the task. Responses focusing on obvious details require less processing effort than the whole responses and consequently are typically more numerous. The ratio of whole responses to detailed responses, including unusual detailed responses (W:D + Dd), is typically 1:1.3. Detailed areas are easy to distinguish on every inkblot except for Card V.

Norm used	High	Low	*M*	*SD*
Exner	> 18	< 8	12.88	3.77
International	> 18	< 2	9.89	5.81
Psychiatric	> 18	<1	9.67	6.00

Possible interpretations of a high D score:
- Tendency to emphasize the practical easy solutions, economical
- Research: Nonsupportive findings: Does not show the minimization of psychopathology in alleged sexual offenders (Wasyliw, Benn, Grossman, & Haywood, 1998)

(*Continued*)

Possible interpretation of a low D score:
■ Impractical, does not take advantage of the easily accomplishable tasks, may tend to work harder at a task than necessary
■ Research: Seen more often with adolescents (Van Patten, Shaffer, Erdberg, & Canfield, 2007)

UNUSUAL DETAIL (Dd)

The unusual detail refers to an area of the inkblot that is not commonly selected, areas that are either small or do not have obvious visual contours. A predilection for such areas implies either perfectionist meticulousness or an idiosyncratic view of the world. Unusual detail responses require considerable scanning and processing effort. The number of unusual detailed responses will, of necessity, go up in records with many responses because the examinee will have exhausted the possible responses that use the entire inkblot and the responses to the obvious sections of the inkblot. The number of unusual detail responses will also rise with the use of white space because many white space responses are coded as unusual details.

Norm used	High	Low	*M*	*SD*
Exner	>3	—	1.16	1.67
International	>8	—	3.33	3.37
Psychiatric	>7	—	2.04	3.70

Possible interpretations of a high Dd score:
■ With high R: Probably resulting from the high energy level and involvement and not from the other possible causes given below
■ Molecular view of the environment, a view that stresses the minutiae or details at the expense of seeing the global picture
■ Obsessive–compulsive and perfectionistic approach to life
■ Peculiar or unique, inclined to look at the world in a way that is different from the way others look at it
■ Guarded or mistrustful, trying to minimize ambiguities
■ With high S: Negativistic
■ Impractical, has difficulty recognizing the obvious

A low Dd score is not interpretable.

WHITE SPACE (S)

The use of white space, which results from the reversal of figure and ground, may be a healthy sign of creativeness and freedom to look at the world in a different manner. Often, however, the use of white space reflects the tendency to reverse the usual view of the world and search for ways of perceiving the environment differently from the way it was presented. White space responses (S responses) are most commonly given to Cards I and II.

Norm used	High	Low	M	SD
Exner	>3	—	1.57	1.28
International	>5	—	2.49	2.15
Psychiatric	>4	—	1.66	1.83

Possible interpretations of a high S score:
- Negativism, oppositional tendency, rebelliousness, wish to look at the world in a way that is different from the way it is presented and the way most people would see it. The tendency may be an asset or a liability depending on how it is used by the individual.
- Difficulty sustaining relationships because of the inclination to be contradictory; intolerant of the usual social compromises
- Research: Associated with lower response quality (Traenkle, 2002) and unconventionality (Petrosky, 2006), not associated with hostility (Martin, MaKinster, & Pfaadt, 1983), correlated with R (Martin, McKinster, & Pfaadt, 1983), associated with more complex perception of the environment (Tegtmeyer & Gordon, 1983)

A low S score is not interpretable.

Popular Responses (P)

A popular response is a response given to a particular card at least once in every three protocols, and it measures how conventional the examinee is. Conventionality is an important aspect of our behavior. For example, the behavior of graduate at a commencement ceremony is almost entirely predictable. The overwhelming majority of the graduating population walks across the stage, shakes the appropriate hands, and receives a diploma. And yet, in almost every commencement exercise I have attended, at least one person does something unexpected—

from coming in with a rubber duck, to displaying a flag, to doing a little dance on stage, to "mooning" the audience. The individuals displaying the unusual behaviors of course know what is expected, but they decide to call attention to themselves through the unusual gesture. Most situations in life are not so prescriptive, and there are people who truly do not know what other individuals would do in a particular situation. These are people who think in a way that is different from the way the rest of the population thinks. By looking at responses that are commonly obtained on the Rorschach, we are able to examine how conventional the person may be.

The designation of a response as a popular response is mostly dictated by the content of the response, but it goes across categories because it requires a particular location. Many P responses occur much more frequently than once in every three protocols; for example, the four-legged animal on the side of Card VIII is seen by 90% of examinees. Because P responses are so common on Cards I, III, V, and VIII, clinicians can often interpret the absence of a P response. Thirteen P responses are possible in the Comprehensive System. The P response is one of the most stable markers of the Rorschach (Exner, Armbruster, & Viglione, 1978; Exner & Weiner, 1982), but it may vary from one culture to another (Bechran, 1998; José Lelé, 2006; Sakuragi, 2006; Sangro, 1997).

Norm used	High	Low	*M*	*SD*
Exner	>9	<4	6.58	1.97
International	>8	<3	5.36	1.84
Psychiatric	>6	<2	4.41	1.66

Possible interpretations of a high P score:
- Conventional and overconforming; knows the expected behavior and is likely to comply
- Not inclined to take actions that show great independence or original thinking
- Banal, stereotyped individual
- Concerned about receiving approval from others; guarded
- Inclined to economize and give only what is needed to complete the task
- Effort to hide personally revealing information
- Research: associated inversely with a scale of rebelliousness (Greenwald, 1991) Nonsupportive findings: Does not show the minimization of psychopathology in alleged sexual offenders (Wasyliw, Benn, Grossman, & Haywood, 1998)

(continued)

> (*Continued*)
>
> Possible interpretations of a low P score:
> ■ Eccentric; may not have a good sense of what most people would do in certain situations; has trouble seeing the world as others see it
> ■ Nonconformist; has difficulty seeing the world in a conventional manner
> ■ Creative person who avoids the common and ordinary
> ■ Possible maladjustment; seen with schizophrenic individuals, obsessive–compulsive individuals, and individuals with schizotypal personalities
> ■ Inclined to make an effort to be different
> ■ Research: May be due to mental deficiency (Hertz, 1940); seen more commonly in adolescence (Van Patten, Shaffer, Erdberg, & Canfield, 2007), with a nonverbal learning disability in children (Dadario, 2002); seen with elderly people approaching death, as they lose interest in their environment

Reflections and Doubles; Egocentricity Index [(3r+(2))/R]

In Greek mythology, Narcissus saw his reflection in a pool of water and fell in love with himself. Unable to quit looking at his own image, he perished. With the Rorschach, people who give an excessive number of reflection responses and doubles are thought to have the same problem as Narcissus: Their self-esteem is too high.

The story of Narcissus notwithstanding, I have trouble seeing a direct link between an inflated self-esteem and a tendency to see reflections and doubles on the Rorschach. The literature on this subject includes many studies that did not support the validity of these markers or of the Egocentricity Index that Exner created with them (Barley, Dorr, & Reid, 1985; Belter, Lipovsky & Finch, 1989; Loving & Russell, 2000; Campos, 2009; Clausel, 1988; Duricko, Norcross, & Buskirk, 1989; Gordon & Tegtmeyer, 1982; Himelstein, 1984; Kahn, 2000; Sacco, 1990; Simon, 1985; Watson & Pantle, 1993). Moreover, reflection responses seem to be associated with the orientation of the inkblot so that such responses are most often obtained with the card rotated 90 degrees to the "portrait" position (Horn, Meyer, & Mihura, 2009). In their review of this literature, Nezworski and Wood (1995) concluded that these variables are probably unrelated to self-focus or self-esteem. I, too, recommend against using these markers.

Reflections norm used	High	Low	M	SD
Exner			.11	.43
International	> 1		.41	.88
Psychiatric	> 1		.18	.61

Doubles norm used	High	Low	M	SD
Exner	> 11	< 6	8.52	2.18
International	> 12	< 2	7.04	3.83

Egocentricity Index norm used	High	Low	M	SD
Exner	> .53	< .26	.40	.09
International	> .62	< .14	.38	.16

Possible interpretations of a high Egocentricity Index score:
- Inflated sense of personal worth
- Other research: Occurs more often with incarcerated juvenile delinquents (Dettmer, 2009), antisocial personalities (C. B. Gacono, Meloy, & Bridges, 2000; C. B. Gacono, Meloy, & Heaven, 1990), sexual homicide perpetrators, and nonviolent pedophiles (C. B. Gacono et al., 2000); associated with the criteria for narcissistic personality disorder (Hilsenroth, Fowler, Padawar, & Handler, 1997)

Possible interpretation of a low Egocentricity Index score:
- Low self-esteem

Organizational Activity

Some of the Rorschach inkblots are more easily integrated into a perception than others. For instance, most people can easily see the entire inkblot on Card V as a bat or a bird, but integrating Card X into a response that uses substantial parts of the inkblot requires more of an effort. Beck (1950) developed a system for estimating the amount of effort the examiner made to produce the responses obtained. He proposed that the organizational activity (Zf) would reveal the amount of effort the examinee was making to generate the responses. However, I have some reservations about this marker. I sometimes find it difficult to decide when segments of the inkblot identified as separate objects are *meaningfully* integrated into a response and merit, as a result, a Z score. Moreover, in most cases I am not sure what the organizational scores say about the examinee. Little recent literature on these markers is available. As a result of these considerations, I do not recommend using this marker.

Norm used	High	Low	M	SD
Exner	> 16	< 8	11.84	2.78
International	> 19	< 6	12.5	4.92

Possible interpretations of a high Zf score:
- Makes much effort in achieving goals and has a high level of intellectual striving High drive and initiative

Possible interpretations of a low Zf score:
- Expends little effort in processing information
- Possibly limited cognitive ability, depression

Developmental Quality

The Developmental Quality represents an attempt to quantify the amount of form that is demanded by a particular response. In my mind this marker (labeled *DQ*) is redundant with some of the determinants. A response that makes a reference to fire because of the color of Card IX, for instance, does not have a high form requirement and would be scored CF (as opposed to FC) as a result. I am not sure why we need another score (DQ = v) to account for the same phenomena. Moreover, much work had to be done to extricate the Developmental Quality from the Form Quality ratings (Exner, 2003); nor is it clear whether the amount of form used by the examinee is related to the perceptual ability of the individual (Ferracuti, Cannoni, Burla, & Lazzari, 1999; Gear, 1996; Ridley, 1987; S. R. Smith, Bistis, Zahka, & Blais, 2007). Although the measure has received some support (e.g., Singh, 2001; Zaccario, 2001), sometimes the expected results were not obtained (Brainard, 2005), and the literature on the subject is limited. Given all of these considerations, I cannot attach too much significance to this score.

DQ+ norm used	High	Low	M	SD
Exner	> 10		7.36	2.23
International	> 11		6.24	3.54

(Continued)

DQo norm used	High	Low	M	SD
Exner	> 19	< 9	13.58	3.67
International	> 24	< 5	14.68	6.74

DQv norm used	High	Low	M	SD
Exner	> 2	—	.98	1.26
International	> 3	—	1.09	1.50

DQv/+ norm used	High	Low	M	SD
Exner	> 1	—	.39	.61
International	> 1	—	.29	.67

Possible interpretations of a high DQ score:
- Bright individual with good perceptual organizational ability
- Research: See above

Possible interpretation of a low DQ score:
- Children, organically impaired, or intellectually limited individual
- Research: See above

Rotations

I recently tested an adolescent whose parents complained that he contradicted everything they said and disregarded all of the house rules, at times for little gain. When I gave him the first card of the Rorschach, he held it from the top and with a flip of the wrist immediately turned it upside down. Although he eventually gave me some responses with the card in the upright position, most of his responses were given with the card upside down. Like the use of the white space, rotations can be a sign of independence or indicate an oppositional attitude. An excessive number of rotations can be interpreted in a manner that is very similar to the excessive use of white space. Turning a card sideways increases the probability of a reflection response. Consequently, the card turns have to be taken into account when interpreting a high count of reflection responses.

Norm used	High	Low	*M*	*SD*
Psychiatric	> 5		1.01	1.83

Possible interpretations of a high Rotation score:
- Flexibility, curiosity, independence
- Negativism, oppositional tendency, rebelliousness, wish to look at the world in a way that is different from the way it is presented and the way most people would see it. The tendency may be an asset or a liability depending on how it is used by the individual.
- Difficulty sustaining relationships because of the inclination to be contradictory, intolerant of the usual social compromises
- Research: Sideways rotation has been associated with an increased number of reflection responses (Horn et al., 2009).

A low rotations score is not interpretable.

Reaction Time

Most clinicians have abandoned Reaction Time (RT) as a measure in the Rorschach. If reaction times are acquired with a stopwatch, the labor involved in acquiring and processing the data for information might be greater than the usefulness of the data in the majority of the cases. When the Rorschach responses are entered into a program such as Hermann, the acquisition and processing of the reaction times is automatic, and the RT measure is occasionally very useful. It has been shown that reaction times have a normal distribution and a considerable range so that some examinees have a shorter reaction time than others (Choca, Van Denburg, & Mouton, 1994). That reaction time study showed a slight gender difference, with men being a bit slower than women, but no differences were found for either age or race. The findings left no doubt that the RT measure has the qualities of an interpretable variable.

A differential RT (achromatic average minus chromatic average) indicates that it took the individual more time to respond to either the achromatic or the chromatic cards than the other. This differential could possibly be out of the ordinary when both the achromatic RT and the chromatic RT are within the normal range, but that would be very unusual. More typically, when the differential is interpretable, either the achromatic or the chromatic RT average is also out of the ordinary. When that happens, if the cause of the high RT is a long delay in one response, the averages themselves are meaningless, and the issue should be handled at the item level (see Chapter 9). Similarly, if a high total RT is due to a high achromatic or chromatic RT, with the other not being out of the ordinary, the high total RT should not be interpreted and the examiner should opt for interpreting the average reaction time that was unusual.

RT total	High	Low	*M*	*SD*
Psychiatric	> 25		12.43	8.76

Possible interpretations of a high RT score:
■ Low energy level, psychomotor retardation, depression
■ Low intellectual ability, confusion over the task
■ Obsessive laboring, having to think carefully over all possible options
■ Guardedness, distrust, having to consider how the different options will be interpreted
■ Resistance, not wanting to do the task
■ Research: higher with depressed individuals (Priyamvada et al., 2009), deprived adolescents (Bhargava & Saxena, 1995), anxious individuals (Vijayakumaran, Ravindran, & Sahasranam, 1994), sex offenders (Prandoni, Jensen, Matranga, & Waison, 1973), and railroad drivers after an accident (Sah, 1989)

A low RT score is not interpretable.
Research: Better reaction times have been found with creative people (Ramachandra, 1994).

RT Achromatic	High	Low	*M*	*SD*
Psychiatric	> 25	—	11.88	9.38

Possible interpretation of a high RT Achromatic score:
■ Having difficulty with depressing stimuli, perhaps as a result of interference from real-life issues

A low RT Achromatic score is not interpretable.

RT Chromatic	High	Low	*M*	*SD*
Psychiatric	> 28	—	12.93	10.12

Possible interpretation of a high RT Chromatic score:
■ Having difficulty with emotional stimuli, perhaps due to interference from real life issues
■ Research: higher with offspring of schizophrenic individuals (Budney, 1996)

A low RT Chromatic score is not interpretable.

RT Differential (average achromatic RT minus average chromatic RT)	High	Low	M	SD
Psychiatric	> |11|		−1.09	8.57

Possible interpretations of a high RT Differential:
- A high positive RT Differential means that the achromatic cards took considerably more time than the chromatic cards. The clinician has to check the mean RT to determine whether either of the two means was high or low; if it is, then the interpretation for that marker should be used.
- If neither mean is out of the ordinary, a *positive* RT Differential may suggest that the examinee has more trouble with stimuli that is not emotionally evoking.
- If neither mean is out of the ordinary, a *positive* RT Differential may also suggest that the examinee has more trouble at the beginning of a task (because the achromatic cards are mostly at the beginning of the Rorschach).
- If neither mean is out of the ordinary, a *negative* RT Differential may suggest that the examinee is energized by emotionally evoking situations.
- If neither mean is out of the ordinary, a *negative* RT Differential may also suggest that the examinee is likely to become fatigued or may have more trouble at the end of a task (because the chromatic cards are mostly at the end of the Rorschach).

A low RT Differential is not interpretable.

Now that we have covered the most general scores obtained from a Rorschach protocol, we can go on to examine other groups of scores, such as scores dealing with determinants (chapter 5), content variables (chapter 6), and the quality of the response (chapter 7).

The Psychogram 5

The core of the Rorschach Structural Summary is represented by the determinants. The determinants reflect the aspects of the inkblots that the examinee takes into account in formulating a response. Perhaps second only to the location of the response, the determinant scores tell us the most about how the individual approaches the world. The distribution of determinants can be placed into a bar graph or psychogram for a visual view. Figure 5.1 provides a psychogram with the expected distribution of determinants.

The highest bar of the psychogram shows the frequency of the responses that were formulated using only the shape of the inkblot. These F responses are responses without any embellishments, responses that include only the elements that are minimally required for a Rorschach response.

On the left side of the psychogram are the movement, texture, vista, and shading responses. These responses are thought to represent the individual's attention to internal psychic functions because movement, texture, vista, and shading elements are mostly not present in the inkblot. These

DOI: 10.1037/14039-005
The Rorschach Inkblot Test: An Interpretive Guide for Clinicians, by J. P. Choca

FIGURE 5.1

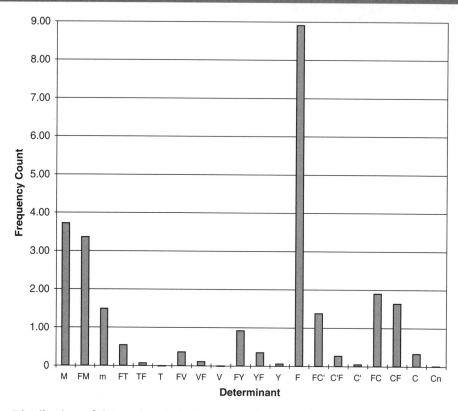

Distribution of determinants in the average protocol.
M = human movement; FM = animal movement; m = inanimate movement;
FT = form dominates texture; TF = texture dominates form; T = pure texture;
FV = form dominates vista; VF = vista dominates form; V = pure vista; FY = form
dominates shading; YF = shading dominates form; Y = pure shading; F = pure form;
FC' = form dominates achromatic color; C'F = achromatic color dominates form;
C' = pure achromatic color; FC = form dominates color; CF = color dominates form;
C' = pure color; Cn = color naming. Data from Meyer, Erdberg, & Schaffer, 2007.

determinants supposedly involve a creation on the part of the examinee, a fabrication coming from the inside of the person, as opposed to something evoked by an actual element of the inkblot. Even though some of these determinants are part of a popular perception (e.g., Card III typically elicits the response of two human figures doing something), the idea that the left side of the psychogram contains internal functions does hold out in most cases, as the research noted below demonstrates.

The right side of the psychogram contains the frequency of the responses based on the color of the inkblot, elements that are clearly part of the inkblot. Because these determinants are evoked by external material, they are likely to reflect the person's response to the outside world. The impact of color on emotion has been known since the founding of psychology and the early work of Wilhelm Wundt and Edward Titchener. Because of this association of color and emotion, these determinants are likely to speak about the person's emotional response to the environment.

The extent to which the person attends to the form of the inkblot is of great importance, even when the response includes movement, texture, vista, shading, or color. This attention to the form indicates that the person is still being guided by boundaries and, as a result, implies a certain amount of control. Let's use color as an example.

A color response may be based predominantly on the shape of the inkblot (FC), or it may be based mostly on color while the shape is still considered (CF), or it may be based entirely on color without consideration of the shape (C). These three types of responses correspond to very different kinds of behaviors. Consider, for instance, alternative responses to an emotionally charged situation, such as a serious traffic accident. The controlled FC response resembles the response of a person who acts in a reasoned and orderly manner (e.g., first doing anything necessary to prevent further accidents, checking on the well-being of the other people involved, calling for help as appropriate, giving and receiving pertinent information, and so on). While responding in this manner, the person may be very aware of his or her disappointment, sadness, anxiety, or anger, but the emotion is controlled, and the behavior is mostly dictated by reason. In contrast, the emotions are more predominant in the less controlled CF response; the individual is likely to focus on his or her experience, thinking or remarking on how terrible the situation is, focusing perhaps on the person who may have been at fault, and so on. Finally, there is the completely emotional response that has no form or control, resembling the C Rorschach response: the person comes out of the car yelling at the individual who was thought to be at fault, the person starts crying or shaking hysterically, and so on.

Several additional points can be made. First, training and social norms have a very definite influence on the control people exert over their behavior. The training of a clinical psychologist includes how to respond to emotionally charged situations or crises in the psychiatric ward, in the office, or on the phone. A dramatic example of what training and experience can accomplish was that of US Air pilot Chesley Sullenberger, who calmly informed the control tower at La Guardia Airport of the failure of both his plane engines and successfully landed the disabled plane on the Hudson River ("Bird Strike," 2009). In the language of the Rorschach, the aim of much of the emergency training of personnel is to convert possible C and CF responses into an FC response. We do want the adrenaline that the C contributes in those situations, and we would not want the unemotional uninvolved F response, even if it were possible; the training and experience serve to support the behavioral control and emphasize the form (F) part of the FC response.

There is something to be said for uncontrolled responses; an excessive amount of control is not psychologically healthy. The ideal is a balance between control and the expression of the drive. A party may not be much of a party without some loosening of controls and having people act in a spontaneous manner; Halloween is not much fun unless you wear a silly costume. In many cultures recreational drugs such as alcohol are used to help lower inhibitions. On the other hand, complete dyscontrol is disruptive, even at a party, sometimes leading to tragic events such as barroom fights or people driving under the influence. The perfect party, in Rorschach parlance, has a reasonable amount of CF but not much pure C.

Social norms clearly govern behavioral controls and the expression of emotion. What may be considered controlled behavior (FC) in one culture may be seen as loosely controlled (CF) or uncontrolled (C) behavior in another culture. The obscenities and gestures that are commonly expressed in the stands of a soccer stadium in Spain would result in arrests in Chicago. Because people are largely a product of their culture, these cultural differences do lead to different personality features and the need to have cultural Rorschach norms (see Chapter 3).

This chapter discusses all of the determinants in more detail, starting with the center of the psychogram or the F bar, and ending with a discussion of blends or responses that use more than one determinant. As in Chapter 4, a table offering possible interpretations of the Rorschach marker follows the discussion of each determinant. These possible interpretations should be considered only as hypotheses; the examiner eventually has to decide whether a specific interpretation applies to a particular examinee. It is also possible that the Rorschach marker may have an explanation that is not offered in the table. Research studies that dealt with the Rorschach marker are cited in the table, regardless of whether these studies lend support to the interpretations.

All of the determinants are used in ratios, indices, and constellations that can provide additional interpretive hypotheses. The simple ratios are covered at the appropriate place in this chapter. The more complex ratios, indices, and constellations are covered in Chapter 8. These are discussed later in order to give the reader a chance to develop an understanding of the basic variables before facing the intricacies of the more complex variables.

Lambda or Pure Form Responses

The frequency of F responses is important enough that a proportional marker has been developed to assess it efficiently. That measure, Lambda, is an index of the psychological willingness to become involved with ambiguous stimuli, and it is also an index of the person's control. Lambda is computed by dividing the frequency of the F responses by the frequency of all other responses (R); in other words, Lambda = Sum F/ (Sum R-Sum F). F responses are more likely with younger children and decrease as age increases (Ames, Learned, Metraux, & Walker, 1952; Ames, Metraux, & Walker, 1971; Exner, Thomas, & Mason, 1985).

Norm used	High	Low	*M*	*SD*
Exner	> 1	< .13	.60	.31
International	> 2	–	.86	.95
Psychiatric	> 4	–	1.25	1.98

Possible interpretations for a high Lambda score:
- Looks at the world in a simplistic way; not willing or able to see complexities
- Conservative in dealing with self and the environment; over-controlled, constricted, insecure, or fearful of involvement; unimaginative; uninvolved
- Defensive and guarded, especially if R is low, not wanting to take a risk at revealing much about himself or herself
- Looks at the world simplistically; does not notice or articulate subtleties of both the external and internal environment; unreflective
- Psychopathology: avoidant, anxious, or depressed
- Research: Seen in individuals with closed head injuries (Exner, Boll, Colligan, Stischer, & Hillman, 1996), with forensic psychiatric patients (L. A. Gacono & Gacono, 2008), with defensive forensic criminals (Conti, 2007), with violent psychopathic individuals (Franks, Sreenivasan, Spray, & Kirkish, 2009), with rapists (Dåderman & Jonson, 2008), in cocaine-dependent individuals (Pinheiro, Da Silva, Wagner, Pinheiro, Da Silva, & Souza, 2008), children with attention deficit hyperactivity disorder (Strickland, 2006; Zhong, Jing, Wang, & Yin, 2007), and veterans with posttraumatic stress disorder (Gray, 2006). Nonsupportive findings: Does not show the minimization of psychopathology in alleged sexual offenders (Wasyliw, Benn, Grossman, & Haywood, 1998).

Possible interpretations for a low Lambda score:
- Looks at the world in an overly complex manner
- Involved with stimuli to the extent that the affect disrupts the person's cognitive functions
- May be excessively open and revealing, without enough ability to inhibit impulses
- Inadequate control over emotions or inner feelings; is often a victim of own needs and conflicts
- Unable to take a detached position or ignore elements in order to focus on the most important aspect
- Difficulty maintaining satisfactory interpersonal relationships

(continued)

(*Continued*)

▪ Research: Positively correlated with self-report measures of psychopathology and clinician ratings of behavioral difficulties (Zaccario, 2001); seen with gifted children (Wideman, 1998)

Many Rorschach practitioners have been using F count or F% instead of Lambda. The interpretation of the scores is the same.

Norm used	High	Low	M	SD
Exner	> 12	< 4	7.95	2.83
International	> 16	< 1	8.92	5.34
Psychiatric	> 19	–	8.68	6.90

Possible interpretations for a high F score:
▪ Looks at the world in a simplistic way; not willing or able to see complexities
▪ Conservative in dealing with self and the environment; over-controlled, constricted, insecure, or fearful of involvement; unimaginative
▪ Defensive and guarded, especially if R is low, not wanting to take a risk at revealing much about himself or herself
▪ Psychopathology: avoidant, anxious, or depressed
▪ Research: Seen in patients with closed head injuries (Exner, Boll, Colligan, Stischer, & Hillman, 1996), with forensic psychiatric patients (L. A. Gacono & Gacono, 2008), with defensive forensic criminals (Conti, 2007), with violent psychopathic individuals (Franks, Sreenivasan, Spray, & Kirkish, 2009), with rapists (Dåderman & Jonson, 2008), in cocaine-dependent individuals (Pinheiro, Da Silva, Wagner, Pinheiro, Da Silva Magalhaes, & Souza, 2008), children with attention-deficit/hyperactivity disorder (Strickland, 2006; Zhong, Jing, Wang, & Yin, 2007), and veterans with posttraumatic stress disorder (Gray, 2006). Nonsupportive findings: Does not show the minimization of psychopathology in alleged sexual offenders (Wasyliw, Benn, Grossman, & Haywood, 1998).

Possible interpretations for a low F score:
▪ Looks at the world in an overly complex manner
▪ Involved with stimuli to the extent that the affect disrupts the person's cognitive functions
▪ May be excessively open and revealing, without enough ability to inhibit impulses
▪ Has inadequate control over emotions or inner feelings; is often a victim of own needs and conflicts
▪ Difficulty maintaining satisfactory interpersonal relationships
▪ Research: Positively correlated with self-report measures of psychopathology and clinician ratings of behavioral difficulties (Zaccario, 2001); seen with gifted children (Wideman, 1998)

Movement Responses

Movement responses are thought to reveal part of one's inner world and appear on the left side of the psychogram. In addition to that projective aspect, movement M responses involve the injection of an action into the response and consequently have an energy or dynamism that is not present in other responses.

The three types of movement (human, animal, and inanimate) reflect very different inner worlds. The human movement (M) count increases dramatically with age, as the frequency of animal movement (FM) count shows a small decrease. The net effect is that the proportion of M to FM responses changes so that, with adults, more human movement is expected than animal movement.

The scoring scheme used for all determinants except movement characterizes the amount of form used by the response. In the case of texture, for instance, responses receive different scores (FT, TF, and T) based on form considerations. This scoring scheme, however, is not followed with movement responses. The reason is that, practically speaking, all responses involving human or animal movement have a definite form demand. (It is hard to see a humanlike creature without respect to shape, even in the case of ghosts or extraterrestrials; monocellular animals can change shapes, but most of us have a shape in mind when we think of an amoeba or a paramecium.) The scoring scheme, therefore, would be applicable only for inanimate movement. Inanimate movement (m) responses without form are so seldom seen that those scores (mF and pure m) are no longer used, and the convention is to score m for what would be Fm if the usual scheme were to be used.

There is, however, a vague similarity between the movement scores and the scheme used for all of the other determinants. Even though the form of the movement responses is practically always the predominant feature, the control implied by the different movement scores varies. As discussed in the next section, the M response typically implies a good amount of control; being more infantile, FM implies more spontaneity and less control; the m points to the control being outside of the person. Consequently, to some degree one could add the movement determinants to the above discussion on form and control. In the previous example of the party, people who have a little CF and also bring a bit of FM would be ideal guests.

The interpretation of the movement responses is complicated by the fact that different kinds of movement are associated with the content of the response. In other words, the rise in the frequency of M is intrinsically tied to a concomitant rise of the number of human figures that are seen on the Rorschach. As individuals mature, they are likely to report seeing more people and more people in motion. The end result is that both of these variables (M and H) are signs of maturity and good adult functioning.

HUMAN MOVEMENT

Like all responses on the left side of the psychogram, M responses are associated with internal process (awareness and interest in one's own internal affairs). Mayman (1977) saw these responses as a representative sample of the person's inner object world, a sort of direct expression of the individual's interpersonal experience. Moreover, the frequency of M responses is typically related to the individual's capacity to think in a deliberate way and to delay gratification in order to accomplish a goal. People with good levels of M responses have been thought to have a creative imagination and to be good at problem-solving. They may show an inner stability that allows them to fall back on their inner resources at times of stress. The marker is also indicative of a good level of empathy with other human beings (Klopfer, Ainsworth, Klopfer, & Holt, 1954).

Norm used	High	Low	M	SD
Exner	>7	<2	4.30	1.95
International	>7	<1	3.73	2.66
Psychiatric	>6	<1	2.79	2.33

Possible interpretations for a high M score:
▪ Appears very mature and adultlike
▪ Intelligent, imaginative individual who is aware and purposeful in his or her actions
▪ Able to consider alternatives in problem-solving situations
▪ Able to delay gratification in the pursuit of a goal
▪ Intellectualized, unable to act before all options are taken into consideration
▪ Research: Increases after active bodily movement is inhibited (Moise, Yinon, Rabinowitz, 1988–1989); related to fantasy and intelligence (Cocking, Dana, & Dana, 1969); represents an adaptive fantasy that is useful for children in stress situations (Donahue & Tuber, 1993); associated with Jung's introverted intuitive personality type (Kopplin, 1999); associated with a 16PF scale of guilt and anxiety (Greenwald, 1991)

Possible interpretations for a low M score:
▪ Appears immature and childish
▪ Has trouble considering alternatives in problem-solving situations
▪ Functions with a trial-and-error approach
▪ Unable to delay gratification to accomplish a goal
▪ Spontaneous, showing freedom to act on the spur of the moment, less likely to think things through than to act on gut reactions and inspiration
▪ Research: Associated with attention-deficit/hyperactivity disorder (Bartell & Solanto, 1995)

ANIMAL MOVEMENT

FM responses represent internal processing that is typically available early in life. There is a tendency for the M count to increase at the expense of the FM count. Because FM is associated with early developments in the internal processing system, it is related to fantasy and spontaneity. There is also a significant relationship between FM responses and intelligence (Sommer, 1957).

Norm used	High	Low	*M*	*SD*
Exner	> 5	< 2	3.74	1.36
International	> 6	< 1	3.37	2.18
Psychiatric	> 5	–	2.57	2.08

Possible interpretations of a high FM score:
- Immaturity; the individual is likely to think and behave in ways that were more appropriate in earlier years
- Interest and thinking more likely to be related to basic needs
- Spontaneous; does not use much reflection or deliberation
- Likely to use fantasy to fulfill needs
- Unable to delay gratification in order to reach goals
- Research: Motorically impaired individuals tend to produce more FM responses (Ihanus, Keinonen, & Vanhamäki, 1992); increases during overt motor activity (Moise et al., 1988–1989)

Possible interpretations of a low FM score:
- Unable to draw from the more primitive interests and drives
- Unable to recognize basic emotional needs
- Unable to use fantasy to satisfy needs
- Possible low intellectual ability
- Research: FM responses decline with elderly people approaching death (Shimonaka & Nakasato, 1991).

HUMAN MOVEMENT:ANIMAL MOVEMENT RATIO

In theory, a good balance between the M and FM values is indicative of a person who is sufficiently mature to have the inner stability that allows the delay of immediate gratification and sufficiently self-accepting to allow the integration of personal needs with effective planning (Klopfer, Ainsworth, Klopfer, & Holt, 1954).

M > 2*FM	M = FM	FM > 2*M
Consider interpretations for high M above	Capable of deferring gratification without undo conflict or inhibition	Consider interpretations for high FM above

INANIMATE MOVEMENT

People differ a great deal in their assessment of the elements of life that they can master and the elements that are beyond their control. Some feel that they can control most important aspects of their lives; others have less of this sense of mastery. Moreover, some people are optimistic about their chances of encountering fewer uncontrollable events, or being less affected by the uncontrollable events (e.g., an earthquake is unlikely to happen, but if it does, my house is unlikely to suffer). In summary, some individuals have a sense of invulnerability, whereas others have a sense of doom.

The elements that are beyond human control are invariably the ones that make us anxious and distressed. On the Rorschach, these elements are represented by the m response. The blowing wind, the moving flames of a fire, and the explosion are common Rorschach responses that speak of forces that cannot be controlled. Although a few of those associations are common, a large number of such responses indicates that the examinee is experiencing life as unpredictable and unmanageable. In other words, the m variable is a sign of distress.

Norm used	High	Low	*M*	*SD*
Exner	>2	–	1.28	.99
International	>3	–	1.50	1.54
Psychiatric	>2	–	.87	1.36

Possible interpretations of a high M score:
- Experiences forces that are beyond one's control
- Sees the world as threatening and unpredictable
- Experiences frustration, tension, and stress
- Has a sense of impotence and helplessness
- Experiences disorganization resulting from a sense of being overwhelmed
- Pathology: anxiety disorder, hostility, suicide potential
- Research: Correlated with the anxiety and hostility scale of the Multiple Affective Adjective Checklist (Greenwald, 1990); associated with anxiety and concentration difficulties (Nesser, 2000); found with adult women in therapy with a history of parental incest (Malone, 1996); seen with self-mutilating adolescents (Kochinski, Smith, Baity, & Hilsenroth, 2008). Nonsupportive research: No elevation found in experimental anxiety-frustration study (Eells & Boswell, 1994).

A low M score is not interpretable.

ACTIVE OR PASSIVE MOVEMENT

In what is undoubtedly the most famous soliloquy of the English language, Hamlet ponders:

> To be, or not to be: that is the question: Whether 'tis nobler in the mind to suffer the slings and arrows of outrageous fortune, or to take arms against a sea of troubles, and by opposing, end them? (Shakespeare, *Hamlet,* Act 3, Scene I)

Hamlet's dilemma, also posed by the well-known Serenity Prayer, is one everyone in a problematic situation faces. As Millon (1990, 1996) has noted, taking action appeals to some personality types; other personality types favor the passive mode. This aspect of one's nature is also related to the sense of mastery or concern for uncontrollable external events discussed in the preceding section.

In addition to personality tendencies, emotional states also lead to different inclinations in terms of taking action or accepting a situation in a passive manner. For example, people who are depressed often lose their motivation to act.

The amount of active and passive movement (a:p) present on a Rorschach protocol likely reflects the approach that the examinee takes toward life and problem solving. A balanced ratio (two action responses for every passive response) implies a flexible style that allows the person to consider both active and passive solutions.

Active movement, norm used	M	SD	Passive movement, norm used	M	SD
Exner	6.44	2.23	Exner	2.90	1.64
International	4.96	3.08	International	3.73	2.65
Psychiatric	3.99	2.89	Psychiatric	1.63	1.74

a > 4*p
- Likely to respond to any situation through action, even when the action may be ineffective or inappropriate
- Has exaggerated sense of mastery
- Pathology: mania, narcissism
- Research: Nonsupportive: not related to the Extraversion Scale of the NEO Five Factor Inventory (Greenwald, 1999)

a = p
- Uncertain about behavior or problem-solving style
- Likely to be ambivalent and indecisive

(continued)

(*Continued*)

a < p
- Likely to respond to any situation through inaction, even when taking action would be more appropriate and effective
- Looks to the outside world to gratify personal needs
- Feels helpless
- Pathology: depression
- Research: Found with transsexual patients (Vermeylen, Bauwens, Lefevre, & Linkowski, 2005) and traumatized girls (Holaday, Armsworth, Swank, & Vincent, 1992). Nonsupportive research: Not found as had been expected with dependent personalities (Campos, 2009)

Texture Responses

Texture (T) responses most typically consist of furry animal skins or fluffy clouds and imply unfulfilled affectional needs. There are some data to show that individuals with one texture response (T = 1) have more secure attachments than people with higher scores (Cassella, 1999). As with all use of achromatic color, there is a depressive or painful aspect to the response. Because the T responses are not common, they are often aggregated (Sum T).

Norm used	High	Low	M	SD
Exner	> 1	–	.95	.61
International	> 2	–	.65	.91
Psychiatric	> 1	–	.44	.86

Possible interpretations of a high T score:
- Desire to be touched or be physically close to others
- Intense need for affection and dependency; sense of longing and loneliness
- Oversensitivity to rejection in interpersonal relationships
- Intense affectional needs may cloud judgment and create a vulnerability to manipulation from others
- Pathology: associated with panic disorders
- Research: Correlated with the Neuroticism Scale of the NEO-Five Factor Inventory (Greenwald, 1999); seen in patients with a history of maternal overprotection (Breecher, 1956), isolating borderline adolescents (Fowler, Brunnschweiler, Swales, & Brock, 2005), ephebophile (sexual preference for adolescent boys) priests (Gerard-Sharp, 2000). Nonsupportive research: A number of studies

(Continued)

have not supported the association of T responses with dependency or affectional needs (e.g., Campos, 2009; Scherpenisse, 2006).

Possible interpretations of a low T score:
- Uninterpretable
- Research: Lower as a group for the more severe psychopathic juveniles (Egozi-Profeta, 1999; C. B. Gacono & Meloy, 1991; Loving & Russell, 2000; Weber, Meloy, & Gacono, 1992)

Vista Responses

Vista responses involve looking at the object from afar, from another perspective, and suggest a tendency to distance oneself from events or persons in everyday life. Like the other determinants on the left side of the psychogram, the Vista (V) responses are associated with inner and introspective functions. More specifically, because they involve shading and distancing oneself, they are thought to be a sign of anxiety, discomfort, or emotional pain. Vista responses occur infrequently, and the VF and V responses can be found in less than 1% of the protocols (Exner, 2003). Consequently, these responses are also typically aggregated (Sum V).

Norm used	High	Low	M	SD
Exner	> 1	–	.28	.61
International	> 1	–	.52	.92
Psychiatric	> 3	–	.72	2.11

Possible interpretations of a high V score:
- Tendency to distance oneself from life situations
- Feelings of inferiority
- Anxiety, emotional pain; painful ruminative introspection that emphasizes the negative aspects of the self
- Tendency to be self-critical and experience guilt
- Chronic preoccupation with negative features of the self
- Possible suicidal risk
- Pathology: depression, anxiety
- Research: Correlated with the Neuroticism Scale of the NEO-Five Factor Inventory (Greenwald, 1999); seen more frequently with patients with negativistic personality traits (Trenerry & Pantle, 1990), patients who commit suicide (Exner & Wylie, 1977; Silberg & Armstrong, 1992), and traumatic injury patients (Epstein, 1998).

A low V score is not interpretable.

Form Dimension

Exner (2003) proposed that the form dimension (FD) score was a measure of a tendency toward introspection. This proposal was based on data that were never published in a peer-reviewed journal and has been questioned by others (Meyer et al., 2011). Given the limited and conflictual literature in existence, I do not support placing any emphasis on this variable.

Norm used	High	Low	M	SD
Exner	> 2	–	1.18	.94
International	> 2	–	1.02	1.19
Psychiatric	> 1	–	.28	.67

Possible interpretations of a high FD score:
▪ Likely to ruminate about the self
▪ Research: As a group, patients with a dissociative disorder scored higher than patients with a borderline personality disorder or psychotic spectrum patients (Brand, Armstrong, Loewenstein, & McNary, 2009); the FD score was higher for private college students than students from a public college (Cai & Shen, 2007). Nonsupporting research: not significant with psychopathic male juvenile delinquents (Loving & Russell, 2000)

Possible interpretations of a low FD score:
▪ Uninterpretable
▪ Research: Seen in the aftermath of traumatic brain injury (Epstein, 1998)

Shading

The shading (Y) responses represent a tendency to focus on inconsistencies of the environment. Shading responses also tend to blur the different parts or boundaries of the inkblot. Consequently, these responses are typically are associated with anxiety and the feeling of helplessness. Because m and Y represent similar issues, they are often interpreted together.

Norm used	High	Low	M	SD
Exner	> 2	–	.61	.96
International	> 3	–	1.34	1.63
Psychiatric	> 1	–	.33	.82

(*Continued*)

Possible interpretations of a high Y score:
- Anxiety
- Painful affect, feeling overwhelmed by life problems
- Depressive resignation to life events; feelings of helplessness, passivity
- Pathology: anxiety, depression, schizophrenia
- Research: Correlated with the Neuroticism Scale of the NEO-Five Factor Inventory (Greenwald, 1999); seen with people subjected to stressful noise (Nesser, 2000), pediatric leukemia survivors (Blackall, 1995), self-mutilating forensic inpatients (Mesirow, 1999), dysthymic adolescents (Weber et al., 1992), anorexic individuals (Small, Teagno, Madero, Gross, & Ebert, 1982), and emotionally disturbed adolescents (Mulder, 1997). Nonsupportive findings includes the positive correlation with the Extraversion Scale of the Eysenck Personality Inventory (De Carolis & Ferracuti, 2005), the lack of elevation found in an experimental anxiety-frustration study (Eells & Boswell, 1994), and other studies included in a review of the literature (G. Frank, 1993).

Possible interpretations of a low Y score:
- Uninterpretable
- Research: Seen with a group of "neurotic" patients (S. Mishra & Gupta, 2008), severe psychopathic individuals (Gacono & Meyer, 1991). Nonsupporting findings included the report that severe psychopathic individuals showed no difference from the less severe group (Rissi, 1998).

Chromatic Color

The most important determinant on the right side of the psychogram is color. As already noted, the color responses on the Rorschach reveal how the individual responds to emotional situations. The evoked affect can be positive as well as negative. Crumpton (1956) showed that the color cards tend to elicit more undesirable affect and aggressive content than the achromatic cards. The issue of the amount of control indicated by the person's Rorschach responses has also been discussed.

FORM-COLOR

These color responses have a predominant shape. The color is used to enhance the response.

Norm used	High	Low	M	SD
Exner	> 6	< 1	3.56	1.88
International	> 4	< 1	1.91	1.70
Psychiatric	> 3	–	1.13	1.37

Possible interpretations of a high FC score:
- Able to experience the emotion but responds in a controlled manner to the excitement
- Able to think and plan in order to respond effectively in an emotionally laden situation
- Research: Seen with Tourette's syndrome patients (Balottin et al., 2009), psoriasis patients (Demma, Cargnel, Nicolini, & Sedona, 2007), and anxiety-free college students (Greenwald, 1991).
- Nonsupportive findings: FC marker was not elevated with externalizing children and adolescents (Jacobs, 2008) or with attention-deficit/hyperactivity disorder adults (Locke, 1999).

Possible interpretations of a low FC score:
- Either does not respond emotionally or responds without enough control
- Research: Seen with victims of domestic violence (Miller, 1999) and highly deprived adolescents (Bhargava & Saxena, 1995).

COLOR FORM

For these responses the shape is less important than the color. A predominance of color form (CF) responses implies less control in an emotionally stimulating situation than the FC response, although the individual is still able to process information with some thoughtfulness.

Norm used	High	Low	M	SD
Exner	> 4	< 1	2.41	1.31
International	> 3	< 1	1.65	1.55
Psychiatric	> 4	–	1.56	1.73

Possible interpretations of a high CF score:
- Driven by the emotion to the extent that the behavior is not very effective
- Tends to be carried away by the drama to the extent that the cognitive controls play a secondary role
- Psychopathology: histrionic, borderline
- Research: Seen with impulsive or aggressive behavior (Finney, 1955; Gardner, 1951; Sommer & Sommer, 1958; Storment & Finney, 1953; Townsend, 1967), with individuals responsible for fatal traffic accidents (Lamournier & de Villemor-Amaral, 2006), with

perpetrators of domestic violence (Miller, 1999), and psoriasis patients (Demma et al., 2007); it is a poor prognostic sign for schizophrenic individuals (Exner & Murillo, 1975). Nonsupportive finding: Not found with people suffering from attention-deficit/hyperactivity disorder (Bartell & Solanto, 1995; Locke, 1999)

Possible interpretations of a low CF score:
- Either does not respond emotionally or responds in a very controlled manner

PURE COLOR

The pure C or open C responses reflect a response to emotionally evocative situations with no thoughtfulness or control involved. The prevalence of pure C responses increases with pathological groups. According to Exner (2003), only 7% of nonpatient records contain a pure C response, with the number increasing to 45% for depressed individuals, 32% for schizophrenic individuals, and 27% for patients with character disorders.

Norm used	High	Low	*M*	*SD*
Exner	> 0		.12	.37
International	> 1		.34	.66
Psychiatric	> 1		.21	.62

Possible interpretations of a high C score:
- Tendency toward impulsive and labile discharge of emotions with no regard for appropriateness
- Likely to have intense emotions
- Possibility of emotional disturbance
- Psychopathology: histrionic, borderline
- Research: Associated with domestic violence (Miller, 1999)

A low C score is not interpretable.

COLOR NAMING

Color-naming (Cn) responses—when the individual is so attracted by the color that the Rorschach task was completely disregarded—are practically never seen; when they do occur, they almost always indicate pathology. This type of response is mostly seen with individuals whose thought process is disorganized and dysfunctional. When calculating the Structural Summary and the ratios, these responses are added to the pure C responses.

Norm used	High	Low	M	SD
Exner	> 0	–	.01	.08
International	> 0	–	.02	.14
Psychiatric	> 0	–	.03	.25

Possible interpretations for a high Cn score:
- Confusion, inability to carry out the task
- Intellectual dysfunction
- Pathology: intellectual deficit, brain damage
- Disorganized and dysfunctional thought process
- Easily overwhelmed by feelings to the point that the feelings cannot be handled

A low Cn response is not interpretable.

SUM COLOR

The Sum Color (SumC) marker is the straight addition of all the color responses. It is mostly used to compare the color responses to the movement responses (see below).

Norm used	High	Low	M	SD
Exner	> 9	< 3	6.09	2.44
International	> 7	< 1	3.91	2.53

Possible interpretation of a high SumC score:
- Emotionally overresponsive
- Pathology: histrionic personality disorder
- Research: Correlated with the histrionic personality of the *DSM–IV* (American Psychiatric Association, 1994; Blais, Hilsenroth, & Fowler, 1998)

Possible interpretation of a low SumC score:
- Low level of emotionality

COLOR RATIO

The color ratio (FC: CF + C) compares the controlled color responses with those that are less controlled. The proper ratio, which indicates that the person is able to experience emotion but has a reasonable control over those emotions, has been associated with the ability to develop problem-solving strategies and benefit from feedback (Pantle, Ebner, & Hynan, 1994).

FC > 2 * (CF + C)	2 * FC < CF + C
May be overly constricted emotionally and have little contact with emotions	Weak control over emotions; the person is labile and overreactive
	Risk of impulsive responding to emotional situations or aggressive acting out
	Affect likely to be poorly modulated, unrestrained, and disorganized
	May have little regard for the adaptiveness or effectiveness of the emotional response
Research: Better treatment prognosis with schizophrenic individuals (Stotsky, 1952)	Research: Seen with incarcerated men (Siemsen, 1999) and in individuals who live with domestic violence (Miller, 1999)

WEIGHTED COLOR SUM

The weighted color sum (WSumC) composite was created to emphasize problems with emotional dyscontrol when they exist. This composite groups all of the color responses together but gives more weight to the responses that reflect less control. The calculation is done as follows: WSumC = 0.5*FC + CF + 1.5*C.

Norm used	High	Low	*M*	*SD*
Exner	> 7	< 2	4.36	1.78
International	> 6	–	3.11	2.17
Psychiatric	> 5	–	2.40	2.00

Possible interpretations of a high WSumC score:
- Likely to be overemotional and to seek external stimulation
- Consider interpretations for high CF and C responses above
- Research: Correlates with the Extroversion Scale of the Eysenck Personality Inventory (De Carolis & Ferracuti, 2005), seen with people who are suggestible and easy to hypnotize (Brenman & Reichard, 1943; Linton, 1954; Steisel, 1952), seen with individuals with panic disorder and agoraphobia (de Ruiter & Cohen, 1992)

Possible interpretations of a low WSumC score:
- Tendency not to be emotional or affectively responsive to outside stimulation
- Research: Seen with individuals with Asperger's disorder and emotional problems (Holaday, Moak, & Shipley, 2001), seen with chronic pain patients (Lorentz, 1995) and children and adolescents who sustained severe burns (Holaday, 1998)

OTHER RATIOS

Several other ratios are used to compare the two sides of the psychogram, such as Experience Actual, Experience Balance or Erlebnistypus, Experience Base, and Experienced Stimulation. Those ratios are covered in Chapter 8.

ACHROMATIC COLOR

Because black is a color, some people may use the blackness of the inkblots in their responses while giving an appropriate number of color responses. For those individuals, the achromatic color responses should be seen as just an extension of their use of color and should be interpreted as part of their emotional response to the environment. When color responses are not present, however, the use of black can be indicative of a toned-down response to color—in other words, an individual who can respond emotionally only in a watered-down manner. Finally, it should be clear from a cursory look at funeral homes that the color black is associated with sadness and morbidity.

ACHROMATIC COLOR SUM

The norms show that examinees typically give one achromatic color response per record. Because of their relatively low frequency, all of the achromatic responses are typically added together into one variable: Sum C' = FC' + C'F + C'.

Norm used	High	Low	M	SD
Exner	> 3	–	1.49	1.16
International	> 4	–	1.75	1.71
Psychiatric	> 2	–	.84	1.37

Possible interpretations of a high Sum C' composite in the absence of an adequate number of color responses:
- Gloomy attitude, presence of negative affect
- Pessimistic attitude
- Psychopathology: negativism, depression

A low Sum C' composite is not interpretable.

Blends

To begin the last section of this chapter, let us consider the thinking process of people discussing an important national issue, such as high immigration rates. Some argue for a simple solution that typically will not work because it leaves many factors out of consideration (e.g., all undocumented immigrants should be deported). In contrast, there are those who want to consider so many aspects at the same time that issue becomes too complex to handle effectively (e.g., the impact of immigration on the economy and crop growers and the impact of deportation on family integrity and welfare and the effect on international relationships and on national systems such as education, taxes, and Social Security and the political consequence of taking a position on this issue). For many tasks, the deferral of action until all angles were covered would result in never taking action at all. More useful than either of those extremes is the thinking process that takes enough factors into consideration to handle a portion of the problem in a reasonably adequate way, even if it is clear that some issues remain. A productive thinking process is neither too simplistic nor too complex.

At this point we have talked about the determinants as if there was only one determinant per response. In actuality, however, approximately 20% of Rorschach responses are *blended,* and have more than one determinant (Exner, 2003). The number and kinds of blends that appear on a record give valuable information about the complexity of the thinking process of that individual.

A blended determinant implies that the individual can appreciate the complexity of the inkblot and is aware that more than one aspect of the inkblot contributed to his or her thinking in a particular response. One issue associated with blends is intellectual capacity: People who are more capable have a better ability to recognize the aspects of the inkblot that suggested the response and to communicate those aspects to the examiner. Research with blends has shown, for instance, that they occur more often with gifted children (Wideman, 1998), with peace negotiators showing integrative complexity (Tibon, 2000), and with children who are more advanced in the Piagetian level of development (Gear, 1996). In reasonably intelligent individuals, the number of blends speaks about the expansiveness or narrowness of their thinking, the flexibility of the person's thinking, and whether they search to discover the variables that influenced their thinking on a response or are content with fulfilling the minimal requirement. For instance, the blended determinant count has been correlated with the Openness to Experience Scale of the NEO-Five Factor Inventory (J.-M. Petot, 2005). Finally, the complexity of the response may also be a measure of the stress, needs, and conflicts experienced by the individual: The more uncomfortable people are in their lives, the higher the level of complexity that is shown in their thinking. Because of the discomfort issue, the color-shading blends have received more attention in the psychological literature than the other possible blends.

Norm used	High	Low	M	SD
Exner	> 8	< 3	5.15	2.08
International	> 8	–	4.01	2.97
Psychiatric	> 4	–	1.54	1.89

Possible interpretations of a high blend score:
- Overly complicated thinking and psychological operations
- Disorganization, confusion, and unpredictability due to overload
- Psychopathology: mania, schizophrenia
- Research: seen with individuals showing a low Lambda on the Rorschach (Konishi, 2003). Nonsupportive studies: not seen with defensive forensic individuals (Conti, 2007), not helpful in a fake-good experimental condition (W. Wood, 2000)

Possible interpretations of a low score:
- Thinking is too narrow; tendency to neglect or ignore the richness and complexity of the environment
- Repression, constriction, guardedness
- Psychopathology: depression
- Research: Seen with depressed adolescents (G. N. Goldman, 2001). Nonsupportive findings: Does not show the minimization of psychopathology in alleged sexual offenders (Wasyliw, Benn, Grossman, & Haywood, 1998)

COLOR-SHADING BLEND

A color-shading blend is one that has a color determinant (FC, CF, or C) and either an achromatic color (FC', C'F, or C'), or a shading (FT, TF, T, FV, VF, V, FY, YF, or Y) determinant. The rationale for this clustering is that these responses combine signs of emotionality (the color) with signs of depression and pain (the achromatic color and shading).

Norm used	High	Low	M	SD
Exner	> 1	–	.45	.68
International	> 1	–	.60	.92
Psychiatric	> 0	–	.23	.31

Possible interpretations of a high color-shading score:
- Thinking process is too complex as a result of anxiety or depression
- Psychopathology: depression
- Research: Seen with suicidal children (D. Petot, 2005)

Interpretation of a low color shading score is not interpretable.

Content 6

I n the film *Take the Money and Run* (Joffe & Allen, 1969), Woody Allen's psychologist becomes quite alarmed when Allen claims to see two elephants making love on a Rorschach card. The camera then moves behind Allen to show the image on the card. The joke was that Allen was indeed looking at a drawing of two elephants copulating.

Nonspecialists typically see the content of the Rorschach response (in the Woody Allen film, the two elephants copulating) as the basis for interpretation. To the Rorschach clinician, however, the content has a minor role in comparison with other variables. Moreover, the content issues are generally examined in a quantitative manner and not in the qualitative way the public would conceive of them. This chapter explores content from a quantitative point of view; a qualitative approach to Rorschach responses is discussed in Chapter 9.

According to Paul Lerner (1991), "there is no area of Rorschach analysis that has been more misused and more underused than content" (p. 145). The theoretical work on

DOI: 10.1037/14039-006
The Rorschach Inkblot Test: An Interpretive Guide for Clinicians, by J. P. Choca

content by people like Mayman (1977) and Phillips and Smith (1953) has been all but forgotten. In fact, there are embarrassingly few articles that deal with content; as a result, this chapter cites mostly theoretical positions.

The Comprehensive System recognizes 29 content categories. Some of these categories are seldom used, and the meaning of most of the categories is unclear. This chapter focuses on the two most important categories: the human and the animal contents. (Other important categories, namely, food, clothing, and somatization, are touched on at the end of the chapter.)

For both human and animal responses, three distinctions are made in both the scoring and interpretation. The distinctions are between a response that involves the entire figure, a response that involves part of the figure, and an association to a figure that is not quite real. The latter, the fantasized figure, can also be seen in whole or in part. The end result is four different scoring categories for both human and animal responses that can be compared and interpreted. Figure 6.1 shows the distribution

FIGURE 6.1

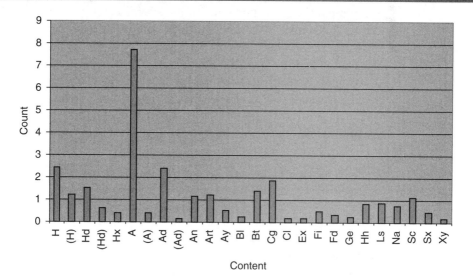

Distribution of the content categories.
H = pure human; (H) = fictional human; Hd = part human; (Hd) = fictional part human; Hx = Human Experience; A = pure animal; (A) = fictional animal; (Ad) = fictional part animal; An = Anatomy; Art = Art; Ay = Anthropology; Bl = Blood; Bt = Botany; Cg = clothing; Cl = Cloud; Ex = Explosion; Fi = Fire; Fd = Food; Ge = Geography; Hh = Household; Ls = Landscape; Na = Nature; Sc = Science; Sx = Sex; Xy = Xray. Data from Meyer et al., 2007.

of the content categories, including human and animal responses, using data from the International Norms.

Human Responses

The number of human responses to the Rorschach inkblots increases until the age of 10 and then remains stable through the life span (Ames, Metraux, & Walker, 1971). All adults are expected to give some human responses. When those are not obtained, it is almost imperative to investigate the finding further, possibly with the Testing the Limits procedure (see Chapter 2), in order to interpret the response correctly.

Generally, the perception of humans is associated with the examinee thinking about people, having the capacity to recognize others as separate entities, and having the ability to establish and maintain good interpersonal relationships. Draguns, Haley, and Phillips (1967) showed that the frequency of human responses is associated with cognitive development and the potential for social relationships. However, there appears to be no relationship between the sense of security in interpersonal attachments and the number of human responses to Rorschach inkblots (Duberstein & Talbot, 1993). There is a positive relationship between the frequency of human contents and treatment response (R. Goldman, 1960; Halpern, 1940; Morris, 1943; Piotrowski & Bricklin, 1961; Stotsky, 1952). Successful treatment has also led to an increase in the number of human responses seen on the Rorschach (Rosso, 2004).

PURE HUMAN

The pure human [H] is the best of the possible human responses in that it typically demands an integration of different parts of the inkblot. A reasonable number of pure human responses suggests that the person thinks about other people with reasonable frequency. Exner (2003) also interpreted the pure human responses as reflecting a healthy self-concept, but the literature appears less supportive of that interpretation.[1]

---

[1]Exner (2003) showed that the number of H increases with the number of overall responses but, because this is invariably true of all scores, it is unclear why that issue would be more relevant with human responses. He repeatedly also emphasized that introversive individuals have higher H scores. Because the label means that Sum M was substantially higher than WSumC, this emphasis is simply highlighting the very obvious relationship between M and H.

Norm used	High	Low	M	SD
Exner	> 5	< 2	3.21	1.71
International	> 5	< 2	2.43	1.89
Psychiatric	> 4	< 2	2.08	1.85

Possible interpretations of a high H count:
- Possibly too interested in interpersonal relationships at the expense of other areas
- May derive too much of his or her self concept from the opinion of others

Possible interpretations of a low H count:
- Not interested or knowledgeable about human interactions
- Distant or separated from others. A private person, this individual is likely not to have a strong and effective social network.

FICTIONAL HUMAN

The fictional human response suggests an unrealistic view of oneself and others. It represents a fanciful or imaginary perception at the expense of the actual characteristics. The fictional human [(H)] response refers to a humanlike figure that is not quite real. The (H) score is mostly interpreted as part of a sum or a ratio.

Norm used	High	Low	M	SD
Exner	> 2	–	1.22	1.02
International	> 3	–	1.22	1.24
Psychiatric	> 2	–	1.78	1.34

PART HUMAN

This score [Hd] is mostly interpreted as part of a composite or a ratio (see Interpersonal Interest sum below). The statistics, however, are as follows:

Norm used	High	Low	M	SD
Exner	> 2	–	.84	1.02
International	> 4	–	1.52	1.71
Psychiatric	> 4	–	1.38	2.31

FICTIONAL PART HUMAN

This score [(Hd)] is mostly interpreted as part of a composite or a ratio (see Interpersonal Interest sum below). The statistics, however, are as follows:

Norm used	High	Low	*M*	*SD*
Exner	> 1	–	.21	.50
International	> 2	–	.64	.92
Psychiatric	> 1	–	.29	.70

INTERPERSONAL INTEREST SUM AND RATIO

The sum of all responses that are associated with human forms, whether in whole, in part, in a fictional form, or some combination of any or all of these, is referred to as the Interpersonal Interest Sum and is denoted as follows: [H + (H) + Hd + (Hd)]. It indicates the interest the examinee has in other human beings and his or her tendency toward human affiliations.

Norm used	High	Low	*M*	*SD*
Exner	> 8	< 3	5.49	1.75
International	> 11	< 1	5.83	3.51
Psychiatric	> 9	–	3.59	4.03

Possible interpretations of a high Interpersonal Interest Sum:
- Possibly too interested in interpersonal relationships at the expense of other areas
- May derive too much of his or her self concept from the opinion of others

Possible interpretations of a low Interpersonal Interest Sum:
- Not interested or knowledgeable about human interactions
- Research: Seen more commonly with children experiencing disruptions in caregiving and attachment (McCarroll, 1998); seen with criminals (Walters, 1953), juvenile delinquents (Ray, 1963; Richardson, 1963), and schizophrenics (Sherman, 1952; Vinson, 1960)

The pure human score is compared to the fictional or part human responses to give the *Interpersonal Interest Ratio,* denoted as follows: H: (H) + Hd + (Hd). This ratio emphasizes the more real and holistic view and experience with others. Both sides of the ratio are expected to be about equal.

High H [> 2:1]	High: (H) + Hd + (Hd) [< 1:2]
Able to see others as distinct entities	Possible unrealistic perception of others
Able to establish and maintain interpersonal relationships	May have fantasized and unrealistic expectations of interpersonal interactions
Experiences people as a whole rather than in fragmented parts	May represent a distancing of the self from others in that other people are only seen in part, or as unreal figures
Research: No studies available	

Animal Responses

Generally, it is easier to see animals on the Rorschach than any other content. Individuals who give a large number of animal associations to inkblots might be inclined to make little effort in the different tasks in their lives. (There is a very high correlation between the number of animal responses and the number of overall responses [Sommer, 1957], partly because in order to give a large number of responses the individual has to see a high number of animals.) Another consideration is that children, of course, are more attracted to animal perceptions than any of the other content categories. The number of animal responses appears to increase up to the age of 13, when roughly half of the Rorschach responses involve animals, and then tapers off (Cotte, 1958). A high number of animals given by an adult would indicate immaturity or lack of social development and sophistication.

PURE ANIMAL

As was true of the human response, the pure animal response [A] is the most highly developed of the possible animal responses. This count is typically translated into a percentile so that A% = Sum A/R. According to Kottenhoff (1965), A% measures stereotyped thought processes, immaturity of temperament, and lack of interest.

Norm used	High	Low	M	SD
Exner	> 11	< 5	7.96	2.25
International	> 12	< 3	7.71	3.18
Psychiatric	> 12	< 3	7.68	3.30

Possible interpretations of a high A count:
- Immature, infantile individual
- Tends to take the easy road without making enough of an effort
- Research: Has a correlation of .63 with depression (Kottenhoff, 1965). Nonsupportive findings: Children and adolescents raised in an environment of enduring interpersonal violence did not show a higher level of A responses (Kamphuis, Turn, Timmermans, & Punamäki, 2008).

Possible interpretations of a low A count:
- Interpretation will depend on what other content area is taking the place of the animal responses.
- Research: Seen with intelligent individuals (Kottenhoff, 1965)

FICTIONAL ANIMAL

This score (A) is mostly interpreted as part of a sum or a ratio (see below). The statistics, however, are as follows:

Norm used	High	Low	M	SD
Exner	> 1	–	.27	.54
International	> 1	–	.42	.73
Psychiatric	> 2	–	.65	1.05

PART ANIMAL

This score [Ad] is mostly interpreted as part of a sum or a ratio (see below). Seeing part of an animal involves a focus on certain elements at the expense of perceiving the entire entity.

Norm used	High	Low	M	SD
Exner	> 4	< 1	2.30	1.20
International	> 5	–	2.41	1.97
Psychiatric	> 3	–	1.34	1.71

FICTIONAL PART ANIMAL

This score (Ad) is mostly interpreted as part of a composite or a ratio. The statistics, however, are as follows:

Norm used	High	Low	M	SD
Exner	> 1	–	.10	.50
International	> 1	–	.16	.45
Psychiatric	> 1	–	.10	.36

FICTIONAL SUM

The summation of all the fictionalized figures provides a measure of how often the individual uses fantasized images and is expressed as follows: (H) + (Hd) + (A) + (Ad).

Norm used	High	Low	M	SD
Psychiatric	> 4	–	1.42	2.26

Possible interpretations of a high Fictional Sum:
- Has trouble relating to the outside world in a real manner
- Needs to distance the world by portraying people and animals as unreal
- Research: No studies found.

A low fictional sum is not interpretable

The Fictional Ratio, expressed as [(H) + (Hd): (A) + (Ad)], examines the mythological or fictionalized human figures in comparison to the animal figures.

Psychiatric norm	M	SD
Human fictional	.83	1.58
Animal fictional	.58	1.09

Possible interpretation of a high human Fictional Ratio
[(H) + (Hd) > 2 *((A) + (Ad))]:
- Has trouble relating to humans in a real and effective manner

Possible interpretation of a high animal Fictional Ratio
[2* ((H) + (Hd)) < (A) + (Ad)]
■ Infantile
■ Has trouble seeing humans and relates to the world in a childish manner

Whole versus Parts Ratio compares the human and animal whole responses to those where only a part was used and is expressed as follows: H + (H) + A + (A): Hd + (Hd) + Ad + (Ad). There are indications that the prevalence of part responses decreases with age (Beizmann, 1957), so an elevation of this marker can be seen as a sign of immaturity.

Psychiatric norm	*M*	*SD*
Whole	8.76	.68
Parts	2.42	3.62

Possible interpretation of a high wholes [> 3:1] ratio:
■ Has trouble seeing the finer details of interactions
■ May relate in a superficial and unsophisticated manner
■ Research: No studies found.

Possible interpretation of a high parts (< 1:3) ratio:
■ May not be able to relate to people or animals as whole objects

Art

The perception of Art (Art) is theoretically associated with a superficial view of the world that emphasizes looks rather than substance. It is often given in responses where the form of the inkblot is less important than another determinant or the over-all impression.

Norm used	High	Low	*M*	*SD*
Exner	> 2	–	.90	.91
International	> 3	–	1.22	1.45
Psychiatric	> 2	–	.36	.82

(continued)

Possible interpretations for a high Art count:
■ Distancing from the experience
■ Focus on external appearances
■ With a low F% or form-based responses (e.g., FC, FC', FT), low level of control

A Low Art count is not interpretable.

Anthropology

The anthropological content (Ay) is associated with having historical or cultural issues in mind. This content may be associated with an interest in learning or an intellectualized view of the world.

Norm used	High	Low	M	SD
Exner	> 1	–	.08	.52
International	> 2	–	.52	.87
Psychiatric	> 1	–	.06	.26

Possible interpretations for a high Ay count:
■ Intellectualization
■ Self-conscious attempt to impress with knowledge

A low Ay count is not interpretable.

Blood

The presence of blood (Bl) is suggestive of injury, danger, or damage. Since it involves a perception in which the form is less important than another determinant, typically color, it is related to controls.

Norm used	High	Low	M	SD
Exner	> 2	–	.90	.91
International	> 3	–	1.22	1.45
Psychiatric	> 2	–	.36	.56

Possible interpretations for a high BI count:
- Feeling in danger, vulnerable, damaged
- Response to traumatic injury or experiencing a traumatic situation
- Sadistic or masochistic pleasure in injuring self or others

A low BI count is not interpretable.

Explosion

This type of response suggest aggressive forces that are out of control. An explosion (Ex) can also be associated with power, excitement, or danger. It is helpful to the flavor of the response (e.g., fireworks may be attached to excitement whereas a nuclear explosion is more damaging and threatening).

Norm used	High	Low	*M*	*SD*
Exner	> 1	–	.20	.40
International	> 1	–	.19	.48
Psychiatric	> 1	–	.14	.45

Possible interpretations for a high Ex count:
- Feeling out of control as in exploding in anger
- Feeling in danger, vulnerable
- Attraction toward danger and excitement

A low Ex count is not interpretable.

Fire

The perception of fire (Fi) invariably places a premium on another determinant, typically color, rather than form. To interpret the response correctly, the clinician has to look beyond the lack of form. Some fires are perceived as being under control (e.g., the exhaust of a space shuttle on Card II), whereas others may not be (e.g., a forest fire on Card IX).

Norm used	High	Low	M	SD
Exner	> 1	–	.20	.40
International	> 1	–	.19	.48
Psychiatric	> 1	–	.14	.45

Possible interpretations for a high Fi count:
- Feeling out of control, as in fiery temper
- Attraction toward danger or excitement

A low Fi count is not interpretable.

Sex

Sex responses (Sx) suggest an interest in sexual matters or possibly sexual confusion. Because sexual matters are not usually brought up with strangers, the topic is sometimes raised for attention or effect.

Norm used	High	Low	M	SD
Exner	> 1	–	.11	.47
International	> 2	–	.47	.94
Psychiatric	> 2	–	.30	1.11

Possible interpretations for a high Sx count:
- Concerned or preoccupied about sexual matters
- Result of sexual trauma
- Sexualized provocativeness, poor internal controls
- Psychopathology: serious decompensation or sexual disturbance, hypomanic or manic state

A low Sx count is not interpretable.

Food

Food (Fd) responses are typically associated with dependency.

Norm used	High	Low	M	SD
Exner	> 1	–	.21	.47
International	> 1	–	.33	.66
Psychiatric	> 1	–	.29	.68

(Continued)

Possible interpretations of a high Fd count:
■ Individual is dependent and needy
■ Inclined to rely on others for direction and support
■ May expect others to be tolerant of their needs
■ Research: Seen more commonly with children experiencing disruptions in care-giving and attachment (McCarroll, 1998); predictive of weight loss in a treatment program (Elfhag, Rössner, Lindgren, Andersson, & Carlsson, 2004). Nonsupportive: Contrary to expectation, it is not seen at all with dependent individuals (Campos, 2009; Stephenson, 1996).

A low Fd count is not interpretable
Research: Seen with panic disorder patients with agoraphobia (de Ruiter & Cohen, 1992)

Clothing

Associations with clothing (Cg) are (in theory, at least) believed to denote a superficial view of the world that emphasizes looks rather than substance.

Norm used	High	Low	*M*	*SD*
Exner	> 3	–	1.41	1.09
International	> 4	–	1.89	1.77
Psychiatric	> 2	–	2.08	1.85

Possible interpretations of a high Cg count:
■ Attention to appearances, superficial image
■ Heavy protective clothes (e.g., shields, armor) may indicate a feeling of vulnerability.
■ Using clothes for disguise may indicate distancing or distrust.
■ Research: Nonsupportive: Children and adolescents raised in an environment of enduring interpersonal violence did not show a higher level of clothing responses (Kamphuis, Turn, Timmermans, & Punamäki, 2008).

A low Cg count is not interpretable.

Isolation Index

The Isolation Index groups all of the nonsocial content categories [II = (2*Cl + 2*Na + Bt + Ge + Ls) / R], and the thinking is that people who focus on those ideas are inclined to isolate themselves. The index has been found to have no correlation with the Social Introversion Scale of the Minnesota Multiphasic Personality Inventory (Simon, 1989).

Norm used	High	Low	M	SD
Exner	> .34	< .06	.19	.09
International	> .41	–	.20	.14
Psychiatric	> .33	–	.12	.14

Possible interpretations for a high Isolation Index score:
- May be withdrawn and alienated
- Research: Seen with residential sexually abused children (Black, 2003) and sexual offending adolescents (Csercsevits, 2000); predictor of violence among conduct disordered adolescents (Reilly, 2002). Nonsupportive: Not found with disruption of caring and attachment in adolescents (McCarroll, 1998)

A low Isolation Index score is not iinterpretable.
Research: Nonsupportive: Not correlated with either the Openness to Experience or Agreeableness scales of the NEO-Five Factor Inventory (Greenwald, 1999)

Somatization

Both of the somatization content areas (Anatomy and Xray) are uncommon. In many Rorschach protocols, there are no such responses. Adding up both of these content areas (An + Xy) gives a count of the interest or preoccupation with the bodily functions.

Norm used	High	Low	M	SD
Exner				
International	> 3	–	1.34	1.54
Psychiatric	> 2	–	.71	1.26

Possible interpretations for a high somatization composite:
- Concerned with bodily functions
- Possible rumination about medical status
- Possible sense of vulnerability
- Research: No studies found

Possible interpretations for a high somatization composite:
- Uninterpretable

Form Quality and Special Scores

7

If you don't think too good, don't think too much.

—*Ted Williams (Boston Slugger)*

A psychology trainee treating a paranoid schizophrenic patient under supervision thought of a bright idea. His delusional patient believed that the FBI was watching him. The patient saw parked cars with people in them in front of the hospital and was convinced that these people were part of a surveillance system aimed at him. The trainee's idea was to take the patient into the street and help him interview the people in the cars. The patient could then convince himself that those people were there for other reasons. The trainee even had a name for the new type of therapy he sought to develop: reality therapy. He argued that the problem with delusional individuals was that they concocted psychotic ideas and never gave themselves the chance to check them out.

The trainee's enthusiasm eventually won over the concerns of the more experienced staff. The trainee was actually allowed to take the patient into the street and have him talk with the people in the cars. Helped by the very

DOI: 10.1037/14039-007
The Rorschach Inkblot Test: An Interpretive Guide for Clinicians, by J. P. Choca

articulate trainee, the patient asked all of his questions and, surprisingly, was able to obtain answers. The trainee's euphoria unfortunately did not last long. Back in the ward, the patient explained to him that FBI agents were very well trained and that one could not expect the agents watching him to tell the truth. Obviously the patient had assimilated the new information into his thinking schemata, but not in the way the trainee had foreseen. Now the patient needed to make some assumptions about the FBI that he did not need before, but once that assimilation was accomplished, the belief system could remain intact. And that was how the trainee's version of reality therapy gained its rightful place in the crowded graveyard of failed psychotherapeutic approaches.

As the trainee learned, the problem with delusions is not that the person does not have a chance to check the reality of the situation, but rather that reality is distorted to fit the fairly immutable convictions the person already has. We can be very creative in our rationale for twisting reality in whatever way serves our needs.

Psychotic patients typically do not reveal themselves well in interviews or personality questionnaires. Whereas patients with anxieties or depressions can accurately tell what ails them, psychotic patients cannot. They do not recognize that their thinking may be disorganized or hard to follow, they may not be aware of how other people judge their ideas, or they may firmly believe that people who disagree with them are wrong. If the patient is delusional and the delusion is plausible (e.g., the business partner is stealing from him, the husband is having an affair), accurate diagnosis may be difficult. It is with this patient population that the Rorschach excels.

The Rorschach is an excellent tool for examining the thinking process of an individual (see Kleiger, 1999). Perhaps the most dramatic and helpful protocols are those that clearly demonstrate a thought process disturbance. Determining whether individuals are delusional is much harder with the Rorschach; however, the presence of a clear thought disturbance coupled with possible delusional thinking argues in favor of a diagnosis of psychosis. Two caveats have to be kept in mind, however:

1. An individual may be delusional and not have a thought disorder. In other words, he or she may hold a very erroneous and irrational conviction while his or her thinking has remained logical, sequential, and free of oddities. This is not very common; however, the current diagnostic system does make provisions for this particular kind of delusion disorder.
2. Many people have a thought disorder and are not psychotic. Thought disorder is possible, even expected, with bipolar affective

disorder (D. Mishra, Kumar, & Prakash, 2009; Osher & Bersudsky, 2007; Serper, 1993; Tai, Haddock, & Bental, 2004). People with other diagnoses, such as attention-deficit/hyperactivity disorder, autism, borderline personality disorder, and anxiety disorders, may also demonstrate a thought disturbance (Abramowitz & Deacon, 2005; Caplan, Guthrie, Tang, Neuchgterlein, & Asarnow, 2001; Lee, Kim, & Kwon, 2005; O'Connell, 1986; Ulloa et al., 2000; van der Gaag, Caplan, van Envgeland, Loman, & Buitelaar, 2005). Moreover, some people who have a thought disturbance do not have any psychiatric disorder.

Identifying a thought disorder is very helpful, even if it does not have a direct diagnostic link. When the Rorschach shows that the person has trouble thinking logically, or that the person's mentation is disorganized, the test is actually revealing a great deal about the person's functioning and how ineffective he or she is in daily life. A person who mixes boundaries, contaminating one perception with another (e.g., the wing of one animal becomes the head of another in the same response), does the same in everyday life, combining two different positions on an issue at the same time. The inability to think in a clear and logical manner is an obvious detriment in the person's capacity to function effectively.

Two types of Rorschach scores are used to examine the thought process: Form Quality and Special Scores.

Form Quality

The Form Quality of the response (FQ score) addresses how well the response complies with the shape of the inkblot. To examine the Form Quality, the clinician takes all of the responses into consideration or selects one particular type of response (e.g., responses that use white space or responses having human movement [M] as determinant). This discussion will start with the Form Quality for the entire protocol (referred to as X) and then proceed to examine other subsets.

POSITIVE FORM QUALITY

The Positive Form Quality (FQx+) response is one of unusually high perceptual quality. Even in excellent protocols of bright individuals, this quality of response is rare.

Norm used	High	Low	M	SD
Exner	> 2	–	.71	.88
International	> 1	–	.21	.68

Possible interpretations of a high FQx+:
- Perceives the world in a highly realistic and overly conventional manner
- Likely to be hypernormal, inflexible, rigid, overly conventional
- In being very conventional, the individual sacrifices creativity and individuality
- Psychopathology: paranoia, depression

A low FQx+= is not interpretable.

ORDINARY FORM QUALITY

Because FQx+ responses are typically infrequent, they are often considered together with ordinary Form Quality (FQxo) responses under the label X+%. Even with the nonpsychiatric population, it is very unusual for a person to have an X+% of 100. According to Exner (2003), the nonpsychiatric average is 77%, and patients with schizophrenia have a mean of 53%. There is a significant negative correlation between X+% and the white space (S) count, suggesting that these are inverse measures of conventionality (Traenkle, 2002). The X+% variable can be helpful in distinguishing between individuals with a borderline personality from schizophrenic patients (Peters & Nunno, 1996), psychotic individuals from nonpsychotic individuals (Peterson & Horowitz, 1990), or substance abusers from nonpsychiatric individuals, the latter suggesting that the substance abusers are more pathological than the nonpsychiatric population (Vanem, Krog, & Hartman, 2008). Children with enuresis score lower than non-enuretic children (Lottenberg Semer & Yazigi, 2009), and children with attention-deficit/hyperactivity disorder also score lower (Zhong, Jing, Wang, & Yin, 2007) on this measure.

Norm used	High	Low	M	SD
Exner	> 21	< 11	16.44	3.44
International	> 16	< 6	11.11	3.74

Possible interpretations of a high FQxo:
- Perceives the world in a realistic and well-grounded manner
- May be hypernormal, inflexible, rigid, overly conventional

> (*Continued*)
>
> ■ In being very conventional, the individual sacrifices creativity and individuality
> ■ Research: Nonsupportive: Not found to be different between schizophrenic and nonpsychiatric groups in Barcelona (Campo, 2000)
>
> Possible interpretations of a low FQxo:
> ■ Perceives the world in an unusual manner
> ■ Perceptions not always consistent with reality
> ■ Unique but at the expense of being able to function in a conventional world
> ■ Psychopathology: cognitive dysfunction, schizophrenia, other form of thought disorder

UNUSUAL FORM QUALITY

Unusual Form Quality (FQxu) responses are perceptions that are seldom seen but that are judged to comply with the shape requirement of the inkblot, in other words, a response that could be seen by others. One issue that is raised by these responses is the extent to which they represent a disregard for convention. Some responses may actually be very creative, so they should not always be taken as less desirable than the ordinary standard.

Norm used	High	Low	*M*	*SD*
Exner	> 6	–	3.49	2.03
International	> 12	–	6.20	3.93

Possible interpretations of a high FQxu score:
■ Tendency to be individualistic
■ Possible disregard for convention and social expectations
■ May have frequent conflicts with others as a result of an unconventional nature
■ Research: Seen more often with sexually offending clergy (G. P. Ryan, Baerwald, & McGlone, 2008), or with adults referred for evaluations of a learning disability or an attention-deficit/hyperactivity disorder (Jones, 2004), or with adolescent boys with disruptive behaviors (Pinto, 1999)

Possible interpretations of a low FQxu score:
■ Uninterpretable
■ Research: Seen with motorists responsible for fatal traffic accidents (Lamounier & de Villemor-Amaral, 2006)

MINUS FORM QUALITY

The variable Minus Form Quality [FQx-] represents responses that disregard the shape of the inkblot. X-% has been shown to be higher with substance abusers than nonpsychiatric individuals (Vanem et al., 2008), suggesting that the substance abusers are more pathological than nonpsychiatric individuals. The perceptual inaccuracies of schizophrenic individuals appear to be related to an inability to filter extraneous information (Perry, Geyer, & Braff, 1999). Individuals who are addicted to opiates and who also suffer from posttraumatic stress disorder have more responses of poor form than addicted individuals who do not suffer from posttraumatic stress disorder (Johnson, 2008).

Norm used	High	Low	M	SD
Exner	> 3	–	1.56	1.20
International	> 9	–	4.43	3.23

Possible interpretations of a high FQx-:
- There is a substantial distortion of reality, enough that the person will have a significant impairment in functioning.
- Psychopathology: schizophrenia, depression, other groups as seen below
- Research: Commonly seen with schizophrenic individuals (Neville, 1995). Other psychiatric groups that have shown perceptual inaccuracies have included children who were prenatally exposed to cocaine (Wagreich, 2008), learning disabled children (Harper & Scott, 1990), bulimic individuals (J. E. Smith, Hillard, Walsh, Kubacki, & Morgan, 1991), sexually abused children and their siblings (Esmail, 1997), hospitalized adolescents (Cragnolino, 2001), and adolescent boys with disruptive behaviors (Pinto, 1999). Nonsupportive evidence: Some studies have not found schizophrenic individuals to score higher (Campo, 2000, Felger, 1996). Transsexual adolescents do not differ significantly in this area from nonpsychiatric individuals (Cohen, de Ruiter, Ringelberg, & Cohen-Kettenis, 1997)

A low FQx- score is not interpretable.

MINUS QUALITY OF WHITE SPACE RESPONSES

The portion of the Form Quality responses that uses white space is referred to as the S-% variable. When this variable has a high percentile, distortions of reality more likely result from anger and negativism than from schizophrenia.

Norm used	High	Low	*M*	*SD*
Exner	> 1	–	.25	.56
International	> 2	–	.87	1.15

Possible interpretations of a high S-%:
- Negativism and anger may be causing a distortion of reality
- Research: Commonly seen in an inpatient adolescent sample (Cragnolino, 2001)

A low S-% is not interpretable.

FORM QUALITY OF HUMAN MOVEMENT RESPONSES

With the typical examinee, the form quality of the responses is the same throughout the protocol. However, sometimes the quality of the responses suffers or improves as the examination progresses (see Chapter 9), and for some examinees the form quality may be different for the achromatic and chromatic cards. It is sometimes useful to compare the form quality of the human movement responses (MQ) to that of the entire protocol. If there were to be a difference in quality between human movement responses and other responses the clinician would have to determine why the human movement responses are of a higher or lower quality than the rest.

MQ+ norm used	High	Low	*M*	*SD*
Exner	> 1	–	.44	.68
International	> 1	–	.12	.43

MQo norm used	High	Low	*M*	*SD*
Exner	> 6	–	3.57	1.84
International	> 4	–	2.26	1.66

MQu norm used	High	Low	*M*	*SD*
Exner	> 1	–	.21	.51
International	> 2	–	.69	.99

MQ- norm used	High	Low	*M*	*SD*
Exner	> 1	–	.07	.27
International	> 2	–	.63	1.05

Special Scores

As discussed above, the FQ score has to do with whether the Rorschach response fits the shape of the inkblot. There are other disturbances of the thinking process that impede good reasoning and that do not involve perceptual inaccuracies. The examinee who saw a butterfly with five testicles on Card II was seeing the usual butterfly at the bottom of the card and had an explanation for the small bumps that are typically disregarded by others. In terms of perceptual accuracy, this response was at least as good if not better than the usual butterfly response. However, the response indicates a problem with the person's thinking (i.e., the explanation of small details in bizarre sexual terms). The Special Scores category of scores is used to flag those instances of faulty reasoning and classify them so that clinicians can describe the kind of life problem the person may demonstrate with his or her thinking. Practically any instance of a Special Score is worth interpreting.

To interpret the Special Scores well, the clinician must consider both quantitative and qualitative aspects. An attempt has been made to blend these two through the use of levels. A Level 1 Special Score (e.g., Deviant Verbalization 1 [DV1]) reflects a minor slippage of the thought process, whereas Level 2 (e.g., DV2) is considered to be more serious. Nevertheless, the clinician still has to consider the kind of thinking process slippage reflected by the finding in order not to overpathologize the individual. A certain person, for instance, may be inclined to overemphasize adjectives, repeatedly describing perceptions with redundant adjectives (e.g., the tiny little bird, the big huge monster). If this is done often, the Special Scores count would be bumped to a very pathological level, even though the infraction of the thinking process may be minor.

R-PAS added a number of Special Scores. This system differentiates two kinds of aggressive responses to separate movement responses from content responses. Three other Special Scores have been added from the literature. The Mutuality of Autonomy—Health (MAH) is scored when "two objects are mutually and autonomously engaged in a reciprocally interactive activity" (Meyer et al., 2011, p. 129). The Mutuality of Autonomy—Pathology (MAP) is scored when an agent or response object is destructive. The Oral Dependence Language (ODL) is scored when verbalizations "are linguistically linked to oral activity and content or interpersonal passivity and dependence" (Meyer et al., 2011, p. 130).

R-PAS distinguishes between *Cognitive Codes* (Deviant Verbalizations or DV, Deviant Response or DR, Incongruous Combination or INC, Fabulized Combination or FAB, Peculiar Logic or PEC, and Contamination or CON) and *Thematic Codes* (Abstract Representation or ABS, Personal Knowledge Justification or PER, Aggressive Movement or AGM, Aggressive Content or AGC, Morbid Content or MOR, Cooperative Movement or COP, Mutuality of Autonomy—Health or MAH, Mutuality of Autonomy—Pathology or MAP, Good Human Representation or GHR, Poor Human Representation or PHR, and Oral Dependency Language or ODL). The Cognitive Codes address the quality of the examinee's thinking, and the way that thinking is communicated. In contrast, the Thematic Themes suggest ideas that are prevalent in the examinee's mind.

One advantage of a performance task like the Rorschach is that it is harder for an examinee to artificially portray a misleading personal image than it would be with a questionnaire. Faking bad on this test is more likely to affect the Special Scores than any of the other measures of the test. It is difficult for an examinee to determine how to artificially change the global scores or the determinants since those variables are interpreted as composites, or even to visualize the advantage of manipulating the responses to change those values. Rather, what often happens in fake bad situations is that the examinees add bizarre wording or unusual themes to their responses. It is therefore important to keep that issue in mind when interpreting certain Rorschach protocols.

COOPERATIVE MOVEMENT

The Cooperative Movement (COP) score is the only Special Score of the Rorschach that is typically a sign of health. When it appears more frequently than expected, however, it must be evaluated in light of other issues. Protocols that also contain an excessive number of aggressive (AG) responses suggest interpersonal problems. The same may be true for protocols showing an excessive number of S responses or a low FQ.

At times a COP response is spoiled by the introduction of an aspect that does not have the same implications for health. One response to Card III may be that two people are in a conflict, which is seen as suggested by the red details of the inkblot. When that material is added to the popular COP response of two people performing a useful task together, the appraisal of the response changes drastically. Soares (2002) showed that more of these spoiled COPs occur with hospitalized psychiatric patients than with nonpatients. COP and AG responses, where both COP and AG were present in the same response, were found to be more frequent with sexually abused adolescent girls when compared to nonabused girls (Ornduff, Centeno, & Kelsey, 1999).

Cultural issues with this variable include the finding that African Americans give fewer COP responses than do White Americans. This finding may suggest that African Americans do not anticipate cooperative interactions with others as a routine event and may feel that members of society are less likely to be responsive to their needs (Presley, Smith, Hilsenroth, & Exner, 2001). Preadolescent children were also found to give fewer COPs than expected (Hamel, 2000).

Norm used	High	Low	M	SD
Exner	> 4	–	2.00	1.38
International	> 2	–	1.07	1.18
Psychiatric	> 1	–	.31	.71

Possible interpretations of a high COP count:
- Likely to be outgoing and have a positive approach to interpersonal relations
- May be perceived as trustworthy, cooperative, and easy to work with
- Positive sign that suggests significant strength, unless spoiled in some way (see comments above)
- Favorable prognosis in psychotherapy
- Research: Correlated with prosocial helping behavior in an experimental study (Alexander, 1995)

Possible interpretations of a low COP count:
- Uninterpretable
- Research: Seen more commonly with children experiencing disruptions in caregiving and attachment (McCarroll, 1998) and sex-offending adolescent males (Csercsevits, 2000). Non-supportive evidence: Children and adolescents raised in an environment of enduring interpersonal violence did not show a lower level of COP (Broeking, 2008; Kamphuis, Turn, Timmermans, & Punamäki, 2008).

ABSTRACT CONTENT

An Abstract Content (ABS) score is typically obtained by individuals who have trouble looking at the world in a clear and logical manner. One type of ABS response is a formless response that typically has M as determinant and human experience (Hx) as content (e.g., "This card represents depression"). The other type of ABS response has a form, such as the response to Card III as a heart that represents the love between the two individuals. (This content score may be a sign of creativity in some individuals; it does not necessarily imply pathology.)

Norm used	High	Low	M	SD
Exner	> 1	–	.16	.43
International	> 1	–	.32	.82
Psychiatric	> 1	–	.23	.76

> (*Continued*)
>
> Possible interpretations of a high ABS count:
> ■ Thought process may be amorphous and unclear, with the person having trouble reasoning in a clear and stepwise fashion.
> ■ This individual may be guided by emotions (check color responses) to the extent that the thought process is too intuitive and does not have enough logic.
>
> A low ABS count is not interpretable.

AGGRESSIVE RESPONSES

Exner's Aggressive response scoring (AG) requires aggressive movement to be present (e.g., an angry person or a bomb exploding). This type, of response may be too restrictive to be helpful, and other Rorschach scorings for aggression have been developed (e.g., Elizur, 1949; C. B. Gacono, Bannatyne-Gacono, Meloy, & Baity, 2005; Holt, 1977). Borrowing from that work, R-PAS distinguishes between Aggressive Movement (AGM), following the Exner guidelines for the AG score, and Aggressive Content (AGC). The AGC Special Score can be used to code any content that is perceived as "dangerous, harmful, injurious, malevolent, or predatory" (Meyer et al., 2011, p. 138). Such content includes weapons, animals that are dangerous to humans, animal parts associated with potential threat such as claws, dangerous environmental forces such as tornadoes, or predatory creatures such as Dracula. In scoring such content the clinician has to distinguish between what the examinee may have perceived as aggressive (e.g., a squid with tentacles) and the nonaggressive use of the content (e.g., a squid as an appetizer). The information in this book applies only to the score of the Comprehensive System.

The AG score was positively correlated with self-reported aggressive potential in college students (Mihura, Nathan-Montano, & Alperin, 2003). Bulimic individuals have been found to have more AG responses than nonbulimic adolescents (J. E. Smith et al., 1991).

Norm used	High	Low	*M*	*SD*
Exner	> 2	–	1.11	1.15
International	> 1	–	.54	.86
Psychiatric	> 1	–	.31	.87

(*continued*)

(*Continued*)

Possible interpretations of a high AG:
■ Likely to view interpersonal interactions as marked by competition or aggression
■ Interactions with others likely to be at least competitive and forceful, if not aggressive and hostile
■ May be identifying with the aggressive action or images, or may be fearful of external dangers
■ Research: Seen more commonly with children experiencing disruptions in caregiving and attachment (McCarroll, 1998). Nonsupportive findings: Physically and sexually abused children do not give a higher number of AG responses (Broeking, 2008; Holaday, Armsworth, Swank, & Vincent, 1992); not seen with women accused of physical child abuse and neglect (Cyrulnik, 2000).

A low AG is not interpretable.

COLOR PROJECTION

Color Projection (CP) responses, the ascription of a chromatic color to an achromatic area of the inkblot, is just as unusual as color-naming responses (see Chapter 5). The response suggests a denial of unpleasant emotions (those evoked by the blackness of the inkblot) and an attempt to substitute those emotions with more pleasant feelings.

Norm used	High	Low	M	SD
Exner	> 0	–	.01	.09
International	> 0	–	.02	.15
Psychiatric	> 0	–	.01	.09

Possible interpretations of a high CP count:
■ Denial of irritating or unpleasant emotions
■ Difficulty dealing with negative feelings
■ Tendency to distort reality in order to deal with negative feelings
■ Lack of insight
■ Psychopathology: hysterical personality, conversion reaction
■ Research: No relevant studies could be found.

A low CP count is not interpretable.

CONTAMINATION

The Contamination (CON) score is given when two or more impressions are fused into one response, so that one response overlaps with another (e.g., the fusing of the popular butterfly with the face on Card I). This score is the most pathological of the inappropriate combination Special Scores.

Norm used	High	Low	*M*	*SD*
Exner	> 0	–	.00	.00
International	> 0	–	.02	.15
Psychiatric	> 1	–	.17	.59

Possible interpretations of a high CON count:
- Likely to mix different concepts together in a pathological manner
- May demonstrate trouble with boundaries and an inability to differentiate and keep separate different ideas or attributes

A low CON count is not interpretable.

DEVIANT VERBALIZATIONS

Deviant Verbalizations (DVs) represent inaccuracies of expression that, when they occur frequently, take away from the person's ability to communicate properly. They consist of neologisms (e.g., "Some bacteria you may see under a telescope") and redundancies (e.g., "a trio of three people"). DVs can be scored at two levels (DV1 and DV2), but even DV2s are probably the least pathological of the Special Scores.

DV1 norm used	High	Low	*M*	*SD*
Exner	> 3	–	.59	.78
International	> 2	–	.65	.99
Psychiatric	> 1	–	.05	.33

DV2 norm used	High	Low	*M*	*SD*
Exner	> 0	–	.00	.06
International	> 0	–	.01	.14
Psychiatric	> 1	–	.13	1.01

Possible interpretation of a high DV count:
- Does not communicate effectively with others
- May appear odd because of some of the words or expressions used
- Egocentric—functions with the apparent belief that others can almost read his or her mind (and know what is meant) even when it is not said

A low DV count is not interpretable.

DEVIANT RESPONSE

Deviant Responses (DRs) are comments that distort the task during the Rorschach administration and consist of two types: inappropriate phrases (e.g., "These could be crabs, but they are not in season") and circumstantial responses (e.g., "This could be a map of Italy, but I don't know much about Italy. I know much more about Cuba.") Because they are a distortion of the task at hand, these instances are a sign of serious mental mismanagement. DRs can be scored at two levels (DR1 and DR2).

DR1 norm used	High	Low	M	SD
Exner	> 3	–	.59	.78
International	> 2	–	.65	.99
Psychiatric	> 1	–	.05	.33

DR2 norm used	High	Low	M	SD
Exner	> 0	–	.00	.06
International	> 0	–	.01	.14
Psychiatric	> 1	–	.13	1.01

Possible interpretations of a high DR count:
- Mentation problems: difficulty staying on task when doing a job; likely to become involved with issues that are extraneous to the task
- Trouble maintaining adequate ideational control
- Thinking is likely to be unfiltered, scattered, and disjointed
- May have trouble with impulse control

A low DR count is not interpretable.

FABULIZED COMBINATIONS

Fabulized Combinations (FAB) are bizarre comments that reflect a significant disregard for reality. They are of two types: implausible relationships between two objects (e.g., "two tigers attacking a submarine") or transparencies (e.g., "two people on an exercise machine, and you can see their hearts pumping"). FABs can be scored at two levels (FAB1 and FAB2).

FAB1 norm used	High	Low	M	SD
Exner	> 1	–	.27	.52
International	> 1	–	.45	.76
Psychiatric	> 1	–	.07	.30

(*Continued*)

FAB2 norm used	High	Low	*M*	*SD*
Exner	> 0	–	.03	.16
International	> 0	–	.08	.31
Psychiatric	> 0	–	.04	.26

Possible interpretations of a high FAB count:
- Likely to show a disregard for reality in daily life
- Thinking may be subject to serious distortions.
- May demonstrate impaired judgment due to poor reality testing

A low FAB count is not interpretable.

INAPPROPRIATE LOGIC

The Inappropriate Logic (ALOG; referred to as Peculiar Logic or PEC in R-PAS) score is used when a spontaneous comment demonstrates an illogical justification for a response, typically on the basis of the placement (e.g., "This must be lettuce because it is next to the rabbit").

ALOG norm used	High	Low	*M*	*SD*
Exner	> 0	–	.04	.20
International	> 0	–	.16	.46
Psychiatric	> 0	–	.08	.33

Possible interpretations of a high ALOG count:
- Thinking process is likely to show illogical reasoning.
- Illogical thinking may be more likely to take place when emotions are involved (check color responses).

A low ALOG count is not interpretable.

INCONGRUOUS COMBINATIONS

Incongruous Combinations (INC) are implausible features that are attributed to a single object (e.g., the *butterfly with five testicles*). They can be scored at two levels (INC1 and INC2).

INC1 norm used	High	Low	*M*	*SD*
Exner	> 1	–	.56	.78
International	> 2	–	.73	.97
Psychiatric	> 1	–	.15	.48

(*continued*)

(Continued)

INC2 norm used	High	Low	M	SD
Exner	> 0	–	.02	.13
International	> 0	–	.10	.33
Psychiatric	> 0	–	.08	.37

Possible interpretations of a high INC count:
- Likely demonstrates bizarre and strained and logic
- May reflect a preoccupation that seriously interferes with the person's thought process

A low INC count is not interpretable.

MORBID CONTENT

Responses coded as Morbid (MOR) include dead or damaged content or a dysphoric attribution to that content (e.g., something characterized as *gloomy* or *sad*). The implication is that the person is feeling damaged or depressed (or both). This variable has a significant correlation with AG content on the Rorschach (Baity & Hilsenroth, 2002) and with the depressive affect seen on the Personality Assessment Inventory (Petrosky, 2005).

Norm used	High	Low	M	SD
Exner	> 2	–	.79	.89
International	> 3	–	1.26	1.43
Psychiatric	> 2	–	.50	1.20

Possible interpretations of a high MOR content count:
- Feels damaged, inferior, or unwanted
- Likely to emphasize negative features about the self
- May see environment as hostile, dangerous, or damaging
- Concerned or preoccupied with negative occurrences such as illness or death
- May have a history of adversities or setbacks
- Pessimistic view of the self and the future
- Expressed enjoyment may indicate an identification with the aggressor
- Psychopathology: posttraumatic stress disorder, depression
- Research: seen with people in treatment for obesity (Elfhag, Barkeling, Carlsson, Lindgren, & Rössner, 2004), psoriatic patients as a result of the "damaged" image of themselves (Demma et al., 2007), women who were victims of paternal incest (Malone, 1996), self-mutilating adolescents (Kochinski, Smith, Baity, & Hilsenroth,

(Continued)

2008), and persons reporting interpersonal difficulties (Schneider, Huprich, & Fuller, 2008). Nonsupportive findings: Marker did not correlate with the Neuroticism Scale of the NEO-Five Factor Personality Inventory (Greenwald, 1999) or with Minnesota Multiphasic Personality Inventory-2 scales (Siemsen, 1999); the marker was not altered in simulated child custody evaluations (Kennelly, 2002); it could not differentiate sexual offenders against minors with rapists of adults (Cohan, 1998).

A low MOR content count is not interpretable.

PERSEVERATION

The Perseveration (PSV) score shows a preoccupation with an issue, an inability to move on after a particular concept has entered the thinking process. The PSV score is used when two almost identical responses are given in a card, or when a previous response is reexamined while the person is responding to a different card, or when the person repeats the same response across different cards.

Norm used	High	Low	*M*	*SD*
Exner	> 0	–	.07	.25
International	> 1	–	.23	.56
Psychiatric	> 2	–	.47	1.20

Possible interpretations of a high PSV count:
- Possible intellectual impairment
- Person may become preoccupied with a concept to the extent that it interferes with the ability to function
- Could be the result of a defensive tactic to stay with one association so that other associations do not need to be given. Possibly a sign of a lack of effort in the tasks the person performs in life
- Research: Partial support for the usefulness of this measure was found with adolescents (Zaccario, 2001).

A low PSV count is not interpretable.

PERSONAL RESPONSES

About half of the adults taking the Rorschach support at least one of their responses with a personal experience, and children give more Personal (PER) responses than adults (Exner, 2003). The PER response represents a way of assuring oneself about the response (as though to provide reassurance that the figure is familiar); it also has an egocentric quality, however, in that the person is basically saying that the response is what it is "because I say so."

Norm used	High	Low	M	SD
Exner	> 2	–	.92	.91
International	> 2	–	.75	1.12
Psychiatric	> 2	–	.45	1.18

Possible interpretations for a high PER response count:
- May be in need of self-assurance in life tasks
- Likely to be egocentric in interactions with others
- May alienate others because of the frequency and forcefulness with which opinions are expressed
- May be indicative of a grandiose, egocentric, or narcissistic quality
- Research: seen more often with mentally ill incarcerated psychopathic individuals scoring high on the Psychopathy Checklist–Revised (Siemsen, 1999), male incarcerated psychiatric patients likely to be violent (Young, Justice, & Erdberg, 1999), or highly psychopathic felons (C. B. Gacono, Meloy, & Heaven, 1990).

A low PER response count is not interpretable.

SIX SPECIAL SCORE SUM

The Six Special Score Sum (Sum6) is a compilation of the count of the six most prominent Special Scores (DV, DR, INC, FAB, CON, and ALOG). This sum is considered to be a good measure of the frequency of slippage in the thinking process.

Norm used	High	Low	M	SD
Exner	> 4	–	1.91	1.47
International	> 6	–	2.75	2.39
Psychiatric	> 3	–	.72	1.79

Possible interpretations of a high Sum6:
- Indicative of a thought disorder
- A tendency for the thought process to be disrupted by extraneous and egocentric intrusions, even if the person is able to see reality in an accurate manner
- Psychopathology: psychosis, schizophrenia
- Research: No relevant studies found

A low Sum6 is not interpretable.

LEVEL 2 SPECIAL SCORES

Special Scores for which a Level 2 is possible—DV, DR, INC, and FAB—are summed to provide the Level 2 (Lvl-2) Special Scores measure. Needless to say, any Lvl 2 score is a bad sign; the higher the score, the more severe the problem.

Norm used	High	Low	M	SD
Exner	> 0	–	.06	.25
International	> 1	–	.25	.62
Psychiatric	> 1	–	.21	1.07

Possible interpretations of a high Lvl-2 score:
- Probable thought disorder
- A tendency for the thought process to be disrupted by extraneous and egocentric intrusions, even if the person is able to see reality in an accurate manner
- Psychopathology: psychosis, schizophrenia

A low Lvl-2 score is not interpretable.

WEIGHTED SUM6

The weighted summary of the six special scores consists of all of the variables of Sum6 but weights the count by the level of the response. In other words, a response scored as DV1 would be counted as 1, and a response scored as DV2 would be counted as 2.

WSum6 can be used to distinguish psychotic from nonpsychotic individuals (Peterson & Horowitz, 1990). The measure has been found to be significantly higher with alcoholic individuals, and even higher with schizophrenic individuals, when these groups were compared with a control group (Vanem et al., 2008). WSum6 can distinguish psychotic individuals from those suffering from a dissociative identity disorder (Brand, Armstrong, Loewenstein, & McNary, 2009).

Norm used	High	Low	M	SD
Exner	> 10	–	4.48	4.08
International	> 19	–	7.63	7.75
Psychiatric	> 13	–	2.68	7.05

(continued)

(*Continued*)

Possible interpretations of a high WSum6:
- Probable thought disorder
- A tendency for the thought process to be disrupted by extraneous and egocentric intrusions, even if the person is able to see reality in an accurate manner
- Psychopathology: psychosis, schizophrenia
- Research: occurs more often with child custody litigants (Bonieskie, 2000), learning disabled children (Brainard, 2005), and hospitalized adolescents (Cragnolino, 2001)

A low WSum6 is not interpretable.

Composites, Complex Ratios, Indices, and Constellations

8

> Any intelligent fool can make things bigger and more complex . . . It takes a touch of genius—and a lot of courage—to move in the opposite direction.
>
> —*Albert Einstein*

In interpreting a Rorschach protocol, it is often useful to group, compare, and contrast different scores or to add scores together that are thought to measure different aspects of the same construct. These contrasts or groupings are referred to as *composites, ratios, indices,* and *constellations*. Some of the simpler ratios were already introduced in previous chapters (e.g., the ratio comparing Whole [W] to Detail in Chapter 4; Human Movement [M] to Animal Movement in Chapter 5). This chapter focuses on ratios, indices, or constellations that are complex in terms of both the logic and the calculations involved.

Complex Rorschach ratios, indices, and constellations are not necessarily more or less useful than simple ratios. For example, the Experience Balance or Erlebnistypus compares the sum of the M score with a weighted sum of the Color responses and is considered to offer an insight into a person's approach to life or style of problem-solving, a finding that can make a good contribution to our understanding of the person. Although these ratios, indices, and constellations do not include any information that has not been

DOI: 10.1037/14039-008
The Rorschach Inkblot Test: An Interpretive Guide for Clinicians, by J. P. Choca

already covered in this book, they may serve to highlight some of the findings in useful ways.

Complex markers raise concerns that should be examined. Even if they enjoy some empirical support, these markers take the examiner away from what is arguably the strength of the Rorschach—the clinician's ability to observe how the individual performs an ambiguous task. Moreover, complex markers typically ascribe one meaning to the different scores involved, even though many of the Rorschach scores can be interpreted in more than one way. Consider, for instance, the Aspirational Index, which takes the W score as a measure of the person's aspiration and M as a measure of psychological resources. However, many other interpretations of the W score are possible (see Chapter 4). If one were to interpret the W count for a particular individual as having some other meaning, then the entire rationale for the Aspirational Index becomes untenable.

Composites and Ratios

This chapter discusses ratios that deal with global scores, ratios from the psychogram, ratios dealing with content, and so on.

EXPERIENCE ACTUAL

The Experience Actual (EA) theoretically represents the person's reactivity, the ability to deal with both the inner and outer world. It is expressed as EA = Sum M + WSumC, where Sum M is the addition of all human movement responses and WSumC is the Weighted Color sum.

Norm used	High	Low	M	SD
Exner	> 11	< 5	8.66	2.38
International	> 12	< 2	6.84	3.76

Possible interpretations of a high EA composite:
- Dilation, capacity to adapt and problem-solve

Possible interpretations of a low EA composite:
- Coarctation, limited resources; coping and problem-solving are ineffective
- Possibly intellectually limited
- Guarded or defensive
- Pathology: depressed or inhibited

EXPERIENCE BALANCE

The Experience Balance (EB), also known by the German word *Erlebnistypus*, represents the relationship between human movement and the weighted sum of the chromatic color responses (Sum M:WSumC). All M and C responses, with the exception of the color naming (Cn) responses, are included in the contrast. This ratio contrasts the extent to which the person is internally oriented as opposed to being responsive to external stimuli. When the value on the left of this ratio is 4 or more points higher than the value on the right, the person is said to have an *introversive style*. When the value on the right is 4 points or higher than the value on the left, the person is said to be *extratensive*. The person who is neither introversive nor extratensive is said to be *ambitensive*.

None of these styles is intrinsically preferable to the others, and none of the styles makes the person more vulnerable to having emotional problems. However, the styles represent very different psychological approaches to life, and each has advantages and disadvantages. The EB is relatively stable with adults, but there may be substantial shifts from one style to another in childhood and early adolescence.

Introversive Sum M > 3 + WSumC	Ambitensive	Extratensive Sum M + 3 < WSumC
Oriented toward the use of inner experience	More flexible in interpersonal relationships	Directs energy toward outside
Likely to satisfy basic needs through intellectual pursuit or fantasy life	Does not have a ready-made approach to coping and may be more likely to vacillate when problem-solving	Likely to satisfy basic needs through interactions with the environment
Cautious, deliberate, and not very physically active	Behavior likely to be more unpredictable or inconsistent than the other styles	Spontaneous; readily reacts to external events
Approaches problem-solving by thinking about the situation and reviewing possible alternatives; unlikely to act prior to reaching an understanding of the situation; thinks more than acts	May be inefficient in problem-solving situations as a result of the above attributes	Approaches problem-solving through trial and error
Attempts to control feelings		Intuitive, likely to use feelings by merging feelings with thinking
Likely able to delay gratification		Has difficulty delaying immediate gratification
Pathology: obsessive–compulsive, dependent, or schizotypal personality; depression	Pathology: bipolar	Pathology: histrionic personality, bipolar manic

EXPERIENCE BALANCE PERVASIVE

The Experience Balance Pervasive (EB Pervasive or EBPer) composite is a measure of the strength of the preferred problem-solving style. It is calculated by dividing the larger of the two sides of the EB by the smallest. Thus, it is either Sum M/WsumC, or WsumC/Sum M. When this composite is 2.5 or greater, the finding indicates a very pervasive style. The preceding exhibit provides a description of the styles.

EXPERIENCE BASE

The Experience Base (eb) ratio compares all nonhuman movement (animal movement [FM] and inanimate movement [m]) determinants to the sum of all shading (Y), texture (T), vista (V), and achromatic color (C') determinants and is expressed as follows: Sum (FM + m): Sum (C' + T + Y + V). The left side of the ratio reflects immature, disorganized, and out-of-control tendencies. The right side of the ratio comprises the response to the gray–black features of the inkblot and is likely to reflect pain and disharmony.

Sum FM + m > 5: C' < 6	Sum FM + m < 6: C' > 5
Immature problem-solving Worried, nervous Pathology: anxiety	Experiencing pain Pathology: depression

EXPERIENCED STIMULATION

The Experienced Stimulation (es) composite is thought to reflect disorganization and the effect of forces that are beyond the person's control. It is calculated by adding together the two sides of the eb ratio: Sum (FM + m) + Sum (C' + T + Y + V).

Norm used	High	Low	M	SD
Exner	> 12	> 4	8.34	2.99
International	> 16	> 2	9.09	5.04

Possible interpretation of a high es composite:
- Low frustration tolerance
- Disorganization, sense of helplessness
- Difficulty being persistent on important tasks
- Pathology: anxiety, depression

Possible interpretation of a low es composite:
- Good tolerance to frustration

DIFFERENCE SCORE

The Difference (D) score is thought to represent the extent to which the person can tolerate frustration. The D score is the difference between the amount of organization and psychological resources the person has, as reflected by EA, and the amount of chaos and helplessness experienced, as represented by es; in other words, D = EA − es. The D composite is then converted to a standard score by means of a table. A low frustration tolerance is the result of the high-scoring es person having limited ability to handle stress.

Norm used	High	Low	M	SD
Exner	>1	<1	−.01	.97
International	>2	<2	−.68	1.48

Possible interpretations of a high D score:
- Has more resources than necessary to deal with the current level of stress
- Overemphasis on being economical
- Tendency to back away from effort

Possible interpretations of a low D score:
- Feels overwhelmed and unable to deal with current stress
- Impulsive and poorly focused, tendency toward disorganization
- Tense, irritable
- Low frustration tolerance
- Pathology: schizophrenia

ADJUSTED D

The Adjusted D (Adj D) is calculated by subtracting the Adjusted es from EA and then converting the result to a standard score by means of the same table used to calculate the D score. In other words, the Adj D is the D score that has been adjusted to take out the effect of current stress.

Norm used	High	Low	M	SD
Exner	>1	<1	.15	.82
International	>1	<1	−.20	1.23

Possible interpretations of a high Adj D score:
- The level of psychological resources is well in excess of the demands experienced by the individual.
- Capacity for control and tolerance for stress

(continued)

(*Continued*)

Possible interpretations of a low Adj D:
- The level of psychological resources is not sufficient to cope with stressful situations.
- Difficulty adjusting to new or stressful situations
- Prone to become distracted, disorganized, impulsive

CONSTRICTION RATIO

The Constriction ratio compares the inhibition or internalization of emotion (Sum C′) to the expression of such emotion (WSumC), so the ratio is Sum C′:WSumC. When emotions are inhibited excessively, the tactic theoretically becomes a painful and disorganizing burden for the individual.

Sum C′ > WsumC	Sum C′ < WSumC
May be inhibiting the release of emotion excessively May experience irritation and other discomforts because of the emotional restraint	Uninterpretable

Indices

The CS has a number of composite variables that are referred to as indices. These are described below.

ASPIRATIONAL INDEX

The Aspirational Index (W:M) denotes a comparison of the person's goals with the resources necessary to achieve them. For this ratio, the W represents the person's aspirations because it is an attempt to integrate everything presented to the person into one construct; the M stands for the person's psychological resources.

3 (or higher): 1	1 (or lower): 1
Overstriver: High aspirations in an individual who does not have the psychological resources to achieve those goals	Understriver: Low aspirations in an individual who would have the necessary resources to strive higher

COMPLEXITY INDEX

The Complexity Index (CI) is a measure of how complex the individual's thinking is, at least as measured by his or her use of determinants. The CI is computed as the proportion of blends in the record: number of Blends/R. (For a discussion of Blends, see Chapter 5.)

High (> .4)	Low (0)
Overly complicated thinking and psychological operations	Thinking is too narrow
Disorganization caused by overload	Repression, constriction, guardedness
Psychopathology: mania, schizophrenia	Psychopathology: depression
Research: Seen with individuals showing a low Lambda on the Rorschach (Konishi, 2003). Nonsupportive findings: Not seen with defensive forensic individuals (Conti, 2007); not helpful in a fake-good experimental condition (W. Wood, 2000)	Research: Seen with depressed adolescents (G. N. Goldman, 2001). Nonsupportive findings: Does not show the minimization of psychopathology in alleged sexual offenders (Wasyliw, Benn, Grossman, & Haywood, 1998)

COPING DEFICIT INDEX

The Coping Deficit Index (CDI) is a global measure that uses measures that are theoretically indicators of coping difficulties. The following exhibit gives the rules for computing the index. Thus, if either EA is less than 6 or the Adj D is less than 0, then that condition is met, and a check mark can be placed in the last column. The operation is then repeated for each of the other rows, taking into consideration the examinee's age. The final step in computing the index is to add all of the check marks of the last column. The index is considered to be elevated when the examinee has met more than four of the conditions.

Condition	Or (alternative condition)	Or (alternative condition)	+
EA < 6	Adj D < 0		
COP < 2 and AG < 2			
For 14 or older: WSumC < 2.5	For 14 or older: Afr < .46		
For 10 to 13: WsumC < 2.5	For 10 to 13: Afr < .53		
For 7 to 9: WSumC < 2.5	For 7 to 9: Afr < .55		
For 5 and 6: WsumC < 2.5	For 5 and 6: Afr < .57		
p > a + 1	Pure H < 2		
SumT > 1	Isolate / R > .24	Fd > 0	

Note. p = passive movement response, a = active movement response, H = pure human, and Fd = food.

(continued)

(*Continued*)

Possible interpretations of a high CDI:
- May have a deficit in adaptive skills, difficulty dealing with everyday requirements
- Possible history of social ineptness, social failures
- May have unsatisfying and meaningless interpersonal relationships
- Research: Seen more often with incarcerated male psychiatric patients who were more likely to be violent (Young, Justice, & Erdberg, 1999)

A low CDI is not interpretable.

DEPENDENCY INDEX

The Dependency Index is designed to measure dependent characteristics of personality: a low value of the Egocentricity Index (Ego Index), a high value of the Sum of texture responses (Sum T), a number of passive movement responses higher than the number of active movement responses plus one (p > a + 1), the presence of food content responses (Fd > 0), and a high number of popular responses (P). It is computed by adding one point for each of these conditions.

Possible interpretations High [> 3]	
Examinee has a dependent personality style, mostly characterized by a low self-esteem, submissiveness, discomfort when left to carry out functions on his or her own. Supporting research: Fowler, Brunnschweiler, Swales, and Brock, 2005 Nonsupporting research: Campos, 2009	Uninterpretable

DEPRESSION INDEX

The Depression Index (DEPI) is supposedly a measure of depression. It is computed similarly to the CDI, by evaluating each of the conditions and placing a check mark in the column on the right. A DEPI of 6 or more is considered elevated.

Condition	Or (alternative condition)	+
FV + VF + V > 0	FD > 2	
Color-shading blends > 0	S > 2	

(Continued)

[3*(Fr + rF) + (2)] / R > .44 and Fr + rF = 0	[3*(Fr + rF) + (2)] / R < .33
For 14 or older: Afr < .46	For 14 or older: Blends < 4
For 10–13: Afr < .53	For 1013: Blends < 4
For 7–9: Afr < .55	For 7–9: Blends < 4
For 5 and 6: Afr < .57	For 5 and 6: Blends < 4
SumShading > FM + m	SumC′ > 2
MOR > 2	2*AB + Art + Ay > 3
	[Bt + 2*Cl + Ge + Ls + 2*Na] / R >
COP < 2	.24

Possible interpretation of a high DEPI:
■ Individual may be depressed
A low DEPI is not interpretable.

Note.   Fr = reflection; Ay = anthropology; Bt = botany; Ge = geography; Ls = landscape; Na = nature.

EGOCENTRICITY INDEX

The Egocentricity Index consists of a percentile grouping of the reflection and pair responses, with the reflection response weighted three times as much as a pair response. The ratio is [3*(Fr + rF) + (2)] / R. For young examinees, it is adjusted by age, as noted on the table. For adults, the mean is .43; the mode is .50 (Exner, 2005).

Age	Index significant if less than	Index significant if more than
5	.55	.83
6	.52	.82
7	.52	.77
8	.48	.74
9	.45	.69
10	.45	.63
11	.45	.58
12	.38	.58
13	.38	.56
14	.37	.54
15	.33	.50
16	.33	.48

HYPERVIGILANCE INDEX

The Hypervigilance Index (HVI) is supposedly a measure of watchfulness or distrust. The first condition must be true (see below), and then at least four of the others.

Condition [1+4]	+
FT + TF + T = 0 This condition must be true	

FT + TF + T = 0   This condition must be true
Zf > 12
Zd > +3.5
S > 3
H + (H) + Hd + (Hd) > 6
(H) + (A) + (Hd) + (Ad) > 3
H + A: Hd + Ad < 4: 1
Cg > 3

Note.   FT = form texture, TF = texture form, Zf = Z frequency, Zd = processing efficiency, (H) = fictional human, Hd = part human, (Hd) = fictional part human, A = pure animal, (A) = fictional animal, Ad = part animal, Cg = clothing

Possible interpretation of a high HVI:
- Individual may be hypervigilant, too concerned about untoward events taking place unexpectedly.

Possible interpretation of a low HVI:
- Uninterpretable

INTELLECTUALIZATION INDEX

The Intellectualization Index (II) is calculated by adding the number of AB Special Scores to the number of two types of content scores. The equation is [II = 2*AB + Art + Ay].

High [> 4]	Low
Tendency to deny affect, never talk about feelings	Uninterpretable
Use of intellectualization and denial as a major defensive tactics	

OBSESSIVE COMPULSIVE STYLE INDEX

The Obsessive Compulsive Style Index (OCS) was designed as a compilation of obsessive–compulsive signs on the Rorschach. Examinees who have an elevated index are expected to be detail oriented and conventional. The computation is explained in the exhibit.

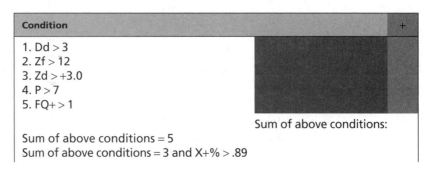

Condition	+
1. Dd > 3	
2. Zf > 12	
3. Zd > +3.0	
4. P > 7	
5. FQ+ > 1	

Sum of above conditions:

Sum of above conditions = 5
Sum of above conditions = 3 and X+% > .89

(*Continued*)

| Sum of above conditions = 2 and FQ+ > 3 |
| FQ+ > 3 and X+% > .89 |

PERCEPTUAL THINKING INDEX

The Perceptual Thinking Index (PTI) is supposedly a measure of thought disturbance.

Condition	Or (Alternative Condition)	+
XA% < .70 and WDA% < .75		
X-% > .29		
LVL2 > 2 and FAB2 > 0		
For 14 or older: R < 17 and WSUM6 > 12	For 14 or older: R > 16 and WSUM6 > 16	
For 11 to 13: R < 17 and WSUM6 > 14	For 11 to 13: R > 16 and WSUM6 > 18	
For 8 to 10: R < 17 and WSUM6 > 15	For 8 to 10: R > 16 and WSUM6 > 19	
For 5 to 7: R < 17 and WSUM6 > 16	For 5 to 7: R > 16 and WSUM6 > 20	
M- > 1	X-% > .40	

Possible interpretation of a high PTI:
- The examinee may have a thought disorder

A low PTI is not interpretable.

SUICIDE CONSTELLATION

The Suicide Constellation (S-CON) was developed by reviewing the Rorschach protocols of adolescents who committed suicide shortly after taking the test (Exner, 2003). The value of the constellation is derived by counting the number of the conditions following the procedure described for the CDI.

Condition	Or (alternate condition)	Condition met (+)
FV + VF + V + FD > 2		
Color-Shading Blends > 0		
3r + [(2) / R] < .31	3r + [(2) / R] > .44	
MOR > 3		
Zd > +3.5	Zd < −3.5	
es > EA		
CF + C > FC		
X+% < .70		
S > 3		
P < 3	P > 8	
Pure H < 2		
R < 17		

Possible interpretation of a high S-CON score:
- Individual may present a suicide risk

A low S-CON score is not interpretable.

Response-Level Interpretations 9

C hapters 4 through 8 of this volume focused on the interpretation of the Structural Summary. Those chapters reviewed the different scores of the Rorschach and adopted a mostly nomothetic approach to their interpretation. In other words, the interpretation of the test rested heavily on the comparison of the score obtained by a particular examinee and the placement of that score on the norms of the test. In contrast, this chapter offers more of an ideographic approach. Interpreting the Rorschach at the response level involves an attempt to figure out why the examinee gave a particular response, to a particular card, at a particular time.

When the Rorschach is administered by mechanistically going through the necessary motions in order to obtain the protocol, it loses some of its value. In the ideal case, the Rorschach clinician is examining the patient's behavior and responses and mentally proposing hypotheses to explain what is happening as the administration proceeds. The response-level exploration is what makes the administration of the Rorschach interesting. The more observant the examiner is

DOI: 10.1037/14039-009
The Rorschach Inkblot Test: An Interpretive Guide for Clinicians, by J. P. Choca
Copyright © 2013 by the American Psychological Association. All rights reserved.

of the behavior and responses of the examinee, the more interesting the task becomes. It is for this reason that some clinicians refer to the Rorschach as the *Rorschach inkblot method* rather than calling it a test (e.g., Weiner, 1994).

This chapter discusses issues involved with the interpretation of an actual response. Interpreting at this level has to be done carefully because this information does not have the stability and robustness of statistics and norms. Nevertheless, when the work is done conscientiously and supported by data from other sources, it is likely to be extremely helpful and enlightening.

Task Approach

The task of generating associations to inkblots is typically a novel situation for examinees because most of them would have never taken the Rorschach before and may have no experience with this type of task. As a result, the test provides an opportunity to learn what an individual does when facing a new situation. Because life is constantly presenting us with new situations, a sense for the approach the examinee is inclined to take is useful information. In some cases, the examinee's approach to new situations may be maladaptive and may be part of his or her dysfunction.

The most common approach to a new task is perhaps best referred to as *compliance:* The examinee accepts the task and is reasonably cooperative, even if he or she is not particularly invested in or excited about the testing. In most cases, that approach can also be inferred to be the examinee's approach to the different aspects of his or her life. At work, for instance, the compliant individual may do the tasks that are required in an effective manner, even when he or she is not particularly motivated or enthusiastic.

By contrast, some examinees become invested in the task; they may be curious and ask questions about the function of the test and how the responses are interpreted. They may put more time and effort into the task, wanting to do their best, giving a good number of responses and embellishing their responses in a rich manner. Such examinees are likely to be more invested in their jobs and to be more motivated to please or to excel as opposed to just meeting the job requirements.

In spite of the energy the invested examinee puts into the task, he or she still recognizes the examiner as the expert, the person who is in charge of the work to be done. The examinee with a controlling approach, on the other hand, wants to take over the direction of the task. This may be done in a positive manner, by noting possible improvements for either the test or the administration, or (and perhaps more commonly) in a negative manner, by finding fault with the procedure, with the examiner, or with both (e.g., "This is a stupid test," "I thought this sort of thing was not done any more," "What kind of professional are you? Can't you find better things to do with your time?"). In a work situation, this type of approach can lead to improvements; the positive controlling approach epitomizes the person who can "think outside the box" and make valuable contributions. However, the negative controlling approach characterizes the kind of worker who may be always complaining about the system or the supervisors in an unproductive way. The latter are the malcontents who use maladaptive oppositional, negativistic, and projective defenses.

Compliant, invested, and controlling individuals want to do the task, even if only because they see themselves as having no other choice. By contrast, the passive–aggressive examinee claims to be cooperating but responds minimally and in an unrevealing manner. The passive–aggressive protocol often leads to one of the well-known test profiles that are discussed in Chapter 10. In the work environment, this approach is maladaptive in that the individual is typically seen as ineffective. Nevertheless, this type of person may have less of a negative effect on the work environment than the employee with a negative controlling approach.

The value of the Rorschach is enriched by clinical observations, and those observations start with insights about how the individual approaches the task. The four approaches described in this section are commonly seen, but many other approaches are possible. The clinician's job is to try to conceptualize the manner of approach that the examinee uses.

Thought Processing

The Rorschach excels in highlighting the peculiarities of the examinee's thinking processes. Few other instruments can be used to examine a person's thinking pattern.

The thinking deficiencies that are discussed in this section span the range from normalcy to severe psychopathology. Some slips of logic are a common occurrence with all individuals and should not be seen as necessarily pathological. In addition to understanding the thinking process involved, therefore, the clinician needs to review the frequency and severity of the deficiency in order to interpret the findings appropriately.

Although perhaps less interesting to the clinician than an uncommon response, the mundane response says a great deal about the individual and should not be disregarded. The examinee who sees a bat or butter-fly on Card I based on the shape of the inkblot is giving the popular response and, barring the possibility of an unexpected comment, is effectively handling the task in the expected way. If all of the responses had the same quality, the examinee should be seen as someone who can think clearly and can perceive the environment in the same way as the vast majority of the population. It is likely that this individual's scores would be mostly or entirely in the normal range. If so, the individual could be additionally characterized as having all of the attributes that those normal scores would imply (e.g., an ability to respond to emotional situations in a controlled manner, good contact with reality).

On the other hand, many responses that are given to the Rorschach reveal thought-processing deficiencies that should be explored and understood. One such pattern is *overinclusiveness,* which was scored as DW in the Klopfer system (Klopfer, Ainsworth, Klopfer, & Holt, 1954). This kind of response typically starts with a readily seen association to an inkblot detail. On Card VIII, for instance, the examinee may see two animals on the side, a popular response to that card. The overinclusive examinee, however, may expand that perception to cover the whole card and see the animals as climbing a tree or a mountain. If the detail of the two animals on the side were removed, the person would not have seen the center of the card as a tree or a mountain. Reality in this case had to be bent for the person to expand the perception to cover the entire inkblot. From the point of view of the quality of the thinking process, the response would have been better had the examinee resisted the overinclusive urge and limited the response to the two animals on the side of the card.

There may be at least two reasons for the overinclusive association. One reason is the card pull of the animals on the side, which stands out. Another reason is the posture of one of the animals, with the front leg raised, which evokes the idea that the animals are in motion. The vertical presentation of the figure suggests that the animal is climbing. The examinee who feels the need to fill the blanks might specify the object the animals are climbing by converting the rest of the inkblot into that object. In this case, the thinking process is an attempt to be as loyal as possible to the animal figures, even at the expense of being inaccurate for the rest of the inkblot. Sometimes that kind of thinking leads examinees to see the animals being pulled up by a creature in the top center of the inkblot. This response includes another example of overinclusion: The examinee might see a hand on D4 that is touching the front paw of the animal. The kind of thought defect portrayed by overinclusive responses is likely to lead the examinee to the fallacy of jumping to conclusions. In other words, the thinking process expands from what is known about a part of reality to cover what is unknown or unclear.

Another process that can lead to overinclusive thinking has to do with the pull that the whole card has for some examinees. The examinee's thinking starts with a response for the entire card, and the details are considered only because they are the building blocks on which the overarching perception is based. The underwater scene on Card X may be a good example. The inquiry for this response may lead the examinee to talk about crabs, eels, seahorses, or part of a coral reef, but those details were not the most important part that the examinee considered in the association. As in the case with all overinclusive responses, the underwater scene bends the reality of the inkblot. One could ask about many details on this inkblot that are not consistent with the underwater scene perception and that would have to be denied or blurred in order to maintain the integrity of the association. Thus, the thinking process is basically the reverse of the previous overinclusion; we have a WD instead of a DW.

To further contrast the two thought processes described, consider the response to Card X of the Eiffel Tower in the top center, with the gardens of the Champs-Élysées in the foreground. The thought process here is likely to be a DW, with the accurate perception being the Eiffel Tower and the gardens being the fill-in. In any event, the WD kind of overinclusion is typical of the holistic thinker who wants to pay attention to the forest rather than the trees. As noted in Chapter 4, such an examinee tends to overorganize the world into a holistic view to such an extent that he or she has trouble accurately seeing the practical elements of reality.

Overinclusions betray a lack of clear boundaries in the person's thinking. In their conversations, such individuals are likely to switch topics, sometimes in a disorganized manner, demonstrating loose associations. The severity of the boundary violations and thinking deficits varies. In the preceding examples, the examinees would be considered to be mildly overinclusive because the extent to which they bent reality to include fill-ins was not atrocious. An examinee who responded to Card X with an association of Napoleon in the taking of La Bastille would be demonstrating more severe pathology. In this case, the original association of the top detail as the Eiffel Tower disappeared to leave a loose association with France and then with Napoleon (the figure in the pink, with a three-corner hat on). Thus, what could have been a DW with a little bending of reality for the Champs-Élysées is now the low-quality response of a psychotic individual.

Some of these overinclusive responses lead to Special Scores (e.g., Contamination, Fabulized Combinations, Incongruous Combinations, and Inappropriate Logic). At times one has to test the limits into the thought process of the examinee with questions that go beyond what would be typically admissible as part of the inquiry in order to reveal the kind of thinking process that led to the association. At times the additional questions prevent scoring a Special Score, but in order to interpret the protocol correctly, such additional explorations may be necessary. The presence of a Special Score, on the other hand, necessitates an understanding of the mechanism leading to the fallacious thinking.

The thought process deficits are likely to affect the interpersonal area. The person whose thinking jumps from a detail fact to an inappropriate conclusion is likely to do the same in social relationships and to develop ideas about people that stretch reality. It would be expected that the pathology that seeps into the interpersonal area is proportional to the severity of the thought process deficits.

Response Sequence

An individual's associations and thinking patterns are triggered by the situation and the properties of the stimulus presented. Consequently, to accurately analyze a Rorschach protocol, the clinician has to keep in mind certain attributes of the situation and the inkblots. This is best done by analyzing the sequence of the responses obtained while keeping in mind the properties of the cards in question.

The responses obtained for the first card may differ in numerous ways from the other responses in the protocol. To some extent the first card represents a training item, the stimulus that is presented so that the individual can "try out" the task at hand. The person's approach to the test that was discussed in the preceding section should begin to be evident in the way the individual handles this card. However, as he or she better conceptualizes what is expected, the questions or clarifications that were needed would have already taken place, and the flavor of the responses obtained may differ. In some cases the examinee approaches the test with a great deal of apprehension. After the examiner accepts a few of the examinee's responses, that apprehension may diminish or go away altogether.

The second card is the first color card. Examinees who have trouble dealing with their emotions may experience a "color shock" that may prevent them from giving an adequate response. On the other hand, examinees may be energized by the emotion or color and may respond to this card with a higher level of enthusiasm or motivation.

Examinees who have trouble dealing with ambiguity will have a hard time with the first four cards of the Rorschach because none of them present a nicely structured stimulus that can be clearly associated with a response. This is particularly true of Card IV, a card that has other attributes (see the section Card Themes) that may also throw off some examinees. Consequently, some examinees may offer poor-quality responses to those cards. These considerations have led clinicians to see Card V as the "recovery card." In other words, examinees who have been giving substandard responses often come back on Card V to give a better response, perhaps the popular response of the bat or butterfly. Because Card V is the easiest card of the Rorschach, a good response is to be expected, and a poor-quality response should be given serious weight in the interpretations.

It is also worthwhile to compare the pattern of responses at the beginning of the test with those at the end to get an idea of what happens with the examinee during the course of a task. Some examinees may invest a great deal of energy and effort at the beginning, but as the work proceeds and the task becomes more routine, they may become bored or may consider the time demanded to be excessive. As the Rorschach continues, such examinees may start reducing the number of responses offered, the amount of elaboration offered with each response, or the quality of the response. Translating this finding into real life, one may suspect that these individuals may start with a great deal of energy and enthusiasm but tire easily.

The opposite pattern is also seen: Examinees may start in a hesitant or tentative manner and become more productive as they gain more confidence with the task. They "warm up to a task" and become more interested and productive as the work proceeds. An idiosyncratic progression, with more or better responses to some cards than to others, should be understood in some manner, perhaps by taking a look at the card structure.

Card Structure

The Rorschach cards have different attributes that may affect the way the examinee responds to them. Half of the cards are black-and-white (achromatic), and half have color (chromatic). The achromatic cards may evoke depressive feelings or morbid thoughts, a mood state that may influence the number and quality of the responses obtained on those cards. The emotions evoked by the chromatic cards, on the other hand, may play a role in energizing the examinee. An appreciable difference between the achromatic and chromatic responses should speak of the effect that the nonemotional and emotional situations have on the examinee. If the response time is noted, a significant difference in average response time should also be considered. More specifically, if the examinee gives a high number of responses to the color cards and responds to those cards very quickly, the finding suggests that he or she may overreact to emotion-inducing situations. Other data would have to be examined to determine whether the emotional reactions of that individual are maladaptive.

Similarly, we can compare the kind of responses obtained with the more ambiguous cards (Cards IV and IX) with the responses obtained on the most unambiguous card (Card V). Some people cope better with life situations that are very structured (e.g., the military) than with those that offer a great deal of freedom (e.g., self-employment); conversely, some individuals are stymied by situations with too many rules and expectations and do better when they have more freedom. If a vast difference is seen between the responses to the structured and those to the unstructured cards, the clinician can consider the type of situation for which the examinee is best suited.

Some of the Rorschach cards are perceptually more difficult than others. Card IX is the most perceptually challenging of the cards. This card has no resemblance to common objects, either in its entirety or when examined by its parts. In contrast, the whole of Card V actually looks like an animal with wings, whereas Card VIII and Card X have details that are seen by most people as resembling animals. For this reason more people have trouble with Card IX than with any of the other cards. Although this card is frequently rejected, it is important to strongly encourage the examinee to give a response because responses to this card reveal how the examinee performs in the challenging life situations. Examinees with low intellectual abilities or cognitive deficits may respond poorly to Card IX (and perform poorly in intellectually demanding life situations).

Card Themes

For different reasons, some of the Rorschach cards are likely to evoke an association to a particular object or mood. A very popular response to Card III, for instance, involves the perception of the two human figures doing something. Card IV, usually perceived to be a large monster, is often linked with masculinity and is sometimes seen as a threatening figure. The soft fur that is typically associated with Card VI can evoke affectional needs, caring, comfort, and intimacy. Card VI is also a sexuality card because it has parts that may remind us of both male and female genitals. Other cards that have parts depicting male or female sexuality include Cards II, III, and VII. Card VII can be associated with femininity because of the gentle-looking women faces typically seen on the top detail. Cards IV and VII have been referred to as the "father" and "mother" cards, respectively (Liaboe & Guy, 1985).

In most cases the themes evoked by the different cards play a role in the kind of response that is obtained, but that role may not be the focus of attention or interpretation. The examinee is typically able to switch from one theme to the next, accommodating to the card pull in his or her response without difficulty. However, some individuals are so disturbed by one theme that they have trouble responding to the card or give a disturbed response to the card.

Response Time

An alleged sexual predator took a much longer time to respond to Card VI than he had taken with the other cards. When this fact was raised in the Testing of Limits procedure, he explained that, after seeing both the male and the female genitalia, he had difficulty disregarding those perceptions and finding a nonsexual response. He had been afraid that if he gave the sexual associations, the responses would be taken as evidence of that he was in fact a sex addict. The longer response time was due to his having to process all that and his having to find another response.

When the test is administered with the help of a program like Hermann, the computer figures out the average chromatic and achromatic reaction time for the individual. In that case, the time taken for any particular response can be compared to the average to see whether it is statistically different. If the examiner does not have the use of such a program and does not use a stopwatch, the determination that a response took more or less time than what had been the usual for the examinee becomes impressionistic and subjective.

A long response time could be due to a number of reasons. It is the examiner's job to investigate why a particular response may have taken more time. Possible reasons may include (a) a reaction to the content of the particular association evoked; (b) the sequence of the response—the more responses an examinee gives to a particular card, the harder the additional responses may be; (c) the complexity of the response—a response that includes several interrelated parts may take a longer time to formulate; and (d) inattention—derailment from the task at hand by attention to other thoughts.

In general, no interpretation is needed for a short response time. As seen in Chapter 4, the mean reaction time for the ten cards is only 12 seconds, so it is virtually impossible to respond significantly faster than the average. Even when the average reaction time for an examinee is much higher than the norm, it is possible that the examinee had two associations simultaneously and had to wait until the examiner handled each in turn.

Content

The content of the response is the Rorschach element that is most often thought by laypeople to be the main focus of interest. Although this is not the case, the content of the response cannot be disregarded. Chapter 6 discussed the nomothetic approach to the content categories. Some response content may be of interpretable interest even if it occurs only once. The interest in that case may be due to the content being particularly unusual or disturbed, or being particularly relevant given the history of the individual.

In the case of psychotic individuals, a response of particularly bad quality may be all the clinician needs to be convinced of the correct diagnosis. At times the response can be so disorganized or so bizarre that a single response is almost pathognomonic of the disorder. This is one of the few times when the inclusion of the verbatim response in the report can be useful in supporting the discussion and diagnostic formulation.

Even with less disturbed examinees, the content of the response may speak in a very relevant way to some aspect of the examinee's history or to a question being investigated. To illustrate: A middle-aged man, depressed and suicidal after learning that his 19-year-old son had hanged himself in a garage, gave the association of a body hanging from a pole to the top portion of Card VI. The clinician did not need any other responses to conclude that the traumatic loss of the son was still very much in his mind and that survivor's guilt was creating a substantial suicidal risk for this individual.

A classic book by Phillips and Smith (1953) offered interpretations for many specific contents, but the offerings were mostly speculative. Some of their interpretations may appear a bit far-fetched today.

Conclusion

Clinicians require information beyond that obtained during the test in order to analyze responses judiciously. As the preceding example illustrated, it was only on the basis of the patient's history and other test evidence of depression and feelings of guilt that the examiner was able to interpret that single response as an ominous sign for that individual.

The Testing the Limits procedure is very useful for the response-level analysis because it allows the clinician to elicit help from the examinee in interpreting a finding. A protocol devoid of movement or color reveals something very important about that examinee and makes it imperative to determine to what extent he or she has to be encouraged before the movement or the color is incorporated into a response. When the movement or color perception is acknowledged, it may be useful to explore why the examinee had not used the determinant previously. For example, one examinee I tested did not use movement because of a realization that none of the inkblots were in motion, and he believed that it would be seen as strange if movement was included. At the same time this person was readily recognizing that some of the figures did look as if they were moving. The findings with that examinee would call for a different interpretation than the findings with the examinee who continued to fight all movement suggestions and who could never be talked into incorporating movement into his or her responses. When examiners evaluate examinees' task approach or thought processing, it is often useful to work with examinees to discover what was in their mind.

Interpretative Process 10

B y now, the reader should have developed a sense for the Rorschach and for the possible meaning of the different scores. This chapter describes the process that may be used to interpret a Rorschach protocol and presents an extended example. Common Rorschach profiles are discussed in Chapter 11; the integration of Rorschach data with other sources of information and the writing of the report is the focus of Chapter 12.

Data Interpretation Process

The four-step interpretative process is outlined in this section. Next, a protocol is interpreted following these steps.

ADMINISTRATION INTERPRETATIVES

Although it is possible to accurately interpret a Rorschach protocol that was administered by someone else, the ideal

DOI: 10.1037/14039-010
The Rorschach Inkblot Test: An Interpretive Guide for Clinicians, by J. P. Choca

situation is for the diagnostician to also be the test administrator. In that case, the interpretative process begins at the time of the administration. As Schachtel (1966) pointed out, how the examinee experiences the test situation is particularly informative because it allows clinicians to understand the pattern of responses that they are likely to obtain. Moreover, the approach to the test can be assumed to reveal the "attitudes, strivings, defenses, needs, fears, wishes and interests" that the person characteristically shows in other life situations (p. 273).

A good diagnostician is constantly working to answer two basic questions: (a) What kind of a person is this examinee? and (b) What can I do to help the examinee reveal the kind of person he or she is? The word *constantly* should be emphasized because the answers to those questions can change from one moment to the next. To those who administer the Rorschach in an automatic manner, the test administration will soon become boring, at least with the run-of-the-mill examinee. As noted in Chapter 2, what keeps the real Rorschach clinician engaged is the spirit of exploration, the use of the instrument as a tool to discover what the examinee is all about. By the time the administration is complete, the experienced Rorschach clinician will already have some sense of what kind of information the test will offer about the examinee.

In addition to the actual responses and the information gleaned during the Testing the Limits procedure, I am inclined to enter any behavioral observations or relevant comments right into the protocol. My first step in interpreting a protocol is to review those salient characteristics, jotting them down on a piece of paper that becomes the basis for the first draft of the report. As discussed in Chapter 2, the manner in which the examinee approached the test is a very important piece of information, something that is more effectively discovered during the administration phase.

ITEM INTERPRETATIVES

The scoring of the protocol is the next step. As the responses are scored, the clinician scores them, all the while keeping in mind the process that was followed in generating the response. Examples of observations made during the test administration that are relevant include the following:

- evidence that the association started with a detail and was expanded into a larger location;
- the process used to integrate determinants (e.g., color) into the form;
- idiosyncratic terms or phrases that the examinee used repeatedly;
- idiosyncratic interests that the examinee demonstrated (e.g., an interest in the symmetry of the two sides);

- an attraction for certain shapes or evidence of avoidance of such shapes (e.g., genital shapes of the inkblot);
- any unique progression that the examinee repeatedly followed in generating responses; and
- any unique content or unrecognized Special Score that recurs (e.g., an examinee's characterization of several details as *scary, dead, happy,* or *weird;* these characterizations may sometimes earn one of the recognized Special Scores, but, in addition, they can be noted as a unique aspect of the person).

These observations should be included in the notes for further integration with the rest of the data (see Chapter 9).

STRUCTURAL SUMMARY INTERPRETATIVES

The Structural Summary is the core of the interpretative process. Values that are out of the ordinary are identified, possible interpretations for the different markers are noted, and the "right" interpretation for the particular individual is selected.

SEQUENCE INTERPRETATIVES

The final step in the interpretative process advocated here involves exploring whether there are any interesting sequence patterns or trends in the protocol (see Chapter 9).

Example: Case Interpretation

The protocol that is interpreted in this section comes from a 20-year-old college student referred for evaluation of possible attentional problems. The examinee's Shipley Vocabulary score was 101, Abstractions was 84, and Blocks was 104, for composite scores of 93 (Vocabulary and Abstractions) and 104 (Vocabulary and Blocks). The Working Memory indices of the Wechsler Adult Intelligence Scale and Wechsler Memory Scale were 99 and 102, respectively. The Processing Speed Index of the Wechsler Adult Intelligence Scale was 98. The Conners Continuous Performance Test was in the nonclinical range, and only two items were out of the ordinary. Needless to say, the intellectual test scores did not uncover a disability in attending to information that was given in an unambiguous and structured manner. Sometimes it is with this kind of case that the Rorschach is most helpful.

The examinee was invested in doing the Rorschach and made a suitable amount of effort. The Rorschach protocol is offered in Exhibit 10.1.

EXHIBIT 10.1

Rorschach Protocol for Case 10.1

1. Card I Reaction Time: 11″
   SCORE=> W o FC′ o A P 1.0a bat
   INQUIRY: the wing span, the body with the 2 eyes
   ANYTHING ELSE? the color
   ANYTHING ELSE? no

2. Card I Reaction Time: 10″
   SCORE=> W o F -(A) 1.0 DR2.INC1
   a three-pronged.... [ct rem what she was going to say] praying mantis,
   a fat one
   INQUIRY: the feelers {a} the eyes {b} they have really long legs {f},
   not feelers, arms
   ANYTHING ELSE? no
   THREE-PRONGED? oh, I am not sure how to explain it. It's as if it had
   three prongs in front {a, e, f} and that's not the way it is supposed
   to be. It is a fat and sort of distorted praying mantis, a weird one

3. Card I Reaction Time: 4″
   SCORE=> D o FMp o (2) Ad2 dog heads
   INQUIRY: the tongue {c}
   ANYTHING ELSE? the eyebrows {d} the ears {e} the long snout {f} they
   look like they r ready to go
   ANYTHING ELSE? no
   READY TO GO? about to jump and run
   ? they have an eager expression
   ANYTHING ELSE? no. They r going in different directions.
   ANYTHING ELSE? no but there are two other dog heads [see #23]

4. Card II Reaction Time: 1″
   SCORE=> W o FMa.FC′.CF o (2) A.Hh 3.0 DR1
   2 elephants
   INQUIRY: trunk {a} ears {b}, they r gray. The red and the white rmd me
   of circus time
   ANYTHING ELSE? no. They r sort of standing up on their hind legs as if
   performing in the circus
   ANYTHING ELSE? no
   RED & WHITE? I dk what those r, maybe decorations or something
   ANYTHING ELSE? no

5. Card II Reaction Time: 3″
   SCORE=> D o FMa.CF o (2) A.An.Bl
   2 infant pigs coming out, with their blood and uterus still connected
   to the umbilical chord {c}

EXHIBIT 10.1 (*Continued*)

```
INQUIRY: this is their feeding from the mother {a}
ANYTHING ELSE? the snout {a}, their eye {f}, huffed feet {g}
ANYTHING ELSE? no
MOTHER? u ct c the mother, she is just assumed to be up on top there
BLOOD & UTERUS? what u c of the uterus is the pink part around the
umbilical chord. The infant pigs are all bloody, u can c the red spots
ANYTHING ELSE? no
```

```
6. Card III  Reaction Time: 2"
   SCORE=> W o Ma.CF o (2) (H).Cg.Hh.An P 4.0 AG.CON
   2 AA dancers
   doing a traditional cooking ceremony with hanging intestines over
   them, stomachs
   INQUIRY: their bodies {a} this is the bowl that they r mixing in {b},
   they r bold {c} but they have breasts {d} their shoes {e} these r the
   hanging intestines, stomachs from the esophagus {f}, these r 2 lungs
   that they r sacrificing into the pot
   ANYTHING ELSE? no
   INTESTINES? the shape & they r red
   AA? they r black
   ANYTHING ELSE? No
   SACRIFICING? Like an African ritual where a young person or animal is
   being offered to the gods
```

```
7. Card IV  Reaction Time: 4"SCORE=> W o FC'.FT o (H) P 2.0 INC1
   the Abominable Snowman in black
   INQUIRY: giant feet, his hands {a}, his head but it is not like Big
   Foot {b} so that's why I called him the Snowman, the fur, layers of
   covering that he has
   ANYTHING ELSE? no
   FUR? the sketching of the ink, the different shadings, it's almost
   feathery
   ANYTHING ELSE? no
   BLACK? The Abominable Snowman is supposed to be white but this one
   is black
   ANYTHING ELSE? no
```

```
8. Card IV  Reaction Time: 6"
   SCORE=> W o Mp o(H).Bt 2.0 AG.PER
   a swamp monster with seaweed all over him
   INQUIRY: instead of fur he has seaweed, he looks mean, his feet look
   like they r made kelp {c}
   ANYTHING ELSE? no
   SEAWEED? it looks like it's on top of him, like almost falling off
   MEAN? the expression on his face {b}
   ANYTHING ELSE? no
```

(*continued*)

EXHIBIT 10.1 (Continued)

9. Card IV Reaction Time: 5"
   SCORE=> W o F-(Ad) 2.0 AG.PSV
   a dragon without a tail
   INQUIRY: I hated this dragon as a kid, it had the head {d}, the big
   body {e} the wings {f} but this is without a tail
   ANYTHING ELSE? no
   HATED? it was a cartoon dragon but I dt like him. It was sort of mean
   and scary
   ANYTHING ELSE? no
   WITHOUT A TAIL? it's been cut off in this drawg
   ANYTHING ELSE? no

10. Card V Reaction Time: 1"
    SCORE=> W o FC' oA P 1.0
    a moth
    INQUIRY: they dt have pretty wings & they r black, blasé, the stubby
    feelers {a}
    ANYTHING ELSE? no

11. Card VI Reaction Time: 11"
    SCORE=> W v FT o Ad.Ay P 2.5
    looks like a raw hide, a cow-skin hide with Indian feathers on top,
    some kd of decoration from a Native Am
    INQUIRY: it looks like fur in here [shadg]
    ANYTHING ELSE? no

12. Card VI Reaction Time: 3"
    SCORE=> Dd F (2) (H)CON
    I c an alien, a skinny alien
    INQUIRY: 2 aliens in one body. There is one head {a} and the second
    head, both with eyes, it is skinny {b}
    ANYTHING ELSE? no
    TWO ALIENS IN ONE BODY? it's like they have morphed together, weird,
    but u can c the 2 heads there
    ANYTHING ELSE? no

13. Card VII Reaction Time: 2"
    SCORE=> W o Ma - (2) H.Sc 1.0 AB.AG.CON
    2 little girls playing with their alter-egos on their back.
    They r evil
    INQUIRY: they have a titter-totter they r playing on {a} alter-ego {b}
    ALTER-EGO? they r twins and they look really nice and happy with their
    pony tails up here {c} & then u have their alter-ego looking the other
    way, the evil side
    ANYTHING ELSE? no

EXHIBIT 10.1 (*Continued*)

14. Card VIII   Reaction Time: 7"
    SCORE=> D o Fma o (2) A.Na.An CON
    2 ground hogs climbing up the side of a cliff, which is really the
    inside of a human body, so you can c the spinal chord and the vertebrae
    INQUIRY: an abstract of the vertebrae there r 3 giant vertebrae {a} {b}
    {c} but there is more {d} and organs {e}
    ANYTHING ELSE? no. There is also a lizzard [see #24]

15. Card IX   Reaction Time: 44"
    SCORE=> D Ma.FMa - (2) A.(H).Sc.Ad.Cg AG.INC2.CON
    2 bears {a} in war with some Civil War fighters, soldiers {b}
    INQUIRY: bear paws {c} tail {d}, they r wearing an Indian headdress {e}
    ANYTHING ELSE? gunmen on their horses {f}, u just c the backs of them
    [horses], that's their rifle, very short ones {g} & they r using deer
    antlers {h}
    ANYTHING ELSE? no
    TESTING OF THE LIMITS: HOW DID U THINK OF THESE THINGS? well, u can c
    how they r there
    IN YOUR MIND, DO THESE THINGS FIT TOGETHER? maybe not commonly but u
    can c how they r all there
    COULD U HAVE DIVIDED THEM? Yeah, but they r together here

16. Card IX   Reaction Time: 2"
    SCORE=> Dd F u (2) Ad
    2 rabbit heads
    INQUIRY: it's hard to c: there is the 2 ears {i} {j} and the eyes {k}
    ANYTHING ELSE? no

17. Card X   Reaction Time: 15"
    SCORE=> D o FC - (2) A
    2 seahorses
    INQUIRY: they r yellow with a red eye
    ANYTHING ELSE? no

18. Card X   Reaction Time: 1"
    SCORE=> D o FMp o (2) A
    2 conch shells with the crabs still living in them
    INQUIRY: u can c the conch shell in the middle and all the legs of the
    crab coming out
    ANYTHING ELSE? no

19. Card X   Reaction Time: 1"
    SCORE=> D o FC o (2) A
    2 regular crabs
    INQUIRY: the body and the legs, 1 big claw
    ANYTHING ELSE? it's kd of brownish
    ANYTHING ELSE? no

(continued)

EXHIBIT 10.1 (*Continued*)

20. Card X Reaction Time: 5″
    SCORE=> D o FC u (2) A
    two yellow tangs, fish
    INQUIRY: rpts
    ANYTHING ELSE? no

21. Card X Reaction Time: 1″
    SCORE=> D v CF u (2) Na
    2 giant pcs of coral
    INQUIRY: they r pink
    ANYTHING ELSE? no

22. Card X Reaction Time: 3″
    SCORE=> D o F - (2) A
    2 sea urchins on top. t is quite beautiful
    INQUIRY: they r on top of the coral
    ANYTHING ELSE? no
    BEAUTIFUL? the whole pic, it has nice colors
    ANYTHING ELSE? no

23. Card I Reaction Time: 5″
    SCORE=> Dd o FMa o Ad AG
    other dog from #3 [This response that was given during the Inquiry]
    INQUIRY: nose {c} ears {d} {h}
    ANYTHING ELSE? he's got something in his mouth {g}, maybe a small
    animal
    ANYTHING ELSE? no
    SMALL ANIMAL? it grabbed something it is going to eat
    ANYTHING ELSE? no

24. Card VIII Reaction Time: 4″
    SCORE=> D o FC - A
    a lizzard [This response that was given during the Inquiry]
    INQUIRY: legs with feet {f}, spikes on his head {g}, eye sockets
    slanted in{h} with the eyeballs {i}
    ANYTHING ELSE? no, it's green
    ANYTHING ELSE? no
    TESTING OF THE LIMITS:
    HELP ME TO SEE THIS . . . rpts parts of inquiry
    ARE U LOOKING AT IT HEAD-ON, LIKE THE FRONT END OF THE ANIMAL? Yes
    ANYTHING ELSE? no

Note. Letters in brackets refer to locations on the location charts.

EXHIBIT 10.1 (*Continued*)

— HERMANN —
Multi-Health Systems. Program written by James Choca, Ph.D.,
and Dan Garside

Rorschach Score Sequence   Page 1
Name: Exhibit 10-1
Date of testing: 12-27-11

Card	No	Time	Scoring							
I	1	11	W	o	FC'	o	A	P	1.0	
I	2	10	W	o	F	−	(A)		1.0	DR2.INC1
I	3	4	D	o	FM	po	(2)Ad			
II	4	1	W	o	FM.FC'.CF	ao	(2)A.Hh		3.0	DR1
II	5	3	D	o	FM.CF	ao	(2)A.An.Bl			
III	6	2	W	o	M.CF	ao	(2)(H).Cg.Hh.AnP		4.0	CON
IV	7	4	W	o	FC'.FT	o	(H)	P	2.0	INC1
IV	8	6	W	o	M	po	(H).Bt		2.0	AG.PER
IV	9	5	W	o	F	−	(Ad)		2.0	AG.PSV
V	10	1	W	o	FC'	o	A	P	1.0	
VI	11	11	W	v	FT	o	Ad.Ay	P	2.5	
VI	12	3	Dd		F		(2)(H)			CON
VII	13	2	W	o	M	a−	(2)H.Sc		1.0	AB.AG.CON
VIII	14	7	D	o	FM	ao	(2)A.Na.An			CON
IX	15	44	D		M.FM	a−	(2)A.(H).Sc.Ad.Cg			AG.INC2.CON
IX	16	2	Dd		F	u	(2)Ad			
X	17	15	D	o	FC	−	(2)A			
X	18	1	D	o	FM	po	(2)A			
X	19	1	D	o	FC	o	(2)A			
X	20	5	D	o	FC	u	(2)A			
X	21	1	D	v	CF	u	(2)Na			
X	22	3	D	o	F	−	(2)A			
I	23	5	Dd	o	FM	ao	Ad			AG
VIII	24	4	D	o	FC	−	A			

(continued)

EXHIBIT 10.1 (Continued)

— HERMANN —

Program written by James Choca, Ph.D., and Dan Garside

Rorschach Structural Summary

Global	n	%	Location	n	%	Determinants	n	%	Contents	n	%	Quality	n	%
R	24		W	10	42	M	4	13	CONT	10		OF ALL		
Rejects	0		D	11	46	FM	7	23	H	1	3	+	0	0
			Dd	3	13	m	0	0	(H)	5	13	o	13	54
P	5	21	DW	0	0	FT	2	7	Hd	0	0	u	3	13
(P)	0	0	S	0	0	TF	0	0	(Hd)	0	0	-	7	29
						T	0	0	Hx	0	0	none	1	0
(2)	15	63	POSITION			FY	0	0	A	12	32	OF F		
Fr	0	0	^	24	100	YF	0	0	(A)	1	3	+	0	0
rF	0	0	<	0	0	Y	0	0	Ad	5	13	o	0	0
3r+(2)		62	>	0	0	FV	0	0	(Ad)	1	3	u	1	20
			v	0	0	VF	0	0	Ab	0	0	-	3	60
RT Ach	6					V	0	0	Al	0	0	none		1000
RT Ch	7					FC'	4	13	An	3	8	OF S		
			DEV QUAL			C'F	0	0	Art	0	0	+	0	0
AFR		71	+	0	0	C'	0	0	Ay	1	3	o	0	0
			o	19	79	FC	4	13	Bl	1	3	u	0	0
			v/+	0	0	CF	4	13	Bt	1	3	-	0	0
Zf	10		v	2	8	C	0	0	Cg	1	3			
						Cn	0	0						

ZSum   19.5

RATIOS

W	10
M	4
W	10
D	11

FD	0
F	5
Blends	5

RATIOS

a	7
p	3
M	4
wtd C	6.0
M+wtd C	10
FM+m	7
Y+T+V+C'	6
&FMmYTVC'	13
FC	4
CF+C	4

Content		
Cl	0	0
Ex	0	17
Fi		
Fd	0	21
Ge		
Hh	5	29
Ls	0	13
Na	5	
Sc	5	
Sx	0	
Vo	0	
Xy	0	
Idio	0	
AB	1	
CP	0	

RATIOS

H+HD	6	
A+AD	19	
H+A	19	
HD+AD	6	
A%		50

none	0	0

SPECIAL SCORES

DV1	0	0
DV2	0	0
DR1	1	4
DR2	1	4
INC1	2	8
INC2	1	4
FAB1	0	0
FAB2	0	0
ALOG	0	0
CON	5	21
		4
AG	5	21
MOR	0	0
CFB	0	0
PER	1	4
COP	0	0
PSV	1	4

In terms of administration interpretatives, two trends seemed note-worthy. For one thing, the examinee tended to be superficial in her associations at first and only clarified her associations in response to further inquiries. Consider, for instance, the exchanges for Response 9 (a dragon without a tail).

INQUIRY

Examinee: I hated this dragon as a kid, it had the head, the big body, the wings, but this is without a tail.

Clinician: Anything else?

Examinee: No.

Clinician: Hated?

Examinee: It was a cartoon dragon but I didn't like him. It was sort of mean and scary.

Clinician: Anything else?

Examinee: No.

Clinician: Without a tail?

Examinee: It's been cut off in this drawing.

Clinician: Anything else?

Examinee: No.

The examinee's original association was somewhat inaccurate in that what she actually had seen was the front end of the dragon. The first Inquiry adds a personal reference (which requires clarification) without shedding light on the association. Only in response to further questioning does a sense for the response become apparent.

A second observation from the test administration involves the concrete and engulfing nature of the examinee's thought process. She is captured by the concrete details. Unlike others who focus on the details while exerting good boundaries and keeping the details separate, however, the examinee puts all of her perceptions together, which results in a bizarre and ineffective response. As an example, consider the interactions in Response 15 (2 bears in war with some Civil War fighters, soldiers):

INQUIRY

Examinee: Bear paws, tail, they are wearing an Indian headdress.

Clinician: Anything else?

Examinee: Gunmen on their horses, you just see the backs of them (horses), that's their rifle, very short ones, and they are using deer antlers.

Clinician: Anything else?

Examinee: No.

Clinician: [Testing the Limits] How did you think of these things?

Examinee: Well, you can see how they are there.

> *Clinician:* In your mind, do these things fit together?
>
> *Examinee:* Maybe not commonly but you can see how they are all there.
>
> *Clinician:* Could you have divided them?
>
> *Examinee:* Yeah, but they are together here.

The details of her response were consistent with the shape of the ink-blot and would have been reasonable responses individually. Moreover, Testing the Limits allowed us to determine that the examinee had recognized that the details of her response did not commonly fit together, but she was still unable to use this good judgment to adjust her response. She was obviously disinclined to abandon some of the details or to convert each of the details into a different response; the grip of the details was so strong that she could not step back and look at the big picture. Consequently, her thinking became scattered and disorganized, resembling a modernistic free-association painting where all kinds of forms are thrown onto the canvas without a unifying theme.

The administration interpretatives in this case led to two hypotheses that must be further confirmed or denied by examining other Rorschach data as well as data from other sources:

- The examinee tends to be superficial at first and communicates in an idiosyncratic manner; she often does not take into consideration what information the other person needs in order to understand what she is trying to convey.
- She tends to put ideas together without regard for good boundaries, spoiling her own productions.

Her phrasing of the dragon as being "without a tail" can be considered during item interpretative. This examinee portrayed several of her figures as distorted or gory. In addition to the dragon, there is the "three-pronged" praying mantis (Card I), the bloody pigs coming out of the uterus (Card II), the stomachs and lungs being sacrificed (Card III), the swamp monster with the seaweed (Card IV), the girls with the alter ego (Card VII), the mountain that is actually the inside of a human body (Card VIII), and two aliens that morphed into one (Card IX). This finding raises the possibility that the examinee sees herself as distorted.

For the Structural Summary interpretatives, a review of the global scores indicates that the examinee gave a reasonable number of responses (24), so she was as productive as would have been expected. She had five Populars and two of her other responses would have been Populars had she not embellished them as much as she did. Thus, this is an individual who is able to see the world as the rest of us see it. She had a high number of pairs, a finding that many Rorschach clinicians would interpret as a high level of narcissism. Her reaction times were within the normal range. Her Affective Ratio suggested that she was energized and may be overproductive in emotionally evoking situations (the color cards).

There appeared to be a balance in her manner of approach to situations, but that impression was achieved by the conversion of many detail (D) responses into wholes (Ws), a conversion accomplished simply by adding them together. If we were to rescore all of those responses, our examinee would have a preponderance of D responses. Consequently, she should be seen as not being very good at holistic thinking, the capacity to see the whole as a unified and coherent unit. The examinee did not use the white space or rotations. If these lows were interpretable, the finding would mean that our examinee tended to look at the world in a fairly conventional way, accepting the way reality is presented to her without much questioning or exploration. However, the average number of white spaces and rotations is so low that an absence of those scores is not interpretable.

The examinee had a reasonable number of movement responses. Although she favored the animal movement, the ratio was not pronounced enough to be interpretable. The active versus passive ratio was acceptable. Her form (F), color (C), and achromatic color (C') responses were significant: There was an excessive number of C responses. One is tempted to add her FC' responses on the achromatic cards to the FC and CF counts because, given the rest of the data, those responses should be seen as a measure of emotionality. For those responses, she notices the black color as she noticed the red for the chromatic cards. In any event, she clearly is inclined to be driven by her emotions in an emotionally evoking situation. She is an intuitive ("feeling") person instead of a thinker. It is noteworthy, however, that she had enough form in her responses so that she would not be seen as an impulsive and emotionally acting out sort of individual.

An examination of the content areas revealed that the examinee had too many fantasized human figures in comparison with her pure human perceptions. The finding suggested trouble perceiving other human beings the way they are, as separate entities with their own feelings, wishes, and agendas. The high animal count also supported the idea that she keeps a distance from others. The indication was that she could have difficulty establishing and maintaining effective human relationships.

As noted, the Rorschach is at its best when we are examining the person's thought process, and this case is no exception. The quality of the responses obtained from this examinee left much to be desired: Seven of her responses (29% of the total) were of poor form quality. In other words, almost one third of the time her perceptions were not consistent with the shape of the inkblot. Even more concerning were the numerous responses that merited a Special Score. As previously discussed, many of the problems seen involved the contamination of one response with another and the incongruous combination of responses. The idiosyncratic nature of her thinking was also shown in the inappropriate phrasing included in some of the responses. The Special Scores also showed aggressive tendencies.

For the sequence interpretatives one can explore trends in this protocol. The first response and the response she gave to Card V were among her best. For these cards, she could give a popular whole response without having to integrate details. It was also noteworthy that the Special Scores disappeared on Card X, even though some of her responses to that card were of poor quality. A possible explanation may be that Card X is so discordant that she did not even try to integrate the distinct elements.

To compose the report for a clinical case, the diagnostician would consider historical data as well as data from the other psychological tests used during the evaluation. An example of an integrated report is offered in Chapter 12. For the purposes of this chapter, the report is limited to the information that has been covered. The report may start by noting that one of the reasons for the referral was the need to assess the patient for a possible attention deficit disorder. Because the patient had a history of psychiatric problems, the full evaluation included the Rorschach. The report would then proceed to give a detailed coverage of the intellectual evaluation leading to the conclusion that the examinee did not have a disability of the attentional function of the type that would be consistent with the current definition of the attention deficit disorder. The report for this examinee might include the following comments:

> Even though the examinee did not demonstrate attention deficits in the intellectual evaluation, the ability to concentrate—like any other intellectual function—is one that the person may or may not use at any particular moment. The thought process revealed on the Rorschach was scattered and disorganized enough that it may rob this individual of the ability to function effectively. For one thing, this examinee tends to be superficial in her communications. She is inclined to use inaccurate terms when she is talking, and she functions in an idiosyncratic mode, often unaware that she has not managed to communicate what she was trying to say to the other person. Her thinking tends to be concrete and she may put ideas together in a loose manner, perhaps jumping from one unrelated topic to the next without much focus. One idea may be put together with another in a way that is incongruous, and diminishes or contaminates both ideas. The lack of poor boundaries in her thinking is likely to expand into her visualization of interpersonal relationships. In other words, the expectations she holds for her role, and the role that others play in her social interactions, may be poorly formed and unstable.
>
> The indications were that the examinee is an emotive individual. Even if she does not act impulsively, she tends to very responsive to emotional stimulation. This tendency may also

contribute to the scattered functioning described above; she may be captured by one emotional situation or another in a disorganizing sort of way. Especially at those times when she becomes emotionally involved, she may lose track of the actual facts of the situation she is facing and think about those situations in a way that is unrealistic or inaccurate. All of this, once more, may contribute to her functioning in an ineffective manner. Given the problems the examinee showed with her thinking process, one must be concerned about a possible decompensation in the future, at times of stress.

Perhaps partly as a result of the examinee's poor functioning and boundary problems, the test results suggested that she has poor self-esteem and does not see herself in a good light in comparison to others. Such views may lead, in turn, to her keeping a distance from others and not having a good social network.

To sum up, the testing showed that the examinee has the intellectual capacity to pay attention. The concerns about the way she functions that brought her to the present evaluation are best understood as having to do with an ineffective thought process that is scattered and disorganized. The examinee is at a point in her life when she needs to accomplish some major goals in order to make a good transition into adulthood. The problems uncovered by the testing are likely to encumber her progress, both in terms of obtaining the needed training and education, and in terms of her establishing the social network she will need later on in life. Consequently, it would be useful for her to be involved in psychotherapy. It would be particularly beneficial if the treatment would lead to her becoming more aware of her thinking process and more thoughtful and focused.

Summary

This chapter offered a navigational map of the steps to be followed in evaluating a Rorschach protocol and drafting the report. What remains to be covered is the increased sophistication that can be derived from being attentive to Rorschach profiles (Chapter 11) and with the integration of Rorschach data with other sources of information as the final steps in the writing of the report (Chapter 12).

Rorschach Profiles | 11

The sophisticated way of interpreting a personality inventory is to consider the score profile rather than the single elevation of scales. For tests such as the Minnesota Multiphasic Personality Inventory (MMPI-2; Butcher, Dahlstrom, Graham, Tellegen, & Kaemmer, 1989) or the Millon Clinical Multiaxial Inventory (MCMI-III; Millon, 1994), more accurate and meaningful descriptions can be generated by considering the set of elevated scales together, because the elevation of one scale can change the character of the elevation of another scale. On the MCMI-III, for instance, the clinical picture of the person with elevations on the Dependent and Avoidant scales looks very different from that of the person with elevations on the Dependent and Compulsive scales. The submissiveness of the first person is accompanied by nervousness and social isolation, whereas the second person will appear less inadequate and more orderly and in control (Choca, 2004).

The same rationale can be applied to the Rorschach. Consider a Rorschach profile with a high number of detailed

DOI: 10.1037/14039-011
The Rorschach Inkblot Test: An Interpretive Guide for Clinicians, by J. P. Choca

associations (D). If the protocol contains 20 responses, the D score could reflect an individual who pays too much attention to details and is more inclined to see the trees rather than the forest. On the other hand, if the protocol contained 75 responses, the high D would not be necessarily interpreted as indicating the individual's manner of approach because it is difficult to give that many responses without obtaining a high D score.

In his interpretative work, Exner (2003) was obviously trying to encourage clinicians to avoid the interpretation of single markers on the Rorschach and to consider instead the entire profile. Unfortunately, this kind of sophistication is even harder to achieve with the Rorschach than with the personality inventories. As noted in Chapter 1 of this volume, the interpretative system Exner proposed is difficult to understand and learn, and it makes many assumptions that may not be true for a particular examinee. Although there is no other profile interpretative system for the Rorschach, seasoned Rorschach clinicians look at the entire protocol and typically do not interpret one Rorschach marker at a time. Such clinicians can look at the entire protocol and see the emergence of a profile, a profile that places the examinee into one of a number of finite categories.

In this chapter, I describe the characteristics of some Rorschach profiles. Although some of these profiles may be associated with a psychiatric diagnosis, no diagnoses are mentioned in these descriptions. As explained in Chapter 1, much of the Rorschach criticism has been earned by those who have tried to sell the Rorschach as the diagnostic instrument that it is not. To arrive at a diagnosis from the fourth edition of the *Diagnostic and Statistical Manual of Mental Disorders (DSM–IV*; American Psychiatric Association, 1994), the clinician has to evaluate each of the criteria for that diagnosis and decide whether the patient meets the criteria. The Rorschach findings can perhaps speak to one or more of the criteria, but that would be about the best that this instrument can do.

Two approaches have been historically used for psychological classification. One approach is to provide the criteria that the individual or the protocol has to meet to be considered an example of that diagnostic group. This approach was followed by some test interpretative cookbooks (e.g., Lachar, 1974) and by the third and fourth editions of the *Diagnostic and Statistical Manual of Mental Disorders (DSM–III*; American Psychiatric Association, 1980; American Psychiatric Association, 1994). The other approach, used in the first and second edition of the *Diagnostic and Statistical Manual of Mental Disorders* (American Psychiatric Association, 1948, 1968), and favored by the proposed fifth edition of the DSM-5 (see http://www.DSM-5.org), is to describe a prototype and require the clinician to judge how closely the individual resembles that prototype. This prototypical approach is the one used in this chapter to discuss the Rorschach profiles.

It should be obvious that there are many more Rorschach profiles than the ones selected for this book. The selected profiles are the ones that, in my experience, come up with more frequency. It should also be noted that no examinee will fit any of the profiles perfectly. Moreover, many protocols represent a mixture of more than one of the profiles described here. The protocol of an adolescent with an oppositional defiant disorder, for instance, may fit both the Rebellious Antagonistic and the Impulsive Over-Emotional profiles below. Nevertheless, these profiles represent patterns of Rorschach scores that occur with some frequency and that can be interpreted in a more sophisticated way than by interpreting single markers.

The clinical approach advocated throughout this book blends empirical data with the more subjective and intuitive recognition of what is going on with the examinee. This chapter again integrates the nomothetic and idiographic elements. A certain amount of insight and clinical judgment is required to use these profiles. The clinician must judge whether the data fit the profile sufficiently closely that the profile can be considered a good reflection of the examinee. Even if it is a good fit, the profile description will undoubtedly need some accommodations: Some material will have to be taken out because it does not apply to a particular examinee, and some findings will have to be added to increase the profile's accuracy and usefulness.

One of the advantages of profiling a protocol is that the clinician is then able to expand what is said about the individual with a description of the profile. However, the report should state clearly that the material refers to what is typically true of similar people and that every point made may not be substantiated with this specific individual.

Guarded Minimal Compliance

The Guarded Minimal Compliance profile is characterized by few responses; in fact, the individual may have to be encouraged or pressured to give the 14 responses that are considered necessary for the test to be valid. The responses are usually superficial and lack embellishments. The type of responses given often consists of the most obvious associations to the shape of the inkblot.

Exhibit 11.1 provides a good example. This protocol was obtained from an adolescent who did not see any personal benefit in taking psychological tests; he had been told that he would be discharged from the psychiatric ward and could go home as soon as the testing was completed. Note that he originally gave only one response per card and had to be encouraged to give an additional four responses. The responses typically revolved around the most obvious aspect of the ink-blot and were either whole or detail responses, depending on where the most obvious aspect was for the particular card. He had a very high number of populars, and there were a couple of repetitive responses. The associations were mostly based only on the shape of the inkblot, although he included movement in cards where the movement was part of the popular response. Most of his responses involved animals, except for the cards where the human figure was easily seen. On the other hand, the responses were of good quality and, outside of the per-severations, there were no Special Scores.

What can the Rorschach tell us about an individual with this pro-file? In the example given in Exhibit 11.1, the clinician acknowledged that the examinee was an adolescent who was eager to go home and who responded in a passive-aggressive way. He was compliant and did what was expected of him in a minimalist manner; he restricted himself to what was barely necessary to complete the task as soon as possible. Similar people may use the same approach in life, never objecting to what is asked of them or taking a stand, but never making enough of an effort to obtain good benefits out of the situation. The Rorschach indicates that the examinee was not oppositional (e.g., no cards were rotated, there was no use of white space), but he could be perceived as unproductive. It may be difficult to establish a strong therapeutic alliance with this individual because he might find it hard to do more than to go through the motions. In other words, he may attend the sessions without making the kind of investment necessary to derive benefit from the sessions.

Cognitive Impairment

The profile of a person with cognitive deficits may resemble the Guarded Minimal Compliance profile. Following Hermann Rorschach's (1921) original claims, some clinicians have proposed using the Rorschach to diagnose neuropsychological problems (Colligan, 1997; Perry & Potterat, 1997; Perry, Potterat, Auslander, Kaplan, & Jeste, 1996). Such use of the Rorschach is not advocated in this book because current neuropsycholog-ical batteries offer much better tools to examine cognitive deficits. Nev-ertheless, it is useful to be aware of the Cognitive-Limited profile because it can be of great diagnostic significance when it appears unexpectedly. Moreover, the Rorschach may be used with neurologically impaired individuals who are also experiencing emotional problems; in those cases the clinician must have a sense of what would have been expected simply as a result of the low intellectual capacity. Needless to say, in such situations it is important to test the individual's intellectual capacity with other appropriate instruments.

The similarities between the Cognitively Impaired and the Guarded Minimal Compliance profiles include the low productivity in terms of the number of responses and the superficiality of the responses. The typical cognitively impaired protocol, however, includes a certain amount of confusion and is more perseverative. High reaction times may reflect struggles to comply with the task. The form quality of the responses may also suffer, and a number of Special Scores may be obtained. The poor-quality responses and Special Scores can typically be seen as resulting from the limited abilities, rather than from a bizarre or psychotic thought process. In the example offered in Exhibit 11.2, for instance, all of the Special Scores are mild deviant verbalizations or perseverations. The other attributes noted here can also be seen in that protocol.

The examinee was a 24-year-old woman who had been arrested for prostitution. She angrily explained to the examiner that the arresting officer claimed she had offered to have sexual intercourse with him for money but that she had not offered any such thing. All she had offered was to perform oral sex for money. The patient did not understand that what she admitted having offered was just as illegal. She had signed a confession at the time of the arrest on the mistaken assumption that she would be allowed to leave after she signed, because the confession cited only oral sex. The patient had trouble understanding why she was still in jail.

As can be seen at the beginning of the Rorschach, and again on Card VII, the examinee tended to misconceive the task: She thought that the inkblots were actual drawings of an object, and that her job was to determine what the object had been before the figure was distorted. She gave the 14 required responses only after being pressured to do so. With one exception, all of her associations involved animals, suggesting immaturity or infantilism. Again with one exception, all of the responses were based entirely on the shape of the inkblot, without any other determinant. However, in contrast to the Guarded Minimal Compliance profile, she obviously wanted to do a good job and frequently offered additional information about her responses. She used the wrong word ("horns") to describe a part of the animal on several occasions, and she could not think of the right name of the animal in other cases. She had few popular responses, and her responses had poor form quality.

The description that may be derived from a Rorschach protocol of this type is that of a simpleminded individual who is easily confused by the complexity of many tasks of daily life. The protocol is characteristic of people who have limited abilities and who, as a result, tend to be minimally productive. Their superficial understandings often do not have enough depth to allow them to function in an effective manner. They are childlike and infantile in their thinking, typically behaving in ways that would be more typical of a much younger person. Such people are emotionally bland, seldom experiencing strong positive or negative emotions. Their lack of intellectual capacity is likely to lead to a distorted view of the environment so that the individual does not see the world the way it is normally seen. At times they may have idiosyncratic ideas or demonstrate unacceptable behaviors as a result of their intellectual limitations.

Over-Controlled Micro-View

Like the two previous profiles, the Over-Controlled Micro-View profile is constricted and has a high form (F) percentile or Lambda. The determinants used are more of the movement and shading variety, rather than achromatic color (C'), and tend to emphasize form (e.g., FC' rather than C'F or C'). In contrast to the previous profiles, however, this profile has a good number of responses. The locations used for those responses are predominantly small details rather than whole perceptions. Much effort is invested on the task; the examinee sometimes checks to see that he or she is doing what is expected. The effort may involve embellishments that do not add new determinants (e.g., the examinee may enumerate different parts of the perception, without adding any elaborations that go beyond the form). Original or unusual responses are typically of good quality.

Individuals with the Over-Controlled Micro-View profile are likely to emphasize the small details, sometimes missing the overall picture. This type of person may focus on the bark of trees rather than the trees or the forest. Such people hold the life assumption that one should work hard to avoid making mistakes, which can be accomplished by maintaining routines and attending to detail. They are inclined to be orderly and plan for the future. They are conscientious, typically preparing well and completing their work on schedule. They tend to be meticulous, dependable, industrious, and persistent. These individuals believe in discipline and practice self-restraint; their emotions are usually kept well under control. The over-control of the emotions tends to give this type of individual a characteristic flavor: They are formal and proper and unlikely to open up and act spontaneously in front of others. They are sometimes seen as perfectionistic, distant, occasionally inflexible, and perhaps indecisive before they have a chance to study all possible alternatives. However, they are often careful, deliberate, righteous, honest, dependable, and hard-working people.

The individual with an Over-Controlled Micro-View profile may have trouble working with some aspects of the environment, and certain situations (e.g., those that change abruptly from one moment to the next in an unpredictable manner, those where following rules does not lead to the desired outcome) can be expected to be particularly stressful. However, controlled individuals are very well suited for situations in which it is important to be accurate and meticulous.

The individual with this profile may find it easier to establish a therapeutic alliance with a professional who is formal, proper, punctual, and predictable. Clinicians who keep a bit of a distance from the patient and allow him or her to control significant parts of the session would also put the person at ease. Explanations of the diagnosis, the nature of the "illness," and the expected course of treatment can hold a special appeal for this person.

Rebellious Antagonism

Individuals with a Rebellious Antagonism profile are likely to make extraneous comments that reveal their attitude toward the testing or life in general. The most blatant are comments about "the stupid tests" or comments expressing the view that the test could not possibly lead to any benefit. Hostile remarks about the examiner or others in the health care professions are sometimes expressed. The protocol itself is typically marked by rotations and the use of white space. Aggressive movement or content Special Scores may be present.

The protocol in Exhibit 11.3, for example, starts with an elephant that is "snickering" after eating the caretaker's lunch, something it knew it "shouldn't have done." Thus, right off the bat the examinee announces that he is sort of a mischievous individual. The protocol is full of movement and color, suggesting a good deal of energy and emotionality. Two responses with inanimate movement betray a certain amount of tension with the environment. The color tends to have little form, indicating a capacity for acting out. On the other hand, the protocol is well organized and is free of bizarre or psychotic elements.

The Rebellious Antagonism profile describes an individual who typically shows a disregard for family or community rules or social norms. Frequently these individuals seem to search for ways of bypassing controls so that they do not have to comply with what is expected of them. They live as though rules were made to be broken and their enjoyment of life depended largely on their ability to circumvent rules that do not please them. Trouble with authority may include a history of legal or disciplinary problems. They emphasize immediate gratification, living mostly for the day. They can be irresponsible, repeatedly failing to live up to their commitments. Self-centered, they are inclined to be unresponsive to the needs of others.

These individuals are often cold or insensitive. They are likely to distrust others and to question others' motives; they assume that they have to be vigilant to protect themselves. They tend to be argumentative and contentious. When crossed, pushed on personal matters, or embarrassed, they become angry, revengeful, abusive, cruel, or vindictive. They typically use projection as a defense, blaming others for anything that goes wrong. People with this profile are likely to be "touchy"; excitable and irritable, they often have a history of treating others in a rough or mean manner and of angrily "flying off the handle" whenever they are confronted or opposed.

Impulsive Over-Emotional

The Impulsive Over-Emotional protocol is characterized by fast reaction times and responses that have to be amended during the inquiry. Whole responses and the common details are favored over the more unusual locations. Color is widely used, with a preference for responses that emphasize color rather than form (i.e., CF and C as opposed to FC).

Exhibit 11.4 gives an example of this type of protocol. The patient was a 30-year-old White divorced man with a history of impulsive behaviors. He was tested in the psychiatric ward after he jabbed a pencil into his left arm because he felt "desperate" about his life situation. He denied suicidal intent and actually ridiculed the idea that anyone would think a person could kill himself by jabbing a pencil into his arm in a psychiatric ward. The action, he explained, was taken impulsively, without thinking about it and without purpose, just the way some people might throw an object against the wall in disgust. In this case, he admitted to feeling shame for being a "loser." Having experienced the physical pain of the wound, he vowed never to hurt himself again. His history, however, was peppered with similar impulsive acts that had cost him jobs and relationships.

Looking at Exhibit 11.4, the reader will notice all of the attributes noted in the first paragraph of this section. It is also noteworthy that many of the responses were given as additional responses, during the Inquiry phase, as opposed to the Free Association. (Those responses appear at the tail end of the protocol.) This tendency may also be the mark of an impulsive person, an individual who does not take the time to be thoughtful and productive from the start but has more ideas that are added later on.

The clinician who treats such patients may note that they are impulsive in their responses, seldom taking the time to think things over before they act. When they are in an emotion-inducing situation, they are blinded by their feelings to the extent that the possible consequences of their behavior are not taken into account. They may be so seduced by an emotion-evoking situation that they behave in unproductive ways.

Thought Disorder

Singer (1977) proposed that people with borderline personality disorder could be diagnosed by comparing their performance on a structured test, such as the Wechsler Adult Intelligence Scale, and on the Rorschach. Although this distinction proved to be too simplistic for the diagnosis of borderline personality disorder (Murray, 1997), Singer's observation is valuable in that there are indeed individuals for whom the distinction holds: People who do well in situations in which the expectations and boundaries are well defined (e.g., military service) but who have a great deal of trouble functioning in situations in which the expectations and requirements are more fluid and ambiguous.

Murray (1992) characterized the Thought Disordered Rorschach as having four attributes: high number of Special Scores, inaccurate perceptions indicated by the poor form quality of the responses, interpersonal ineptness as reflected in by unreal human perceptions or responses with poor human movement, and inadequate controls denoted by responses in which other determinants (e.g., color) were more important than the form (e.g., CF or C as opposed to FC).

A fifth attribute can be identified: poor boundaries. In the context of the Rorschach, poor boundary responses mix one perception with another. In the milder forms, a response expands the original perception to include something else in the inkblot (e.g., the perception of the two bongo players on Card III [D1] is expanded to include two guitars that are hanging as decorations in the background [D2]). In this example the examinee does not seem able to focus on the original perception and brings in other perceptions into the mix. More severe boundary problems are seen with people who combine more distant perceptions (e.g., the bongo players on Card III are related in some way to the two people high-fiving each other on Card II) or combine perceptions in a peculiar manner (e.g., the bongo players shared love of music is shown by the red heart suspended between the two of them).

Murray (1992) labeled individuals demonstrating his four attributes as *psychotic*. That label may not be accurate for this type of Rorschach protocol if *psychotic* is understood to refer to a delusional individual. The *thought disorder* label is a better term for what is described here. As already noted in Chapter 9, many individuals show a thought process disturbance even if they are not schizophrenic or otherwise psychotic. Perhaps the most outstanding strength of the Rorschach is the instrument's capacity to reveal difficulties with the thinking process. The negative impact that such contaminated thinking has on the person's ability to adjust and cope with the environment cannot be overestimated.

Exhibit 11.5 shows an example of such a thought-disordered individual. This protocol was obtained from a 25-year-old woman who had run away from the halfway house in which she had been living. She was picked up by the police in a confused state.

The Thought Disorder protocol characterizes an individual whose thinking is disorganized. Individuals with thought disorder may jump from one topic to the next and explain themselves poorly, so that they cannot be clearly understood. They may misinterpret neutral events as actions that relate to them in a very specific way or that have some sort of special meaning. They may be prone to misinterpreting the statements or actions of others. They tend to be eccentric in appearance, thinking, or verbal expression, and they may have habits that others find peculiar. At times their emotional reactions may seem odd or inappropriate. They may report unusual perceptions or experiences and express strange beliefs. Finally, such people may mix their own personal idiosyncrasies with other material in their conversations.

Morbid Dysphoria

The Dysphoria protocol is typically constricted in that it may have a high F% or Lambda. In contrast with other constricted protocols (i.e., the Guarded Minimal Compliance, Cognitive Impairment, Over-controlled-Micro-View), however, this protocol contains a great deal of emotion. The emotion may be partly expressed through the use of black colors and shading. The contents include morbid perceptions, such as deformed animals or human beings, road kill, death, and destruction. Although not necessarily short, the protocol is labored, with the examinee having to make an effort to complete the task. The Reaction Time is typically high for the entire protocol.

Sometimes the Rorschach becomes particularly helpful when individuals are in denial or have a reason to hide their true feelings. Exhibit 11.6 provides a good example of a person who was obviously sad and morbid in her outlook on life. Yet, when taking the psychiatric questionnaires, she answered the items so that she appeared to be close to the picture of mental health.

The protocol starts in a very tentative way, as if the examinee were very unsure of herself ("kind of looks like a bat" with the examinee's "guessing" that she saw the bat because the card was black). The tentativeness also translates into a very labored performance with extremely long reaction times. In many instances it took several minutes before she was able to offer a free association. When asked about this long initial reaction time, she revealed that an effort was required for her to say that she "can't think of anything" (comment in Response 4).

Six of the 19 responses obtained were driven by the blackness of the inkblot. Yet the protocol showed a great deal of emotion in terms of a good number of color responses. Morbid thoughts frequently entered the examinee's thinking in the form of "dead," "squashed," "burnt," an animal that is "almost a skeleton," creatures that are "hurt badly," and dead people who are still squirting blood.

In describing this type of protocol, the clinician can talk about an individual who is feeling sad and demonstrating a dysphoric mood. Such people typically have a pessimistic outlook in life. They show a diminished interest in their daily activities and do not derive much pleasure from their current involvements. Life may become a burden, an unwanted task that has little personal meaning. They may find it difficult to make decisions, even about minor matters. They typically see their situation as difficult, occasionally struggling with the issue of whether life is worth living. Individuals with similar test profiles typically experience vegetative symptoms, such as fatigue or a low energy level. They may move at a slow pace.

Hyper-energized Euphoria

The Hyper-energized Euphoria protocol is the flip side of the Morbid-Dysphoria protocol. The individual with this protocol gives an excessive number of responses in a very jovial and effortless manner. A great deal of emotionality and movement may also be expressed through the use of color and personal embellishments. The average Reaction Time may be short. Typically much is added to responses already given during the Inquiry, and responses are added as the testing proceeds. Although the protocol may include rotations and the use of white space, those scores can be seen as part of the individual's effort to be more productive, as opposed to being oppositional or negativistic.

Exhibit 11.7 provides an example. The first thing to note is the large number of responses, indicating the examinee's hyperproductivity. The examinee's reaction time was about half of the average, which indicates that the majority of the responses were given fairly quickly, without much time for thinking. There was an abundance of whole responses suggesting a tendency to jump at the most obvious ideas. The engulfing of the surface holistic view included much use of the white space. Her use of the white space, however, is not in the spirit of an oppositional reversal of the figure–ground perspective but in the spirit of including whatever could be fitted into the whole. (Only one response was given with the card rotated.)

With this profile, the high number of responses inflates the number of determinants. To adjust the 44 responses that were obtained to the usual 22, the number of determinants may be cut in half. Even with that adjustment, the record contains a high amount of movement and color (FM, m, CF), indicating a great deal of psychological energy and activity. The high FM suggested the childish nature of this person's responding, perhaps partly due to her mental state at the time of the testing. The inanimate movement perhaps betrayed a high level of tension in her interactions with the environment. The reasonable F count and the balance between movement and color showed some capacity for control. This was not the case, however, when the examinee was dealing with emotional stimuli. The color balance showed a potential for much acting out; she had no controlled color responses, whereas she gave nine of the less controlled (CF + C) color responses.

The clinical characterization of this profile may center on the person's overproductiveness, elevated mood, and tendency toward expansiveness or grandiosity. Such people are typically overenergized and overly talkative, sometimes speaking fast in a pressured sort of way. At times they become overly invested in a project or in pleasurable activities, and they can no longer follow a reasonable daily schedule. No longer able to moderate their activities, they become too driven by their goals to conduct their business effectively.

As seen in this chapter, there are recognizable profiles, characterized by a pattern of Rorschach attributes, that can be helpful to the clinician in the use of this test.

EXHIBIT 11.1

Rorschach Protocol of a Minimally Compliant Adolescent

Rorschach Protocol

----

1. Card I Reaction Time: 0″
   SCORE=> W o F o A P
   cd b a bat
   INQUIRY: here is the body and the wings
   ANYTHING ELSE? no
   Is this the way it works? Are we going to have to do this for every card?

2. Card II Reaction Time: 6″
   SCORE=> D o FMa o (2)(A)
   here r 2 bears playing patty-cake
   INQUIRY: head, u c the paws touching
   ANYTHING ELSE? no
   THEY R PLAYING PATTY-CAKE? Well, that's what it looks like! They
   must be cartoon characters
   ANYTHING ELSE? no
   LOCATION: D1 + D2

3. Card III Reaction Time: 14″
   SCORE=> D o Ma o (2)H P
   2 waiters setting up a table at a restaurant
   INQUIRY: Here r the heads, they r leaning back
   >? no
   LOCATION: D1

4. Card IV Reaction Time: 5″
   SCORE=> D o F o (A) P
   This is Godzilla
   INQUIRY: the head up here and the big feet
   ANYTHING ELSE? no
   LOCATION: D7

5. Card V Reaction Time: 6″
   SCORE=> W o F o A P
   Here u have a bat
   INQUIRY: the head and the wings, the feet
   ANYTHING ELSE? no

6. Card VI Reaction Time: 12″
   SCORE=> W o F o A P
   An animal skin rug
   INQUIRY: this is what is left of the head and the legs
   >? no

(continued)

EXHIBIT 11.1 (Continued)

7. Card VII Reaction Time: 8″
   SCORE=> D o F o (2)Hd.Cg P
   2 Indian girls
   INQUIRY: they have a feather in their head
   >? no
   LOCATION: D1

8. Card VIII Reaction Time: 7″
   SCORE=> D o F o (2)A P
   2 mountain lions
   INQUIRY: the head and the feet
   >? no
   LOCATION: D1

9. Card IX Reaction Time: 28″
   SCORE=> W CF u Art
   This is nothing. I cannot see anything here. [Patient told that
   at least one response was needed in every card] Well, maybe one of
   those modern art paintings that is just colors.
   INQUIRY: this is just colors. An abstract painting
   >? no

10. Card X Reaction Time: 46″
    SCORE=> D o F o A P
    a crab
    INQUIRY: just the legs and the body
    >? no
    LOCATION: D1

11. Card I Reaction Time: 92″
    SCORE=> W o F o A PSV
    [pt told that he did not give enough responses for the test to be
    valid. He was given the cards and told to pick cards and give
    at least 4 more responses]
    This cd also b a butterfly
    INQUIRY: well, I dk, a bat or a butterfly, an animal with wings

12. Card II Reaction Time: 15″
    SCORE=> D ma o Sc
    here u have a space shuttle taking off
    INQUIRY: this part is the exhaust
    >? no
    LOCATION: DS5 + D3

13. Card II Reaction Time: 9″
    SCORE=> D o Ma o (2)(H).Cg PSV
    or 2 people dressed in a holloween costume
    INQUIRY: they have a mask on or something. They r hi-fiving each other
    >? no
    LOCATION: D1 + D2

EXHIBIT 11.1 *(Continued)*

```
14. Card X Reaction Time: 29"
    SCORE=>  D  o  F  o  A
    Here u have a green snake. Now, that should b enough, no?
    INQUIRY: well, it just looks like it
    >? no
    LOCATION: D4
```

— HERMANN —

Multi-Health Systems. Program written by James Choca, Ph.D.,
and Dan Garside

Rorschach Score Sequence

Card	No	Time	Scoring						
I	1	0	W	o	F	o	A	P	
II	2	6	D	o	FMa	o	(2)(A)		
III	3	14	D	o	Ma	o	(2)H	P	
IV	4	5	D	o	F	o	(A)	P	
V	5	6	W	o	F	o	A	P	
VI	6	12	W	o	F	o	(A)	P	
VII	7	8	D	o	F	o	(2)Hd.Cg	P	
VIII	8	7	D	o	F	o	(2)A	P	
IX	9	28	W		CF	u	Art		
X	10	46	D	o	F	o	A	P	
I	11	92	W	o	F	o	A		PSV
II	12	15	D		ma	o	Sc		
II	13	9	D	o	Ma	o	(2)(H).Cg		PSV
X	14	29	D	o	F	o	A		

(continued)

EXHIBIT 11.1 (Continued)

Program written by James Choca, Ph.D., and Dan Garside

— HERMANN —

Rorschach Structural Summary

Global	n	%	Location	n	%	Determinants	n	%	Contents	n	%	Quality	n	%
R	14		W	5	36	M	2	14	CONT	5		OF ALL		
Rejects	0		D	9	64	FM	1	7				+	0	0
			Dd	0	0	m	1	7	H	1	6	o	13	93
P	8	57	DW	0	0	FT	0	0	(H)	1	6	u	1	7
(P)	0	0	S	0	0	TF	0	0	Hd	1	6	-	0	0
						T	0	0	(Hd)	0	0	none	0	0
(2)	5	36	POSITION			FY	0	0	Hx	0	0			
Fr	0	0	^	14	100	YF	0	0	A	6	38	OF F		
rF	0	0	<	0	0	Y	0	0	(A)	3	19	+	0	0
3r+(2)		36	>	0	0	FV	0	0	Ad	0	0	o	9	100
			v	0	0	VF	0	0	(Ad)	0	0	u	0	0
						V	0	0	Ab	0	0	-	0	0
RT Ach	20					FC'	0	0	Al	0	0	none	0	0
RT Ch	19					C'F	0	0	An	0	0			
			DEV QUAL			C'	0	0	Art	1	6	OF S		
AFR	40		+	0	0	FC	0	0	Ay	0	0	+	0	0
			o	12	86	CF	1	7	Bl	0	0	o	0	0
			v/+	0	0	C	0	0	Bt	0	0	u	0	0
Zf	0		v	0	0	Cn	0	0	Cg	2	13	-	0	0
ZSum	0.0					FD	0	0	Cl	0	0	none	0	0
						F	9	64	Ex	0	0			

RATIOS					RATIOS			SPECIAL SCORES	
W	5	Blends	0	Fi	0			DV1	0	0
M	2			Fd	0	0		DV2	0	0
		RATIOS		Ge				DR1	0	0
W	5	a	4	Hh				DR2	0	0
D	9	p	0	Ls	29			INC1	0	0
		M	2	Na	0			INC2	6	0
		wtd C	1.0	Sc	1			FAB1	0	0
				Sx	0			FAB2	0	0
		M+wtd C	3	Vo	0			ALOG	0	0
				Xy	0			CON	0	0
		FM+m	2	Idio	0			AB	0	0
		Y+T+V+C'	0	RATIOS				CP	0	0
				H+HD	3			AG	0	0
		&FMmYTVC'	2	A+AD	9			MOR	0	0
								CFB	0	0
		FC	0	H+A	11			PER	0	0
		CF+C	1	HD+AD	1			COP	0	0
				A%	56			PSV	2	14

EXHIBIT 11.2

Rorschach Protocol of an Adult Woman With Cognitive Impairment

Rorschach Protocol

----

1. Card I Reaction Time: 24″
   SCORE=> W o F o A P
   I am sorry, I dk what this is
   INSTRUCTIONS ARE REPEATED EMPHASIZING THE FACT THAT THESE ARE INKBLOTS
   this is like a bat
   INQUIRY: this shape over here [DdS30]
   ? and the wings [D2]
   ANYTHING ELSE? this [Dd22]
   ? that's because it has eyes there
   ANYTHING ELSE? no
   THIS SHAPE [DdS30]? I dk, that's part of the bat
   WAHT PART? I dk
   ANYTHING ELSE? no
   LOCATION: W

2. Card II Reaction Time: 36″
   SCORE=> W o F - A DV1
   this is like a butterfly
   INQUIRY: bec of the wings [D1]
   ANYTHING ELSE? the little horns here [D2]
   ANYTHING ELSE? this over here [Dd25]
   ? that's like the tail
   ANYTHING ELSE? no
   LOCATION: W

3. Card III Reaction Time: 60″
   SCORE=> D F (H) (P)
   extra-terrestials
   INQUIRY: the head [Dd32] and the body [Dd22]
   ANYTHING ELSE? the feet [D5]
   ANYTHING ELSE? no
   LOCATION: D9

4. Card IV Reaction Time: 97″
   SCORE=> D F u A
   it has the shape of a toad
   INQUIRY: because it is this way [touches D7]
   ? because of the feet [D6]
   & this over here [touches D7]
   ? it's like the body
   ANYTHING ELSE? the head [D3]
   ANYTHING ELSE? the legs [D6]
   ANYTHING ELSE? no
   LOCATION: D7

EXHIBIT 11.2 *(Continued)*

5. Card IV Reaction Time: 15″
   SCORE=> W o FM a- A
   it looks like a monkey
   INQUIRY: it's like is standg up, it's walking, & this is the tail
   [D1]
   ANYTHING ELSE? everything else
   ? this is the monkey [ind W]
   ANYTHING ELSE? no
   LOCATION: W

6. Card V Reaction Time: 28″
   SCORE=> W o F o A P DV1
   this is like a bat
   INQUIRY: teh wings [D4] and the head [D6]
   ANYTHING ELSE? this thing here [D9]
   ? that's like the tail
   ANYTHING ELSE? the little horns [Dd34]
   ANYTHING ELSE? no
   LOCATION: W

7. Card VI Reaction Time: 40″
   SCORE=> D F o A
   this is like a spider
   INQUIRY: the shape of this thing here [D3]
   ANYTHING ELSE? no
   LOCATION: D3

8. Card VII Reaction Time: 68″
   SCORE=> W o F - A
   I dk what this is, they have changed it too much
   ? I dk what it used to be before
   INSTRUCTIONS REPEATED WITH THE EMPHASIS THAT THESE R INKBLOTS
   it looks like an animal that is in the water but I ct find exaclty
   what kd
   INQUIRY: rpts
   >? I dk
   LOCATION: W
   >? I dk
   WHAT KD OF AN ANIMAL? I dt rem, I dk how it is called
   >? it is something like a crab

9. Card VIII Reaction Time: 38″
   SCORE=> D F u A
   this looks like a spider
   INQUIRY: this part here [D4]
   >? by the shape of it
   ANYTHING ELSE? this here [Dd22]
   >? it's like the legs of the spider

(continued)

EXHIBIT 11.2 (Continued)

ANYTHING ELSE? no
LOCATION: D4

10. Card VIII Reaction Time: 37"
SCORE=> D F - A
it also has the shape of an animal that is in the water
INQUIRY: rpts
>? I dk
WHAT KD OF AN ANIMAL? one from the water
>? I dk the name, like a fish
LOCATION: D1

11. Card IX Reaction Time: 31"
SCORE=> W o F - A PSV
an animal from the water
INQUIRY: everything here
>? it looks like the body of a fish
ANYTHING ELSE? this thing here [D5]
? like the spine
ANYTHING ELSE? no
LOCATION: W

12. Card X Reaction Time: 20"
SCORE=> D F u A
an animal from the water
INQUIRY: this thing here looks like a shrimp [D9]
>? this thing here [ind Dd in top section]
? the eyes
ANYTHING ELSE? no
LOCATION: D9

13. Card X Reaction Time: 32"
SCORE=> Rejected
this has the shape of a shrimp
INQUIRY: this is the one I just gave u
WAS THE SHRIMP WHAT YOU MEANT BY AN ANIMAL FROM THE WATER? Yes

14. Card I Reaction Time: 44"
SCORE=> W o F o A PSV
EXPLAINED THAT AT LEAST ONE MORE RESPONSE IS NEEDED. GIVEN THE CHOICE
OF CARDS
a butterfly
INQUIRY: the body [D4] amd the wings [D2]
ANYTHING ELSE? no
LOCATION: W

15. Card X Reaction Time: 7"
SCORE=> D F o A
AFTER THE INQUIRY IT WAS EXPLANED THAT - BECAUSE R#13 TURNED OUT

EXHIBIT 11.2 *(Continued)*

TO BE THE SAME AS R#12, WE STILL NEED ANOTHER RESPONSE
this looks like an octupus
INQUIRY: bec of all the legs
ANYTHING ELSE? no
LOCATION: D1

— HERMANN —
Multi-Health Systems. Program written by James Choca, Ph.D.,
and Dan Garside

Rorschach Score Sequence

Card	No	Time	Scoring						
I	1	24	W	o	F	o	A	P	
II	2	36	W	o	F	–	A		DV1
III	3	60	D		F	o	(H)	(P)	
IV	4	97	D		F	u	A		
IV	5	15	W	o	FMa	–	A		
V	6	28	W	o	F	o	A	P	DV1
VI	7	40	D		F	o	A		
VII	8	68	W	o	F	–	A		
VIII	9	38	D		F	u	A		
VIII	10	37	D		F	–	A		
IX	11	31	W	o	F	–	A		PSV
X	12	20	D		F	u	A		
X	13	32	Rejected						
I	14	44	W	o	F	o	A		PSV
X	15	7	D		F	o	A		

Note. — HERMANN —
Multi-Health Systems. Program written by James Choca, Ph.D., and Dan Garside

(continued)

EXHIBIT 11.2 (Continued)

— HERMANN —

Rorschach Structural Summary

Global

	n	%
R	14	
Rejects	0	
P	2	14
(P)	1	7
(2)	0	0
Fr	0	0
rF	0	0
3r+(2)	0	
RT Ach	45	
RT Ch	33	
AFR	56	
Zf	0	
ZSum	0.0	

Location

	n	%
W	7	50
D	7	50
Dd	0	0
DW	0	0
S	0	0
POSITION		
^	14	100
<	0	0
>	0	0
v	0	0
DEV QUAL		
+	0	0
o	7	50
v/+	0	0
v	0	0

Determinants

	n	%
M	0	0
FM	1	7
m	0	0
FT	0	0
TF	0	0
T		
FY	0	0
YF	0	0
Y	0	0
FV	0	0
VF	0	0
V	0	0
FC'		
C'F		
C'		
FC	0	0
CF	0	0
C		
Cn		
FD	0	0
F	9	64

Contents

	n	%
CONT	2	0
H	0	0
(H)	1	7
Hd	0	0
(Hd)	0	0
Hx	0	0
A	13	93
(A)	0	0
Ad	0	0
(Ad)	0	0
Ab	0	0
Al	0	0
An	0	0
Art	0	0
Ay	0	0
Bl	0	0
Bt	0	0
Cg	0	0
Cl	0	0
Ex	0	0

Quality

	n	%
OF ALL		
+	0	0
o	5	36
u	3	21
-	5	36
none	1	0
OF F		
+	0	0
o	5	38
u	3	23
-	4	31
none	1	000
OF S		
+	0	0
o	0	0
u	0	0
-	0	0
none	0	0

RATIOS				Blends	0		Fi	0		SPECIAL SCORES	0	0
W	7			RATIOS			Fd	0		DV1	2	14
M	0			a	1		Ge	0		DV2	0	0
				p	0		Hh	7		DR1	0	0
W	7						Ls	0		DR2	0	0
D	7			M	0		Na	0		INC1	0	0
				wtd C	0.0		Sc	0		INC2	0	0
							Sx	0		FAB1	0	0
				M+wtd C	0		Vo	0		FAB2	0	0
							Xy	0		ALOG	0	0
				FM+m	1		Idio	0		CON	0	0
				Y+T+V+C'	0					AB		
							RATIOS			CP		
				&FMmYTVC'	1		H+HD	1		AG	0	0
							A+AD	13		MOR	0	0
				FC	0					CFB	0	0
				CF+C	0		H+A	14		PER	0	0
							HD+AD	0		COP	0	0
							A%	93		PSV	2	14

EXHIBIT 11.3

Rorschach Protocol of Teenage Girl With Substance Abuse Issues

Rorschach Protocol

----

1. Card I Reaction Time: 5″
   SCORE=> W o FM ao A P
   kd of like a butterfly
   INQUIRY: u can see it with the wings fully expanded in flight
   >? here is the body and the wings
   ANYTHING ELSE? no
   LOCATION: W

2. Card I Reaction Time: 5″
   SCORE=> Dd o FM.FC′ (2)A
   cd b 2 bears
   INQUIRY: just the head, they r howling in different directions, lookg
   away from each other
   ANYTHING ELSE? no, they r black
   ANYTHING ELSE? no
   LOCATION: Dd28

3. Card II Reaction Time: 1″
   SCORE=> D o FM.FC ao A
   a butterfly
   INQUIRY: it's red, with the wings outstretched, like it is takg off
   from the place where she had rested
   ANYTHING ELSE? no
   LOCATION: D3

4. Card III Reaction Time: 6″
   SCORE=> D o FM.FC ao A
   another butterfly
   INQUIRY: it is red
   ANYTHING ELSE? it is flitterg here in the cn
   ANYTHING ELSE? no
   LOCATION: D3

5. Card IV Reaction Time: 7″
   SCORE=> D o M.FD a H P
   one of those Russian dancers, when they kick their feet out
   INQUIRY: u c the feet kickg out
   ANYTHING ELSE? the head is kd of small so u r lookg at him from the
   bm
   ANYTHING ELSE? no
   LOCATION: D7

6. Card V Reaction Time: 5″
   SCORE=> W o FM.FC′.FD ao A P
   bat

EXHIBIT 11.3 *(Continued)*

INQUIRY: head {D6} & feet {D9}. It is flyg and u r lookg at it from above
FROM ABOVE? well the face is lookg down
ANYTHING ELSE? no, it is black
ANYTHING ELSE? no
LOCATION: W

7. Card VI Reaction Time: 1″
   SCORE=> D o FM ao (A)
   a weird bug of some sort
   INQUIRY: u have the wings and the head, it is takg off from this thing {Dd31}
   WEIRD? Well it is just strange looking, like something out of a cartoon
   LOCATION: D3

8. Card VI Reaction Time: 5″
   SCORE=> W v YF u Bt V
   v maybe a leaf
   INQUIRY: the way the inside looks, all dried up, with what used to be the vein in here {D12}
   ANYTHING ELSE? no
   LOCATION: W

9. Card VII Reaction Time: 7″
   SCORE=> D o M ao (2)Hd P
   2 ladies kissg
   faces
   INQUIRY: well, they r about to kiss, iwth their mouths pockered up
   ANYTHING ELSE? no
   LOCATION: D9

10. Card VIII Reaction Time: 2″
    SCORE=> D o FM.FC ao A P
    a badger
    INQUIRY: it is of a strange color, but it looks like it
    ANYTHING ELSE? it's climbg a mountain or something
    ANYTHING ELSE? no
    LOCATION: D1

11. Card IX Reaction Time: 3″
    SCORE=> W v FM.CF a- (A).Fd
    v maybe a weird bug, if u hold it upsidedown
    INQUIRY: it's got a green front and orange back {D2}. It is eating something up here {D9}
    BUG? just the way it looks
    ANYTHING ELSE? no
    EATING? it just looks like some red meat
    ANYTHING ELSE? no
    LOCATION: W

(continued)

EXHIBIT 11.3 (*Continued*)

12. Card X Reaction Time: 13″
    SCORE=> D o FC ao A
    a cricket
    INQUIRY: it's brown
    ANYTHING ELSE? no
    LOCATION: D7

13. Card II Reaction Time: 6″
    SCORE=> D o FM.CF ao (2)A.Bl AG
    2 bears fightg
    INQUIRY: their faces r all red {D2} & they have blood on themselves
    {nside detail + D3}
    ANYTHING ELSE? they r sort of spitting {small Dds betw the D2s}
    ANYTHING ELSE? no
    LOCATION: W

14. Card II Reaction Time: 12″
    SCORE=> D So m.CF a Sc.Fi
    the space shuttle takg off
    INQUIRY: here is the shuttle and here is the exhaust, red fuel that it
    is spitting out
    ANYTHING ELSE? no
    LOCATION: DS5 + D3

15. Card III Reaction Time: 6″
    SCORE=> W v/+M.CF (2)H.Hx.Hh P
    it's a party
    INQUIRY: 2 ppl playg the drums {D1} but u c decorations everywhere
    DECORATIONS? they have bright colors
    ANYTHING ELSE? there is life everywhere here, I like it. This is my
    favorite
    ANYTHING ELSE? no
    LOCATION: W

16. Card III Reaction Time: 2″
    SCORE=> W v CF u Art
    cd b an abstract painting
    INQUIRY: they have that sort of undescript shapes and the colors
    ANYTHING ELSE? no
    LOCATION: W

17. Card VIII Reaction Time: 22″
    SCORE=> W v CF u Art
    a coat of arms
    INQUIRY: with all of the colors, it looks like an emblem of some sort
    ANYTHING ELSE? no

18. Card VIII Reaction Time: 5″
    SCORE=> W v C u Na V
    the colors of a sunrise

EXHIBIT 11.3 (*Continued*)

INQUIRY: it just looks like the colors being reflected all over the place
ANYTHING ELSE? no
LOCATION: W

19. Card IX   Reaction Time: 3″
    SCORE=> W v C u Na
    ^ this looks like another sunset
    INQUIRY: just the colors
    ANYTHING ELSE? no

20. Card X   Reaction Time: 12″
    SCORE=> W v FM.CF a Na
    Under the sea scene
    INQUIRY: animals of all different colors moving around
    ANYTHING ELSE? no
    LOCATION: W

21. Card X   Reaction Time: 3″
    SCORE=> W v CF o Ls
    The Eiffel Tower and the gardens in front
    INQUIRY: this is the tower {D11} and the rest is the garden with all
    the colorful flowers
    ANYTHING ELSE? no

22. Card X   Reaction Time: 2″
    SCORE=> W v CF u Art
    Miro painting
    INQUIRY: all of the colors, sort of abstract
    ANYTHING ELSE? no
    LOCATION: W

23. Card X   Reaction Time: 3″
    SCORE=> W v C Hx
    It's happiness
    INQUIRY: it is just very colorful, happy colors. I like this one too.
    ANYTHING ELSE? no
    LOCATION: W

(*continued*)

EXHIBIT 11.3 (*Continued*)

— HERMANN —
Multi-Health Systems. Program written by James Choca, Ph.D.,
and Dan Garside

Rorschach Score Sequence
Name: Exhibit

Card	No	Time	Scoring							
I	1	5	W	o	FM	ao	A	P		
I	2	15	Dd	o	FM.FC'		(2) A			
II	3	11	D	o	FM.FC	ao	A			
III	4	12	D	o	FM.FC	ao	A			
IV	5	27	D	o	M.FD	a	H	P		
V	6	5	W	o	FM.FC'.FD	ao	A	P		
VI	7	11	D	o	FM	ao	(A)			
VI	8	5	W	v	YF	u	Bt			V
VII	9	7	D	o	M	ao	(2) Hd	P		
VIII	10	22	D	o	FM.FC	ao	A	P		
IX	11	31	W	v	FM.CF	a-	(A).Fd			
X	12	13	D	o	FC	ao	A			
II	13	46	D	o	FM.CF	ao	(2) A.Bl		AG	
II	14	12	D	So	m.CF	a	Sc.Fi			
III	15	26	W	v/+	M.CF		(2) H.Hx.Hh	P		
III	16	2	W	v	CF	u	Art			
VIII	17	22	W	v	CF	u	Art			
VIII	18	45	W	v	C	u	Na			V
IX	19	3	W	v	C	u	Na			
X	20	12	W	v	FM.CF	a	Na			
X	21	3	W	v	CF	o	Ls			
X	22	2	W	v	CF	u	Art			
X	23	3	W	v	C					

EXHIBIT 11.3 (Continued)

— HERMANN —

Program written by James Choca, Ph.D., and Dan Garside

Rorschach Structural Summary
Name: Exhibit

Global

	n	%
R	23	
Rejects	0	
P	6	26
(P)	0	0
(2)	4	17
Fr	0	0
rF	0	0
3r+(2)		17
RT Ach	11	
RT Ch	17	
AFR		77
Zf	0	
ZSum	0.0	

Location

	n	%
W	13	57
D	9	39
Dd	1	4
DW	0	0
S	1	4
POSITION		
^	21	91
<	0	0
>	0	0
v	2	9
DEV QUAL		
+	0	0
o	12	52
v/+	1	4
v	10	43

Determinants

	n	%
M	3	9
FM	10	29
m	1	3
FT	0	0
TF	0	0
T	0	0
FY	0	0
YF	1	3
Y	0	0
FV	0	0
VF	0	0
V	0	0
FC'	2	6
C'F	0	0
C'	0	0
FC	4	11
CF	9	26
C	3	9
Cn	0	0
FD	2	6
F	0	0
Blends	11	48

Contents

	n	%
CONT	12	
H	2	7
(H)	0	0
Hd	1	4
(Hd)	0	0
Hx	2	7
A	8	29
(A)	2	7
Ad	0	0
(Ad)	0	0
Ab	0	0
Al	2	6
An	0	0
Art	3	11
Ay	0	0
Bl	1	4
Bt	1	4
Cg	0	0
Cl	2	6
Ex	0	0
Fi	1	4
Fd	1	4

Quality

	n	%
OF ALL	12	
+	0	0
o	10	43
u	6	26
-	1	4
none	6	0
OF F		
+	8	29
o	2	7
u	0	0
-	0	0
none	0	0
OF S		
+	3	11
o	0	0
u	1	4
-	1	4
none	0	0
SPECIAL SCORES	4	
DV1	1	4

(continued)

EXHIBIT 11.3 (Continued)

Global		Location			Determinants			Contents			Quality		
n	%	n	%		n	%		n	%		n	%	
		RATIOS			RATIOS			Ge	0	0	DV2	0	0
		W	13	a	13	57		Hh	1	4	DR1	0	0
		M	3	p	0	0		Ls	1	4	DR2	0	0
								Na	3	11	INC1	0	0
		W	13	M	3			Sc	1	4	INC2	0	0
		D	9	wtd C	5.5			Sx	0	0	FAB1	0	0
								Vo	0	0	FAB2	0	0
								Xy	0	0	ALOG	0	0
				M+wtd C	18			Idio	0	0	CON	0	0
											AB	0	0
				FM+m	11			RATIOS			CP	0	0
				Y+T+V+C'	3			H+HD	3		AG	1	4
				&FMmYTVC'	14			A+AD	10		MOR	0	0
											CFB	0	0
											PER	0	0
				FC	4			H+A	12		COP	0	0
				CF+C	12			HD+AD	1		PSV	0	0
								A%	36				

EXHIBIT 11.4

Rorschach Protocol of an Impulsive and Overly Emotional Man

Rorschach Protocol

- -

1. Card I Reaction Time: 5"
   SCORE=> W o FM ao A P
   kd of like a butterfly
   INQUIRY: u can see it with the wings fully expanded in flight
   >? here is the body and the wings
   ANYTHING ELSE? no
   LOCATION: W

2. Card I Reaction Time: 5"
   SCORE=> Dd o FM.FC' (2)A
   cd b 2 bears
   INQUIRY: just the head, they r howling in different directions, lookg
   away from each other
   ANYTHING ELSE? no, they r black
   ANYTHING ELSE? no
   LOCATION: Dd28

3. Card II Reaction Time: 1"
   SCORE=> D o FM.FC ao A
   a butterfly
   INQUIRY: it's red, with the wings outstretched, like it is takg off
   from the place where she had rested
   ANYTHING ELSE? no
   LOCATION: D3

4. Card III Reaction Time: 6"
   SCORE=> D o FM.FC ao A
   another butterfly
   INQUIRY: it is red
   ANYTHING ELSE? it is flitterg here in the cn
   ANYTHING ELSE? no
   LOCATION: D3

5. Card IV Reaction Time: 7"
   SCORE=> D o M.FD a H P
   one of those Russian dancers, when they kick their feet out
   INQUIRY: u c the feet kickg out
   ANYTHING ELSE? the head is kd of small so u r lookg at him from the bm
   ANYTHING ELSE? no
   LOCATION: D7

6. Card V Reaction Time: 5"
   SCORE=> W o FM.FC'.FD ao A P
   bat

(continued)

EXHIBIT 11.4 (Continued)

INQUIRY: head {D6} & feet {D9}. It is flyg and u r lookg at it from above
FROM ABOVE? well the face is lookg down
ANYTHING ELSE? no, it is black
ANYTHING ELSE? no
LOCATION: W

7. Card VI Reaction Time: 1"
SCORE=> D o FM ao (A)
a weird bug of some sort
INQUIRY: u have the wings and the head, it is takg off from this thing {Dd31}
WEIRD? Well it is just strange looking, like something out of a cartoon
LOCATION: D3

8. Card VI Reaction Time: 5"
SCORE=> W v YF u Bt V
v maybe a leaf
INQUIRY: the way the inside looks, all dried up, with what used to be the vein in here {D12}
ANYTHING ELSE? no
LOCATION: W

9. Card VII Reaction Time: 7"
SCORE=> D o M ao (2)Hd P
2 ladies kissg
faces
INQUIRY: well, they r about to kiss, iwth their mouths pockered up
ANYTHING ELSE? no
LOCATION: D9

10. Card VIII Reaction Time: 2"
SCORE=> D o FM.FC ao A P
a badger
INQUIRY: it is of a strange color, but it looks like it
ANYTHING ELSE? it's climbg a mountain or something
ANYTHING ELSE? no
LOCATION: D1

11. Card IX Reaction Time: 3"
SCORE=> W v FM.CF a- (A).Fd
v maybe a weird bug, if u hold it upsidedown
INQUIRY: it's got a green front and orange back {D2}. It is eating something up here {D9}
BUG? just the way it looks
ANYTHING ELSE? no
EATING? it just looks like some red meat
ANYTHING ELSE? no
LOCATION: W

EXHIBIT 11.4 (*Continued*)

12. Card X Reaction Time: 13″
    SCORE=> D o FC ao A
    a cricket
    INQUIRY: it's brown
    ANYTHING ELSE? no
    LOCATION: D7

13. Card II Reaction Time: 6″
    SCORE=> D o FM.CF ao (2)A.Bl AG
    2 bears fightg
    INQUIRY: their faces r all red {D2} & they have blood on themselves
    {nside detail + D3}
    ANYTHING ELSE? they r sort of spitting {small Dds betw the D2s}
    ANYTHING ELSE? no
    LOCATION: W

14. Card II Reaction Time: 12″
    SCORE=> D So m.CF a Sc.Fi
    the space shuttle takg off
    INQUIRY: here is the shuttle and here is the exhaust, red fuel that
    it is spitting out
    ANYTHING ELSE? no
    LOCATION: DS5 + D3

15. Card III Reaction Time: 6″
    SCORE=> W v/+M.CF (2)H.Hx.Hh P
    it's a party
    INQUIRY: 2 ppl playg the drums {D1} but u c decorations
    everywhere
    DECORATIONS? they have bright colors
    ANYTHING ELSE? there is life everywhere here, I like it. This is
    my favorite
    ANYTHING ELSE? no
    LOCATION: W

16. Card III Reaction Time: 2″
    SCORE=> W v CF u Art
    cd b an abstract painting
    INQUIRY: they have that sort of undescript shapes and the colors
    ANYTHING ELSE? no
    LOCATION: W

17. Card VIII Reaction Time: 22″
    SCORE=> W v CF u Art
    a coat of arms
    INQUIRY: with all of the colors, it looks like an emblem of some
    sort
    ANYTHING ELSE? no

(continued)

EXHIBIT 11.4 (*Continued*)

18. Card VIII Reaction Time: 5″
    SCORE=> W v C u Na V
    the colors of a sunrise
    INQUIRY: it just looks like the colors being reflected all over the
    place
    ANYTHING ELSE? no
    LOCATION: W

19. Card IX Reaction Time: 3″
    SCORE=> W v C u Na
    ^ this looks like another sunset
    INQUIRY: just the colors
    ANYTHING ELSE? no

20. Card X Reaction Time: 12″
    SCORE=> W v FM.CF a Na
    Under the sea scene
    INQUIRY: animals of all different colors moving around
    ANYTHING ELSE? no
    LOCATION: W

21. Card X Reaction Time: 3″
    SCORE=> W v CF o Ls
    The Eiffel Tower and the gardens in front
    INQUIRY: this is the tower {D11} and the rest is the garden with
    all the colorful flowers
    ANYTHING ELSE? no

22. Card X Reaction Time: 2″
    SCORE=> W v CF u Art
    Miro painting
    INQUIRY: all of the colors, sort of abstract
    ANYTHING ELSE? no
    LOCATION: W

23. Card X Reaction Time: 3″
    SCORE=> W v C Hx
    It's happiness
    INQUIRY: it is just very colorful, happy colors. I like this one
    too.
    ANYTHING ELSE? no
    LOCATION: W

EXHIBIT 11.4 (*Continued*)

— HERMANN —
Multi-Health Systems. Program written by James Choca, Ph.D.,
and Dan Garside

Rorschach Score Sequence
Name: Exhibit

Card	No	Time	Scoring						
I	1	5	W	o	FM	ao	A	P	
I	2	15	Dd	o	FM.FC'		(2)A		
II	3	11	D	o	FM.FC	ao	A		
III	4	12	D	o	FM.FC	ao	A		
IV	5	27	D	o	M.FD	a	H	P	
V	6	5	W	o	FM.FC'.FD	ao	A	P	
VI	7	11	D	o	FM	ao	(A)		
VI	8	5	W	v	YF	u	Bt		V
VII	9	7	D	o	M	ao	(2)Hd	P	
VIII	10	22	D	o	FM.FC	ao	A	P	
IX	11	31	W	v	FM.CF	a-	(A).Fd		
X	12	13	D	o	FC	ao	A		
II	13	46	D	o	FM.CF	ao	(2)A.Bl		AG
II	14	12	D	So	m.CF	a	Sc.Fi		
III	15	26	W	v/+	M.CF		(2)H.Hx.Hh	P	
III	16	2	W	v	CF	u	Art		
VIII	17	22	W	v	CF	u	Art		
VIII	18	45	W	v	C	u	Na		V
IX	19	3	W	v	C	u	Na		
X	20	12	W	v	FM.CF	a	Na		
X	21	3	W	v	CF	o	Ls		
X	22	2	W	v	CF	u	Art		
X	23	3	W	v	C		Hx		

(continued)

EXHIBIT 11.4 (Continued)

– HERMANN –

Program written by James Choca, Ph.D., and Dan Garside

Rorschach Structural Summary
Name: Exhibit

Global

	n	%
R	23	
Rejects	0	
P	6	26
(P)	0	0
(2)	4	17
Fr	0	0
rF	0	0
3r+(2)		17
RT Ach	11	
RT Ch	17	
AFR	17	
Zf	0	0
ZSum	0.0	

Location

	n	%
W	13	57
D	9	39
Dd	1	4
DW	0	0
S	1	4

POSITION

	n	%
^	21	91
<	0	0
>	0	0
V	2	9

DEV QUAL

	n
+	0
o	12
v/+	1
v	10

Determinants

	n	%
M	3	9
FM	10	29
m	1	3
FT	0	0
TF	0	0
T	0	0
FY	0	0
YF	1	3
Y	0	0
FV	0	0
VF	0	0
V	0	0
FC'	2	6
C'F	0	0
C'	0	0
FC	4	11
CF	9	26
C	3	9
Cn	0	0
FD	2	6
F	0	0

Contents

	n	%
CONT	12	9
H	2	7
(H)	0	0
Hd	1	4
(Hd)	0	0
Hx	2	7
A	8	29
(A)	2	7
Ad	0	0
(Ad)	0	0
Ab	0	0
Al	0	0
An	0	0
Art	3	11
Ay	0	0
Bl	1	4
Bt	1	4
Cg	0	0
Cl	0	0
Ex	0	0

Quality

	n	%
OF ALL		
+	0	0
o	10	43
u	6	26
-	1	4
none	6	0
OF F		
+	0	0
o	0	0
u	0	0
-	0	0
none	0	0
OF S		
+	0	0
o	1	4
u	1	4
-	0	0
none	1	1

RATIOS
W	13
M	3

Blends	11	48

RATIOS
a	13	57
p	0	0

M	3
wtd C	5.5

W	13
D	9

M+wtd C	18

FM+m	11
Y+T+V+C'	3

&FMmYTVC'	14

FC	4
CF+C	12

Content				SPECIAL SCORES		
Fi	1	4		DV1	0	0
Fd	1	4		DV2	0	0
Ge	0	0		DR1	0	0
Hh	1	4		DR2	0	0
Ls	1	4		INC1	0	0
Na	3	11		INC2	0	0
Sc	1	4		FAB1	0	0
Sx	0	0		FAB2	0	0
Vo	0	0		ALOG	0	0
Xy	0	0		CON	0	0
Idio	0	0		AB	0	0
				CP	0	0
RATIOS				AG	1	4
H+HD	3			MOR	0	0
A+AD	10			CFB	0	0
				PER	0	0
H+A	12			COP	0	0
HD+AD	1			PSV	0	0
A%	36					

Note. -- HERMANN --
Multi-Health Systems. Program written by James Choca, Ph.D., and Dan Garside.

EXHIBIT 11.5

Rorschach Protocol of a Thought-Disordered Woman

Rorschach Protocol

----

1. Card I Reaction Time: 0″
   SCORE=> W o F o A 1.0
   an animal
   INQUIRY: a spider or something
   ? I dk it just looks like an animal

2. Card I Reaction Time: 5″
   SCORE=> W o F - (H) 1.0
   a wolf
   1/2 wolf and 1/2 person
   INQUIRY: its got the eyes of a wolf {Dds30}
   PERSON? here in the middle {D4}

3. Card II Reaction Time: 30″
   SCORE=> W o F - (2)H.A 4.5 CON
   2 ppl greeting each other & they have dogs and their dogs r the same
   kd of dogs. One man is very old, his shadow looks very old and tired,
   but his outward appearance is very young. The other man is older
   but his shadow is bright and young. And they r joined together, only
   half of each
   INQUIRY: ppl {D2} dogs {bm right or left corner}, shadows {D1},
   joined together {D4}
   HALF OF EACH? u only c the top half

4. Card II Reaction Time: 12″
   SCORE=> WS o M a- (2)H.Hh 4.5 PSV.ABS
   2 Chinese ppl doing a dance with a little lava lamp. Actually doing
   that Russian dance where they r dancing on their butts, kicking out
   their feet. They still have that lava lamp. That's keeping them
   together.
   The lava goes through their knees.
   INQUIRY: lava lamp {DS5}, lava {D3}

5. Card III Reaction Time: 6″
   SCORE=> W o M a- (2)H.A.Sx 5.5 CON
   Oh, those r lovers. No, I take that back, they r the same sexes.
   There is 2 ppl & they look like they r dancg around. There is a bow
   tie or a butterfly btw them & is flittering down. On the outside
   of each of them, it looks like there is 2 monkeys, they r just
   gliding,
   & they r following the backs of these men dancg.
   INQUIRY: rpts

6. Card IV Reaction Time: 5″
   SCORE=> W o F - (H) P 2.0 DV2

EXHIBIT 11.5 (*Continued*)

this card feels heavy, I dt like this one. This is a giant, a monster,
this is something u ct defeat. I dt like this one, take it. It's
2 heavy.
INQUIRY: no, I don't want to c that again.

7. Card V Reaction Time: 2″
   SCORE=> W o F - A.Hd.Hd 1.0 CON.FAB2
   a butterfly
   with ears & feet, tail maybe. On each side of them, there is 2 men
   laughing. Under one of the sides, where the man is laughing, in the
   upside-down position, he is crying. On the other side also. On the
   top of the wings, there is the man laughing jovially. Underneath,
   in the same wing, still part of the same man, he is crying.
   INQUIRY: ears {Dd31} man laughing {Dd33+Dd35}, man crying {Dd25}

8. Card VI Reaction Time: 32″
   SCORE=> Dd o F o An.Sx DV2
   this looks like a clitoris. Parts of it on here {D12}. It's kind
   of, u ever see Pink Floyd? that's where u will see that and some
   of the other pictures.
   INQUIRY: You have to see Pink Floyd to understand. He was crazy
   ? No, I ct tell u any more

9. Card VII Reaction Time: 6″
   SCORE=> D o M ao (2)Hd P
   that's cute. That looks like 2 little girls out of a scene of a Walt
   Disney pic, Fantasia, & they r doing a little dance
   INQUIRY: their hands like this

10. Card VIII Reaction Time: 21″
    SCORE=> WS o FM a- A.H.Bt.Hd 4.5 AG.FAB2
    2 leopards and there is an aligator, there is 2 ppl, there is a tree,
    there is 2 lion heads. The aligator is holding up the leopards, helping
    them up the tree, with one claw in each paw. The back of the leopard
    is on the man's stomach to try to reach the very bm of the tree,
    to try to get up there. Why he is trying to get up there, I dk bec
    the aligator's mouth is open and if he gets up there, the aligator
    is going to eat them. And the lions on the bm are just waiting for
    that to happen. This has me confused bec these r not lion's feet
    these r ppl feet. The leopards r noted for, they can jump. One jump
    and they wld b that aligator's meal. But if they did it together,
    the aligator couldnt close his mouth, but then I dk what would happen
    to the leopards.
    INQUIRY: leopards {D1}, aligators {Dd22}, tree {D4}
    2 ppl {Dd33}, lion heads {Dd33}
    open mouth of the aligator {S between Dd22 and D3}

(continued)

EXHIBIT 11.5 *(Continued)*

11. Card IX Reaction Time: 13″
    SCORE=> D o F - (2)A V
    First I see sea horses, here, with eyes, except they are not really
    sea horses. v
    INQUIRY: Eyes {white space below Dd26}
    LOCATION: D3

12. Card IX Reaction Time: 3″
    SCORE=> W o FM a- A 5.5
    v now I c a jazz band
    ^ this is a base, not an electric base player, a regular one.
    a bear > here is playing the trombone. The longer u look at them,
    the more u r going to c. They r going to be different, even though
    at first they look the same.
    INQUIRY: base {D3}, bear with trombone {D1}

13. Card X Reaction Time: 45″
    SCORE=> W v C Art
    maybe this is when all of those are combined. They all have the same
    colors, cause these colors are somewhere in those
    INQUIRY: its like a study of color, sort of a painting

14. Card X Reaction Time: 1″
    SCORE=> D o F o (2)(A)
    funny crabs with one head. Like cartoons.
    they have funny long heads {top of D11}
    INQUIRY:rpts
    LOCATION: D11

15. Card X Reaction Time: 10″
    SCORE=> W o FM po (2)A 5.5 AG
    these r crabs 2 but they r not funny, they are mean. I dk if u can
    find the same animals as in the other ones, but I wdt b surprise
    INQUIRY: rpts
    MEAN? they look dangerous
    LOCATION: D1

16. Card X Reaction Time: 3″
    SCORE=> D o F o (2)A DV1 V
    here v are the sea horses. You know with the sea horses, the men
    give birth to the babies and raise the babies, I think it's great.
    LOCATION: D4

17. Card X Reaction Time: 12″
    SCORE=> D o M ao H DV1.CON
    here is a man that is stupidfied. He is a loud, voistrous loud mouth,
    jap, jap, jap, jap, jap
    Now I only take him to here {mid of D9} and this is where it is
    stupidfied

EXHIBIT 11.5 (*Continued*)

but then u go up and u c that they have the same expression on their
face {Dd25}, how did u get them to do that? [looks surprised]
INQUIRY: (feels that the lower face and the upper face are of the
same man and have the same expression. Is again surprised that the
examiner was able to get the 2 faces in the inkblot to have the same
expression)
LOCATION: D9

18. Card X Reaction Time: 1″
    SCORE=> D o F o Cg.Sx
    and this is like my bra
    INQUIRY: well, do I have to describe it any further?
    LOCATION: D6

19. Card X Reaction Time: 0″
    SCORE=> D o M.FM a- H.A AG
    and this is taking a bite out of him, the man that is japping.
    INQUIRY: some sort of animal like a crab. This man has to watch out.
    MAN? This guy here {D15}
    ? just the way he looks
    LOCATION: D7 for crab

                         — HERMANN —
       Multi-Health Systems. Program written by James Choca, Ph.D.,
                          and Dan Garside
                    Rorschach Score Sequence
                       Name: Exhibit

Card	No	Time	Scoring								
I	1	0	W	o	F	o	A		1.0		
I	2	5	W	o	F	-	(H)		1.0		
II	3	30	W	o	F	-	(2)H.A		4.5	CON	
II	4	12	WS	o	M	a-	(2)H.Hh		4.5	PSV.ABS	
III	5	6	W	o	M	a-	(2)H.A.Sx		5.5	CON	
IV	6	5	W	o	F	-	(H)	P	2.0	DV2	
V	7	2	W	o	F	-	A.Hd.Hd		1.0	CON.FAB2	
VI	8	32	Dd	o	F	o	An.Sx			DV2	
VII	9	6	D	o	M	ao	(2)Hd	P			
VIII	10	21	WS	o	FM	a-	A.H.Bt.Hd		4.5	AG.FAB2	
IX	11	13	D	o	F	-	(2)A				V
IX	12	3	W	o	FM	a-	A		5.5		
X	13	45	W	v	C		Art				
X	14	1	D	o	F	o	(2)(A)				
X	15	10	W	o	FM	po	(2)A		5.5	AG	
X	16	3	D	o	F	o	(2)A			DV1	V
X	17	12	D	o	M	ao	H			DV1.CON	
X	18	1	D	o	F	o	Cg.Sx				
X	19	0	D	o	M.FM	a-	H.A			AG	

(*continued*)

EXHIBIT 11.5 (Continued)

— HERMANN —

Program written by James Choca, Ph.D., and Dan Garside

Rorschach Structural Summary

Name: Exhibit

Date of Analysis: 01-17-11

Global

	n	%
R	19	
Rejects	0	
P	2	11
(P)	1	0
(2)	8	42
Fr	0	0
rF	0	0
3r+(2)		42
RT Ach	8	
RT Ch	12	
AFR		111
Zf	10	
ZSum	35.0	

Location

	n	%
W	11	58
D	7	37
Dd	1	5
DW	0	0
S	2	10
POSITION		
^	17	89
<	0	0
>	0	0
v	2	11
DEV QUAL		
+	0	0
o	18	95
v/+	0	0
v	1	5

Determinants

	n	%
M	4	21
FM	4	21
m	0	0
FT	0	0
TF	0	0
T	0	0
FY	0	0
YF	0	0
Y	0	0
FV	0	0
VF	0	0
V	0	0
FC'	0	0
C'F	0	0
C'	0	0
FC	0	0
CF	1	5
C	0	0
Cn	0	0
FD	0	0
F	10	53

Contents

	n	%
CONT	8	
H	5	17
(H)	2	7
Hd	4	13
(Hd)	0	0
Hx	0	0
A	10	33
(A)	1	3
Ad	0	0
(Ad)	0	0
Ab	0	0
Al	0	0
An	1	3
Art	1	3
Ay	0	0
Bl	0	0
Bt	1	3
Cg	1	3
Cl	0	0
Ex	0	0
Fi	0	0

Quality

	n	%
OF ALL	8	
+	0	0
o	8	40
u	0	0
-	10	47
none	1	0
OF F	10	33
+	0	0
o	4	40
u	0	0
-	6	60
none	0	0
SPECIAL SCORES	0	0

RATIOS

W	11
M	4
W	11
D	7

Blends	0
RATIOS	
a	7
p	1
M	4
wtd C	1.5
M+wtd C	6
FM+m	4
Y+T+V+C'	0
&FMmYTVC'	4
FC	0
CF+C	1

Fd	0
Ge	0
Hh	1
Ls	37
Na	5
Sc	3
Sx	10
Vo	0
Xy	0
Idio	0
RATIOS	
H+HD	11
A+AD	11
H+A	18
HD+AD	4
A%	37
	37

DV1	2	11
DV2	2	11
DR1	0	0
DR2	0	0
INC1	0	0
INC2	0	0
FAB1	0	0
FAB2	2	11
ALOG	0	0
CON	4	21
AB	0	0
CP	0	0
AG	3	16
MOR	0	0
CFB	0	0
PER	0	0
COP	0	0
PSV	1	5

Note. -- HERMANN --
Multi-Health Systems. Program written by James Choca, Ph.D., and Dan Garside

EXHIBIT 11.6

Rorschach Protocol of a Woman With Morbid and Dysphoria

```
                          Rorschach Protocol
---------------------------------------------------------------------------
1. Card I  Reaction Time: 87″
   SCORE=>  W  o  FC'  o  A  P  1.0
   kd of looks like a bat
   INQUIRY: the wings
   ANYTHING ELSE? I guess just bec it's black
   ANYTHING ELSE? no

2. Card I  Reaction Time: 166″
   SCORE=>  W  So  F  o  (Ad)
   the cat in Alice in Wonderland
   INQUIRY: eyes and grin
   ANYTHING ELSE? the shape of it
   ANYTHING ELSE? no

3. Card I  Reaction Time: 224″
   SCORE=>  W  v  m  pu  Bt  MOR
   v trees that have been burnt
   INQUIRY: this is the tallest tree and these are the trees on the
   other side and they have been on fire bec of all the bumps and crevices
   there
   ANYTHING ELSE? no
   LOCATION: W

4. Card II  Reaction Time: 239″
   SCORE=>  D  So  C'F  o  Na  >
   > cave, the rocks here, & then is reflected in the water
   INQUIRY: the color and kd of like it's not perfect, a little jagged.
   Here it looks like a stalactite {a}
   ANYTHING ELSE? no

5. Card II  Reaction Time: 411″
   SCORE=>  W  Sv  m.CF  pu  Hd.Bl  AG.MOR
   like a pc of human anatomy that got shot and is bleedg all over the
   place
   INQUIRY: the bullet hole {DS5} is here. I ct make out what part of
   anatomy it was but someone got shot bad
   ANYTHING ELSE? no
   BLEEDG? U can c the red stains everywhere
   LOCATION: W

6. Card III  Reaction Time: 320″
   SCORE=>  D  So  FC.FC'  o  Ad  V
   v>v^>^v 1/2 of a spider, like a black widow, bec they have those
   red marks on them
   TOLD SHE WAS TAKING TOO LONG, AND ASKED WHY. PT SAYS SHE CAN'T THINK
```

EXHIBIT 11.6 *(Continued)*

OF ANYTHING
INQUIRY: it's got a mouth {a}, & the eyes {b}. The black widow is
black and has the red mark

7. Card IV Reaction Time: 351"
   SCORE=> W v C'F o Cl V
   v>v^v looks like there is a fire & there is a dark black smoke that
   is lighter at the top

8. Card IV Reaction Time: 333"
   SCORE=> W v F u (A) MOR
   v^ like a dead bug
   INQUIRY: the shape, like a squashed butterfly
   ANYTHING ELSE? no
   LOCATION: W

9. Card IV Reaction Time: 305"
   SCORE=> W v m.DF ao Hh.Na
   a boat with the water splashing around in the wake of the boat
   INQUIRY: here is the boat {a} and the rest is the water splashing
   ANYTHING ELSE? it gets smaller here {a} and bigger as it goes out.

10. Card V Reaction Time: 459"
    SCORE=> W o FC' o A P 1.0
    v^ a moth
    INQUIRY: wings, very fuzzy type antennas
    ANYTHING ELSE? they r dark colors
    ANYTHING ELSE? no

11. Card V Reaction Time: 122"
    SCORE=> W o F o (A) P MOR
    a butterfly that got burnt up
    INQUIRY: the little antennas, the wings, like a skeleton almost,
    kd of fried

12. Card V Reaction Time: 183"
    SCORE=> D o m a o (H) MOR
    [this is very confusing] like somebody got hurt, hurt bad
    INQUIRY: Right here, somebody got hit in the head, or hit by a car,
    and is layg down like this
    ? u c the person is not in good shape
    ? just the way it looks
    ANYTHING ELSE? no
    LOCATION: D7

13. Card VI Reaction Time: 255"
    SCORE=> W v F u Bt V
    v^v some really weird flower
    INQUIRY: that's the stem {a}, & that's the flower {b}

(continued)

EXHIBIT 11.6 (Continued)

ANYTHING ELSE? those cd b leaves on the stem
ANYTHING ELSE? no

14. Card VII Reaction Time: 227"
    SCORE=> D o M po (2)(Hd) P
    an Indian with one feather in the head, they r stearg at each other
    INQUIRY: the outline of someone's face
    ANYTHING ELSE? no

15. Card VIII Reaction Time: 214"
    SCORE=> W v/+FM.Fr.CF ao A P 4.5 <
    < some kd of animal, walking on rocks, by the water and there is
    the reflection. That's very pretty, I like the colors

16. Card IX Reaction Time: 363"
    SCORE=> W v CF o Na >
    >v> the northern lights or something bec of the colors
    INQUIRY: it dt look like it has a definite shape

17. Card IX Reaction Time: 101"
    SCORE=> W v m.CF a - Bl MOR
    dead ppl after a fight
    INQUIRY: the blood is squirting over here {D9}, like somebody got
    shot and is bleeding down
    ARE U SEEN THE PERSON? no, just the stuff that is left over and the
    blood
    ANYTHING ELSE? no

18. Card X Reaction Time: 335"
    SCORE=> W v m.CF ao Fi.Cl V
    v rmds me of the Fourth of July
    INQUIRY: bright colors that look like fireworks
    ANYTHING ELSE? that looks like smoke {a} coming from this firework
    here {b}
    ANYTHING ELSE? no

19. Card X Reaction Time: 460"
    SCORE=> W v/+FC o (A).Hh 5.5
    a Chinese celebration. That looks like a dragon and then the colors.
    INQUIRY: they have bright colors & that is one of those dragons they
    use {c} because it has like eyes {d}

Note. Letters in brackets refer to locations on the location charts.

EXHIBIT 11.6 *(Continued)*

— HERMANN —

Multi-Health Systems. Program written by James Choca, Ph.D.,
and Dan Garside

Rorschach Score Sequence   Page 1

Name: Exhibit

Card	No	Time	Scoring								
I	1	87	W	o	FC'	o	A	P	1.0		
I	2	166	W	So	F	o	(Ad)				
I	3	224	W	v	m	pu	Bt			MOR	
II	4	239	D	So	C'F	o	Na				>
II	5	411	W	Sv	m.CF	pu	Hd.Bl			AG.MOR	
III	6	320	D	So	FC.FC'	o	Ad				V
IV	7	351	W	v	C'F	o	Cl				V
IV	8	333	W	v	F	u	(A)			MOR	
IV	9	305	W	v	m.DF	ao	Hh.Na				
V	10	459	W	o	FC'	o	A	P	1.0		
V	11	122	W	o	F	o	(A)	P		MOR	
V	12	183	D	o	m	ao	(H)			MOR	
VI	13	255	W	v	F	u	Bt				V
VII	14	227	D	o	M	po	(2)(Hd)	P			
VIII	15	214	W	v/+	FM.Fr.CF	ao	A	P	4.5		<
IX	16	363	W	v	CF	o	Na				>
IX	17	101	W	v	m.CF	a-	(H).Bl			MOR	
X	18	335	W	v	m.CF	ao	Fi.Cl				V
X	19	460	W	v/+	FC	o	(A).Hh		5.5		

(continued)

EXHIBIT 11.6 (Continued)

— HERMANN —

Program written by James Choca, Ph.D., and Dan Garside

Rorschach Structural Summary
Name: Exhibit

Global	n	%	Location	n	%	Determinants	n	%	Contents	n	%	Quality	n	%
R	19		W	15	79	M	1	4	CONT	8		OF ALL		
Rejects	0		D	4	21	FM	1	4	H	0	0	+	0	0
			Dd	0	0	m	6	24	(H)	2	8	o	14	74
P	5	26	DW	0	0	FT	0	0	Hd	1	4	u	4	21
(P)	0	0	S	4	21	TF	0	0	(Hd)	1	4	-	1	5
						T	0	0	Hx	0	0	none	0	0
(2)	1	5				FY	0	0	A	3	13			
Fr	1	4	POSITION			YF	0	0	(A)	3	13	OF F		
rF	0	0	^	12	63	Y	0	0	Ad	1	4	+	0	0
3r+(2)		21	<	1	5	FV	0	0	(Ad)	1	4	o	3	60
			>	2	11	VF	0	0	Ab	0	0	u	2	40
			v	4	21	V	0	0	Al	0	0	-	0	0
RT Ach	347					FC'	3	12	An	0	0	none	0	0
RT Ch	305					C'F	2	8	Art	0	0			
						C'	0	0	Ay	0	0	OF S		
AFR		36	DEV QUAL			FC	2	8	Bl	2	9	+	0	0
			+	0	0	CF	5	20	Bt	2	9	o	3	75
			o	8	42	C	0	0	Cg	0	0	u	1	25
			v/+	2	11	Cn	0	0	Cl	2	9	-	0	0
Zf	4		v	9	47	FD	0	0	Ex	0	0	none	0	0
ZSum	12.0					F	5	20	Fi	1	4	SPECIAL SCORES		

RATIOS		Blends	5		Fd		26		DV1	0	0
W	15	RATIOS			Ge				DV2	0	0
M	0	a	3		Hh				DR1	2	9
		p	3		Ls		16		DR2	0	0
W	15	M	0		Na		16		INC1	3	13
D	4	wtd C	6.0		Sc				INC2	0	0
					Sx				FAB1	0	0
		M+wtd C	6		Vo				FAB2	0	0
					Xy				ALOG	0	0
		FM+m	6		Idio		6		CON	0	0
		Y+T+V+C'	5								
					RATIOS				AB	0	0
		&FMmYTVC'	11		H+HD		3		CP	0	0
					A+AD		8		AG	1	5
		FC	2						MOR	6	32
		CF+C	5		H+A		7		CFB	0	0
					HD+AD		4		PER	0	0
					A%		35		COP	0	0
									PSV	0	0

Note. -- HERMANN --
Multi-Health Systems. Program written by James Choca, Ph.D., and Dan Garside

EXHIBIT 11.7

Rorschach Protocol of a Man in a Manic State

Rorschach Protocol

---

1. Card I Reaction Time: 0″
   SCORE=> W o F o A P
   giant moth
   INQUIRY: basically the wing span, the little appendices up in the
   front, and the teeth. You ever saw the movie Moth? They had little
   parts like that
   ANYTHING ELSE? no

2. Card I Reaction Time: 1″
   SCORE=> W S o F o (Hd)
   Jack-o-lantern, smiling
   INQUIRY: like looking at a jack-o-lantern, the way it is carved,
   but from the face, is very close to it (Anything else?) no, u can
   c the ears & everything else
   ANYTHING ELSE? no

3. Card I Reaction Time: 3″
   SCORE=> W o FMa - Ad
   a dog with the tongue stikg out
   INQUIRY: just the front part below the chin, u c the tongue stikg
   out, the ears drooped
   ANYTHING ELSE? no
   LOCATION: W

4. Card I Reaction Time: 9″
   SCORE=> W S o FC′ o Ad 3.5
   the face of a dog or an animal, something snouty
   INQUIRY: the eyes here (S), the snout, the ears, the jowls in through
   here (side). The rest of the white, (S on top) is the coloring on
   the fur.

5. Card I Reaction Time: 10″
   SCORE=> W v F u (H) V
   v the old Dart Fader game. This is the creature that came from the
   upper
   part of the screen that I could never hit
   INQUIRY: I was just kidding
   >? the mask that Dart Fader uses in the game
   ANYTHING ELSE? no

6. Card II Reaction Time: 1″
   SCORE=> W S o Mp.mp.CF o(2)H.Bl 4.5 AG.MOR
   someone who got stabbed
   INQUIRY: 2 people here & a person in the mid who got stabbed & there
   is all the blood down here

EXHIBIT 11.7 (*Continued*)

ANYTHING ELSE? no
BLOOD? the orange color & the way it's drippg down
ANYTHING ELSE? no

7. Card II Reaction Time: 5"
   SCORE=> D S v/+ ma.CF o Hh.Ex
   rocketship ready to take off
   INQUIRY: the cn part using the black as a background & the red as
   the fuel spewing out
   ANYTHING ELSE? no
   LOCATION: W minus the top red

8. Card II Reaction Time: 9"
   SCORE=> W S v CF o Hh.Bt
   a lantern seen through trees
   INQUIRY: I was seeing an old fashioned railroad lantern, with the
   color
   lenses, out in the country, you are seen the light, the red being
   the light, seen through the foliage

9. Card II Reaction Time: 7"
   SCORE=> W v mp.CF.FD o Hh.Ls CON
   lookg down on a jet from above
   INQUIRY: the point here, the stubby wings, and the landscape. If
   you r looking down & u c the red sand, mountains thru here
   ANYTHING ELSE? no

10. Card II Reaction Time: 1"
    SCORE=> W v CF u Ls
    some type of desert landscape, red sand
    INQUIRY: this is below the plane

11. Card II Reaction Time: 2"
    SCORE=> W S v/+ FMa.Fr.CF.FD o A.Hh 4.5
    a raccoon trying paw through a plate glass window (laughs)
    INQUIRY: tail, feet, ears, paw, its reflection on the window. I can
    see the full reflection with a lot of height to it, so it wd b a
    big window
    ANYTHING ELSE? no
    LOCATION: W
    I am seeing height, an expansive area above and below the raccoon,
    the glass is continuing down here (cn white), I see a distance here.
    The red could be nothing more than draperies, or anything reflected
    on the window

12. Card II Reaction Time: 15"
    SCORE=> W v Ma - (2)H.Cg
    I am thinking of a Japanese Kabuki play

(*continued*)

EXHIBIT 11.7 (Continued)

INQUIRY: the shape right in here, when u c the male Japanese Kabuki
dancers, they have the hair done like this & the kimono that usually
flares out, the hands (top). It's some type of action
LOCATION: the whole thing. I started by looking at the cn & worked
my way out from there
REST? The Japanese dress, flaring out, the dress is usually bulky

13. Card III Reaction Time: 5"
SCORE=> D o Ma o(2)H.Hh P
a couple of dancers
INQUIRY: 2 different people on both sides with a table in the mid
or something like that
ANYTHING ELSE? the way their legs r positioned, their hands r on this
particular table, dancg face-2-face
ANYTHING ELSE? no
LOCATION: black sections

14. Card III Reaction Time: 1"
SCORE=> D o Ma o(2)H PSV
a couple of people playg the piano
INQUIRY: a musical instrument
ANYTHING ELSE? no
LOCATION: black

15. Card III Reaction Time: 3"
SCORE=> D o Ma o(2)H.Hd PSV.AG.MOR
a couple of people beating on someone's head
INQUIRY: be the same thing almost, the facial expression of the
person
down below. It almost look like they r enjoying it
ANYTHING ELSE? no

16. Card III Reaction Time: 8"
SCORE=> W o Ma o (2)H.Ls 5.5
African village scene
INQUIRY: a sense of the color, a sameness, a house here (red outside),
a house here, color in the background. This could be doing laundry,
or it could be like a mixing bowl where they mill the corn. The reason
for being African is the pronounced shapes. I can see the shape here
without much hair. Breasts, thin bodies, healthy but thin. A sense
of community here.
ANYTHING ELSE? no

17. Card IV Reaction Time: 18"
SCORE=> W o FD o (A) P
like a giant monster from a prehistoric movie
INQUIRY: the whole pic, it makes it look like there is a tail down
below
ANYTHING ELSE? u got the arms up above. On top of the pic,
u got little slits for eyes. The way the feet are shaped, extra large

which is the way that most of them seem to be
ANYTHING ELSE? no

18. Card IV Reaction Time: 5″
    SCORE=> W v/+ F o Ad.Na AB.AG.MOR
    also looks like a serpent, scary enough to represent death
    INQUIRY: got the head stikg out of a rock formation down below. You
    can almost c the different tusks on the serpent, the different eyes,
    and the nostrils
    ANYTHING ELSE? no

19. Card IV Reaction Time: 5″
    SCORE=> W o FMp.FD o A.Bt 4.0
    a bear sitting on a tree stump
    INQUIRY: the bulk of the body, the lg feet, just the stump
    (Anything else?) the bulk, as though you r looking up towards it
    from laying down on the ground.

20. Card IV Reaction Time: 8″
    SCORE=> W v FMp o A.Bt
    A lion peering through a bush
    INQUIRY: if u look at the shadows in here, u c the cat ears, the
    snout, the nose, somewhat of the feet in thru here. A leafy tangle
    along the side of it.
    ANYTHING ELSE? no

21. Card V Reaction Time: 3″
    SCORE=> W o F o A P
    a moth
    INQUIRY: it's a moth, it looks like a moth, the wings, a tropical
    moth with a little bit of a tail on it, the antennae
    ANYTHING ELSE? no

22. Card V Reaction Time: 8″
    SCORE=> W v Ma -(2)H AG.MOR
    someone strangling 2 people
    INQUIRY: sort of like the person in the mid has them around the neck,
    dragging them on the ground
    ANYTHING ELSE? no

23. Card V Reaction Time: 1″
    SCORE=> W o F o A PSV
    giant bat
    INQUIRY: u can c the 2 appendages up above, the 2 little feet and
    the wings themselves
    ANYTHING ELSE? no
    GIANT? It just looks big

(*continued*)

EXHIBIT 11.7 (*Continued*)

24. Card V Reaction Time: 7"
    SCORE=> W v F Na AB
    looks like the pic of power, just by itself, just power, being in
    control
    INQUIRY: rpts. The bat image, the bat rmds u of power, and the idea
    of the person grabbg the 2 others, like that person being in command
    ANYTHING ELSE? no

25. Card VI Reaction Time: 12"
    SCORE=> D o F o (Ad) P
    animal skin
    INQUIRY: basically the bm half, a skin that has been taken off a
    good size animal
    ANYTHING ELSE? the tail part here rmds me of someone splitting the
    thing
    down the mid
    ANYTHING ELSE? no

26. Card VI Reaction Time: 7"
    SCORE=> D v mp u Hh
    weather vane
    INQUIRY: the top part, being able to spin around
    ANYTHING ELSE? no

27. Card VI   Reaction Time: 9"
    SCORE=> D o F - (2)Ad
    it also looks to the point, like we have 2 wolf heads, right next
    to each other
    INQUIRY: down at the bm, with the nose & everything else, on both
    Sides
    ANYTHING ELSE? no

28. Card VI Reaction Time: 7"
    SCORE=> W S v mp.FC'.FD o Ls.Cl
    looking down on a river gorge with a stream running through it
    INQUIRY: is like a view from above, thru a break in the clouds, the
    clouds being the white. You can c the thin white line, narrowing,
    thinning out, got a couple of sand banks on the side of it. The part
    where the gorge comes in, is the darker part, with water marks.
    ANYTHING ELSE? no

29. Card VII Reaction Time: 7"
    SCORE=> D o F o (2)Hd.Cg P
    2 indians
    INQUIRY: heads at the top here. The feathers on top of the head,
    younger indians that only have one or two feathers each
    ANYTHING ELSE? no

30. Card VII Reaction Time: 9"
    SCORE=> W S v F Na AB.AG.MOR

EXHIBIT 11.7 (*Continued*)

looks almost like death because it looks like they r going to fall
into a pit here
INQUIRY: they r at the point where they are ready to totter down
to the bm of the pit here
THEY? anybody, the Indians maybe, the other heads r very vicious,
ready to attack, but the most vicious part is the pit
ANYTHING ELSE? no

31. Card VII   Reaction Time: 9"
    SCORE=>   D   o   FMa   o(2)Ad   AG
    a couple of boar heads, it looks like they r very angry
    INQUIRY: just the pic of a boar, the nose, the expression, the eye,
    & the jaw
    ANYTHING ELSE? no

32. Card VII   Reaction Time: 1"
    SCORE=>   W   v   Ma.Fr   u   (H).Cg
    a young woman in a turn-of-the-century dress admiring herself in
    the mirror
    INQUIRY: is easy to c the head, the features, the turn-of-the-century
    dress has a plume that they used to wear, and the bustles the used
    to wear. Since is the exact thing on the other side, I was thinking
    it was a mirror. Not so much admiring but looking thoughtfully into
    the mirror. She likes what she sees, the chin is up, not down.
    ANYTHING ELSE? no

33. Card VIII   Reaction Time: 8"
    SCORE=>   D   o   FMa   o   A   P
    2 bears climbg a mountain
    INQUIRY: they r climbg up to the top
    BEARS? the outside fig
    ANYTHING ELSE? no

34. Card VIII   Reaction Time: 1"
    SCORE=>   D   o   FMa   u(2)A   AG
    2 wild animals trying to devour each other down at the bm
    INQUIRY: rpts. one animal being here & 1 animal being here
    ANYTHING ELSE? no

35. Card VIII   Reaction Time: 7"
    SCORE=>   D   v   FMa   -   A   AG
    prehistoric animal trying to get rid of the 2 bears
    INQUIRY: trying to shove the bears away
    ANIMAL? the formation of the skull & the different appendages that r
    stikg out
    ANYTHING ELSE? no

36. Card VIII   Reaction Time: 5"
    SCORE=>   W   o   FMa.Fr   o   A.Ls   4.5

(*continued*)

EXHIBIT 11.7 (Continued)

a musk rat walking along the river bank. A clear stream, seen its own reflection, I mean, being reflected into the water rather than seen its own reflection
INQUIRY: this could be a tree leaning down into the water, this could be some rat shells, something with a redish color, the other side could be the reflection into the water.
ANYTHING ELSE? the archeology part is the bones here, and some sort of claw decaying a little bit. This could be something left with the body, a pot (bm) like the clay pots the Indians wd put in with the body. It has been burried, there is an orderliness to it.
NOTE: Scoring here pertains to the original response. The enlarged perception will be scored below.

37. Card VIII Reaction Time: 3″
SCORE=> W v/+ FMa.Fr.CF o A.An.Hh 4.5
could be also an animal in a cave with artifacts. I see a skeleton and could be claws in front of it. I see the animal going into an old cave
INQUIRY: see #36

38. Card IX Reaction Time: 8″
SCORE=> D v Ma - Hd.A MOR.AG
an animal being crushed at the bm
INQUIRY: these (green) r the feet, crushing the animal at the bm
ANYTHING ELSE? no

39. Card IX Reaction Time: 3″
SCORE=> W v C o Hh
also looks like there is a shining light at the bm so that a glowing light shines through
INQUIRY: at the top! It comes through the green here & it comes at the top & shines out
ANYTHING ELSE? no

40. Card IX Reaction Time: 1″
SCORE=> D o FMa u (2)(A) AG
a couple of goblins that are hooked up in a nice little fight
INQUIRY: rpts. The expression on their face. It look like they were close to each other at one time but there is a bitter look on their face right now
ANYTHING ELSE? no

41. Card IX Reaction Time: 7″
SCORE=> W v ma u Ex
Armageddon, something violent but exactly what, I ct say
There is some violence in here, something disturbing.
INQUIRY: there is no real form as u look at it, no sense of order, no straight lines, no curbs. You wd think of the atomic bomb as u c it raising or a volcano erupting. The raggedness along the ages,

EXHIBIT 11.7 (*Continued*)

some sort of explosion.
EXPLOSION? the up trust. This is calmer (bm) than it is in here top)
ANYTHING ELSE? the smearing of the lines, is like movement
ANYTHING ELSE? no

42. Card X Reaction Time: 13″
    SCORE=> D o FMa o (2)A AG
    a couple of crabs engaged in combat
    INQUIRY: all their different appendages stikg out. They look like they
    r ready to go after each other, even though they r not there yet
    ANYTHING ELSE? no

43. Card X Reaction Time: 10″
    SCORE=> D o FM ao (2)A AG
    several other animals that are in combat for positioning for the
    cn pc here, everyone just fighting everyone in this scene, no matter
    who it is
    INQUIRY: these 2 (grey) basically they r right next to each other &
    it looks like they r butting heads with each other
    ANYTHING ELSE? no

44. Card X Reaction Time: 9″
    SCORE=> W v CF o Ls
    the ocean, like a coral reef, crabs and sea weeds, the coral itself.
    INQUIRY: crabs, tropical fish (yellow, orange). You see them thru
    the water and u dt see any real shape. You got your algae, green
    here
    ANYTHING ELSE? the crabs here (brown). This area is some skeletal-
    like thing
    that has been gnawed. Very peaceful, a natural type setting.

(*continued*)

EXHIBIT 11.7 (Continued)

— HERMANN —
Multi-Health Systems. Program written by James Choca, Ph.D.,
and Dan Garside
Rorschach Score Sequence

Card	No	Time	Scoring									
I	1	0	W	o	F		o		A	P	
I	2	1	WS	o	F		o		(Hd)		
I	3	3	W	o	FM	p	-		Ad		
I	4	9	WS	o	FC'		o		Ad		
I	5	10	W	v	F		u		(H)		V
II	6	1	WS	o	M.m.CF	p	o	(2)	H.Bl	AG.MOR	
II	7	5	DS	v/+	m.CF	a	o		Hh.Ex		
II	8	9	WS	v	CF		o		Hh.Bt		
II	9	7	W	v	m.CF.FD	p	o		Hh.Ls	CON	
II	10	1	W	v	CF		u		Ls		
II	11	2	WS	v/+	FM.Fr.CF.Fd	a	o		A.Hh		
II	12	15	W	v	M	a	-	(2)	H.Cg		
III	13	5	D	o	M	a	o	(2)	H.Hh	P	
III	14	1	D	o	M	a	o	(2)	H	PSV	
III	15	3	D	o	M	a	o	(2)	H.Hd	PSV.AG.MOR	
III	16	8	W	o	M	a	o	(2)	H.Ls		
IV	17	18	W	o	FD		o		(A)	P	
IV	18	5	W	v/+	F		o		Ad.Na	AB.AG.MOR	
IV	19	5	W	o	FM.FD	p	o		A.Bt		
IV	20	8	W	v	FM	p	o		A.Bt		
V	21	3	W	o	F		o		A	P	
V	22	8	W	v	M	a	-	(2)	H	AG.MOR	
V	23	1	W	o	F		o		A		
V	24	7	W	v	F				Na	AB	
VI	25	12	D	o	F		o		(Ad)	P	
VI	26	7	D	v	m	p	u		Hh		
VI	27	9	D	o	F		-	(2)	Ad		
VI	28	7	WS	v	m.FC'.FD	p	o		Ls.Cl		
VII	29	7	D	o	F		o	(2)	Hd.Cg	P	
VII	30	9	WS	v	F				Na	AB.AG.MOR	
VII	31	9	D	o	FM	a	o	(2)	Ad	AG	
VII	32	1	W	v	M.Fr	a	u		(H).Cg		
VIII	33	8	D	o	FM	a	o		A	P	
VIII	34	1	D	v	FM	a	u	(2)	A	AG	
VIII	35	7	D	v	FM	a	-		A	AG	
VIII	36	5	W	o	FM.Fr	a	o		A.Ls		
VIII	37	3	W	v/+	FM.Fr.CF	a	o		A.An.Hh		
IX	38	8	D	v	M	a	-		Hd.A	MOR.AG	
IX	39	3	W	v	C				Hh		
IX	40	1	D	o	FM	a	u	(2)	A)	AG	
IX	41	7	W	v	m	a	u		Ex		
X	42	13	D	o	FM	a	o	(2)	A	AG	
X	43	10	D	o	FM	a	o	(2)	A	AG	
X	44	9	W	v	CF		o		Ls		

EXHIBIT 11.7 (Continued)

— HERMANN —

Program written by James Choca, Ph.D., and Dan Garside

Rorschach Structural Summary

Global	n	%	Location	n	%	Determinants	n	%	Contents	n	%	Quality	n	%
R	44		W	28	64	M	9	15	CONT	11		OF ALL		
Rejects	0		D	16	36	FM	13	22	H	7	11	+	0	0
			Dd	0	0	m	6	10	(H)	2	3	o	29	66
P	7	16	DW	0	0	FT	0	0	Hd	3	5	u	7	16
(P)	0	0	S	8	18	TF	0	0	(Hd)	1	2	-	6	14
						T	0	0	A	14	22	OF F		
(2)	14	32	POSITION			FY	0	0	(A)	2	4	+	0	0
Fr	4	7	^	43	98	YF	0	0	Ad	5	8	o	7	58
rF	0	0	<	0	0	Y	0	0	(Ad)	1	2	u	1	8
3r+(2)		59	>	0	0	FV	0	0	Ab	0	0	-	2	17
			v	1	2	VF	0	0	Al	0	0			
RT Ach	6					V	2	3	An	1	2	DV1	0	0
RT Ch	5					FC'	0	0	Art	0	0	DV2	0	0
			DEV QUAL			C'F	0	0	Ay	0	0	INC1	0	0
AFR		38	+	0	0	C'	0	0	Bl	1	2	INC2	0	0
			o	22	50	FC	0	0	Bt	3	5	DR1	0	0
			v/+	4	9	CF	8	14	Cg	3	5	DR2	0	0
Zf	15		v	18	41	C	1	2	Cl	1	2	FAB1	0	0
ZSum	46					Cn	0	0	Ex	2	3	FAB2	0	0
						FD	5	8	Fi	0	0	ALOG	0	0
						F	12	20	Fd	0	0			

(continued)

EXHIBIT 11.7 (Continued)

— HERMANN —

Program written by James Choca, Ph.D., and Dan Garside

Rorschach Structural Summary

Global		Location		Determinants		Contents		Quality	
n	%	n	%	n	%	n	%	n	%	
		RATIOS		Blends 9	20	Ge 0	0	CON 1	2	
				RATIOS		Hh 8	13	AB 1	2	
		W 28		a 20	46	Ls 6	10	CP 0	0	
		M 9		p 6	13	Na 3	5	AG 12	27	
				M 9		Sc 0	0	MOR 6	13	
		W 28		wtd C 9.5		Sx 0	0	CFB 0	0	
		D 16		M+wtd C 18		Vo 0	0	PER 0	0	
				FM+m 18		Xy 0	0			
				Y+T+V+C' 2		RATIOS		COP 0	0	
				&FMmYTVC' 20		H+HD 13		PSV 2	5	
				FC 0		A+AD 22				
				CF+C 9		H+A 25				
						HD+AD 10				
						A% 35				

Psychological Test Report 12

B y now, the reader has read about the different approaches to the Rorschach (Chapters 1 and 2), the fundamentals of interpretation (Chapter 3), and the interpretations associated with the different Rorschach scores and responses (Chapters 4–9) and he or she has walked through the steps that may be followed when interpreting a Rorschach protocol (Chapters 10 and 11). This chapter focuses on what is typically the final product of the clinician's diagnostic work: the psychological test report.

Because the test report is the part that is most often seen by others, it is important to write a report that is nicely formatted, easy to read and understand, and effective. This chapter reviews the information that is typically included in a report, the basics of good practice in report writing, the process that is followed, and the organizational schemes that can be used for the discussion section.

DOI: 10.1037/14039-012
The Rorschach Inkblot Test: An Interpretive Guide for Clinicians, by J. P. Choca

Information to be Included

A good report typically contains the presenting complaint or reason for the referral, background information (history of the presenting complaints, medical history, social history, educational history, occupational history), behavioral observations, results of a mental status examination, test results, diagnostic formulation, and recommendations.

Psychological test reports are written, by necessity, in a pejorative and uncomplimentary fashion. Even the terms used typically have a negative connotation. Ask a group of people to raise a hand if they see themselves as "agreeable" or "cooperative," and you will see many hands being raised. Ask the same group to indicate if they are "dependent" or "submissive," and you are likely to get only a hand or two. Yet these words refer to the same personality trait: When the label used to describe an attribute sounds socially appealing, the label loses its discriminative value in characterizing some individuals and not others. The interest in sending an individual for testing is to find out *what is wrong;* if the referral source wanted a list of indiscriminate descriptions, he or she would check the person's horoscope. Consequently, an effective test report necessarily focuses on negative elements.

Nevertheless, as highlighted by the very popular positive psychology movement (see, e.g., Csikszentmihalyi, 2008; Seligman, 2011; Seligman & Csikszentmihalyi, 2000), there is something to be said for pointing out the positive attributes or strengths that the person brings into the mix. When the Rorschach shows a good balance between holistic and detailed thinking, when the examinee has a healthy number of human and cooperative movement responses, when the Rorschach responses are of good form quality, when the protocol does not contain pathological Special Scores—all of these findings should be cited in the report. Such information not only serves to exclude many problem areas that should not be of concern but, more important, tells the reader of the individual's strengths that can be marshalled for the areas that require work.

Basics of Good Practice

Most clinicians develop a personal style of writing that may be unique, but this should be done within certain parameters. To start with, a psychological report should be written in a professional manner. Without being stodgy, the language should not be so informal that it would appear uneducated or unsophisticated. The report should be as readable and interesting as possible. Abbreviations and esoteric terms should be avoided as much as possible. Because our work is controlled by the Health Insurance Portability and Accountability Act (HIPAA), it is likely that the examinee will read the report; this should be kept in mind when writing it.

One way to make the report interesting is to focus on the examinee rather than on the tests used. Some readers may be interested in learning something about the instruments that were used, but those are likely to be in the minority. In contrast, all readers of a psychological test report are interested in learning something about the examinee, or they would not be reading the report. Keeping this in mind, the clinician can address the attributes of the examinee rather than facts about the tests. For example, the statement "The Rorschach protocol had many responses where color was used in an uncontrolled manner" is meaningful only to those of us who are well versed in the use of the Rorschach. A better statement of the same information would be "The Rorschach indicates that Mr. Smith is likely to be carried away by his emotions in emotionally charged situations, to be impulsive, and not to be thoughtful and controlled enough."

The report should be organized so that every paragraph handles a specific issue. At times the beginning of the paragraph may be designed to reveal what the paragraph is all about. A paragraph that starts with "Supporting Mrs. Smith's complaints of depression, the findings pointed to her being . . . " obviously sets the stage for addressing the findings about the person's depression. Paragraphs should also follow logically from one to the next. In describing the individual's personality, for instance, each paragraph may address a different element of the person's personality in an orderly manner.

Test reports should make the readers aware that statements are based on test data. The test report would become unreadable if every statement were to be anchored on all the pieces of data that provide the foundation for that statement. On the other hand, it should be made clear that the statements are not just impressionistic or intuitive feelings that the clinician has about the examinee and that they can be substantiated with the test findings. Phrases like "according to the Rorschach" or "the stories of the Thematic Apperception Test suggested that . . . " can provide the foundation for statements without burdening the report.

Findings are obviously associated with different levels of confidence, and statements should communicate the clinician's level of confidence. The person's IQ, for instance, is so scientifically determined that the range in which it varies can be determined 95% of the time. Most other data cannot be ensured with that level of accuracy. The phrasing in a report should have some transparency, letting the reader know how confident we can be with a particular stipulation. Note the difference in the confidence portrayed by the following statements: "The patient's depression was obvious throughout the testing; he demonstrated . . ."

and "Perhaps as a result of the abuses the patient received during childhood, she appeared to have reached adulthood with a flawed borderline personality." The first statement indicates that there can be little doubt about the person's depression; the second allows for the possibility that it may not be true.

Although many psychological reports are written in the present tense (e.g., "Mr. Smith has an anger management problem"), there are advantages to the use of the past tense. Psychological evaluations are, at best, a good rendition of how the examinee was at the time of the testing. When clinicians have the opportunity to test the same individual on more than one occasion, they see examinees who have changed a great deal and those who have not. The use of the past tense serves to keep both the reader and the writer cognizant of the fact that the clinical picture may not be very stable.

The Process

A good metaphor for the task of writing a psychological test report may be that of putting a jigsaw puzzle together: By the time the clinician starts planning and writing the report, he or she has numerous bits of information about the examinee (the puzzle pieces), and the task is to put all of those pieces together to form a coherent picture of the individual.

The pieces of this puzzle include, first and foremost, the reasons for referral, the presenting complaints, and the history. Taking a good history is imperative because the history gives the foundation for the test interpretations. If there are parts of the history that the clinician does not understand, it is necessary to clarify them. A good clinician often has to be educated about areas that are outside his or her expertise, whether these are the details of a medical illness, the requirements of a particular occupation, or the finer points of law in a forensic case. Part of being competent diagnosticians is gathering the necessary information about all of the important aspects of the case. Mature clinicians are not afraid to address questions to the patient, the relatives, the physicians, or anyone else.

It is often useful to search for information on the web or in one of the reference systems (e.g., PsycINFO). I remember doing a neuropsychological evaluation of a woman who insisted that her hypomanic state had been the result of a head trauma sustained in a motor vehicle accident. Both the treating psychiatrist and the neurologist had disregarded that piece of information and were seeing the psychiatric and the neurological complaints as different issues. Much to my surprise, I was able to find journal articles showing that hypomanic states following head injuries are not that uncommon. Those of us who are psychologists are trained to appreciate the value of data and typically have access to the appropriate search engines that allow retrieval and review of the available scientific information. Consequently, one of the contributions we can make to the care of an individual is to add relevant data that may not have been taken into consideration.

The relative importance that the different pieces will have in the final report is typically decided on a case-by-case basis. The test battery often includes some measure of intellectual ability, one or more questionnaires or personality inventories, and the projective tests. If the person's intellectual capacity is very limited, for instance, the cognitive findings might drive much of the report because they are important in explaining the person's behavior. In another case, the findings from one of the inventories may be so enlightening that the clinician would have needed very little else to be able to write a good report. In still another case, the projective protocols may be the rich and revealing part of the puzzle and should then be emphasized. Finally, in many cases each of these elements makes a more-or-less equal contribution to an understanding of the examinee, and the sources used for the report may be more balanced.

Putting the puzzle together demands that the clinician integrate the different sources of information. Much of the history and the questionnaires or personality inventories offer data on the person's self-evaluation. These are the sources clinicians typically rely on to describe the symptoms or the way the individual feels. Although elements of an individual's personality may be seen in practically all instruments used, the personality inventories are much more adept than other data sources at giving us that kind of information.

The projective tests provide a glimpse of the individual in action. The Rorschach is particularly well suited to reveal how the individual approaches ambiguous situations in life, and life is full of ambiguities. The amount of energy the individual is likely to invest in life activities is likely to be more tangible in this instrument than in any other. This test is undoubtedly the best instrument to use to examine the person's thinking processes, both in terms of its qualities and effectiveness. As far as the thinking content, the test may reveal preoccupations or other anomalies that may be of interest and value.

Most clinicians expect the Thematic Apperception Test (Murray, 1943) to say something about the person's needs and aspirations. Interpersonal relations and conflicts, and how well the person can differentiate between the views and feelings of different people, are also areas where this test may excel. Locus of control, morbidity, suicidality, expected outcomes, grandiosity, or low self-esteem can be often abstracted from the examinee's stories (for more information, see Aronow, Weiss, & Reznikoff, 2001; Bellak & Abrams, 1993; Cramer, 1996; Teglasi, 2010).

A final but no less important source of report data is the clinician's observations of the subtle aspects of examinee thought and behavior. Those observations should be an integral and important source of data.

The information derived from these various sources may support, complement, or conflict with one another. When the information from these sources is consistent, clinicians can draw strong conclusions and make authoritative statements. If a patient complains of depression and the personality inventory shows a depressive profile, signs of dysphoria are seen on the Rorschach (e.g., a low number of responses, a high frequency of morbid content), and the stories of the Thematic Apperception Test have a sad and pessimistic flavor, then the findings of depression are convincing.

Often the sources of information complement one another: The findings do not necessarily address the same attribute, but the different attributes that emerge fit together well. For example, a clinician may have the following data for an examinee: a personality inventory that reveals a schizotypal personality, Rorschach findings that show the poor form quality and Special Scores, and Thematic Apperception Test stories that suggest an inability to distinguish people as different entities. These pieces of the puzzle contain different aspects of the picture, but they would be consistent with a diagnosis of schizophrenia.

When the different sources of information appear to be in conflict, the clinician has to resolve the conflict prior to writing the report. Conflicts are invariably teaching us something about the individual, even in cases where the final resolution may involve the discrediting of one source of information as invalid. In the case of an adolescent who is intent on being discharged from the hospital, the personality inventory that looks like the picture of mental health has something to say about the patient's motivation and the possible use of malingering, denial or suppression in order to solve problems. The individual who performs well on a structured task (e.g., an intelligence test) but does poorly on the projectives may be revealing what happens when he or she faces an ambiguous task. In all such cases much is learned from inconsistent data.

Organizational Schemes

Several organizational schemes are commonly used to write the discussion of the test results. These schemes vary in their level of sophistication and readability.

Perhaps the least sophisticated scheme involves the description of the different findings, taken one at a time. This is the kind of report a computer could be programmed to generate. The report would focus first on the number of responses, for instance, and offer different interpretations if the number of responses is in the average range or if it is higher or lower than expected. Although perhaps closer to the data than any other scheme, this type of report is not very useful, especially to the nonspecialist.

A second scheme that is used fairly often is the function scheme. The clinician would have to have a preconceived idea of the important functions that should be discussed in a report and how they should be organized. These preconceived ideas could be derived from the clinician's psychological theory framework or be based on the factors or areas the test has been shown to be measuring. Thus, a psychoanalytical clinician following the Menninger tradition may want to discuss ego defenses, conflicts, symptom formation, adaptation, thinking, affect, and judgment and may develop a particular order for organizing these topics in the report. The system that Exner (2003) followed was derived from his own interpretive system and reviewed the different functions that the Rorschach measures. Although much more sophisticated than the single description approach, the function scheme still involves a cookie-cutter model that is less than optimal. Even when the function report is written in such a way that the examinee is the subject of the report, its real focus is still the test or the clinician's theory rather than the examinee.

A better option than the ones discussed above is an individualized personal scheme. This approach views the examinee as a unique individual and tailors the discussion to the examinee without relying on a standard template. Here the clinician is free to communicate his or her sense of the examinee much in the way that a writer may portray the protagonist of a story. In some cases the discussion may be driven by some characteristics that the examinee was found to have. In other cases it may be the referral problem that becomes the core of the discussion, or some other issue. This scheme may be seen as the most meaningful because it is completely centered on the examinee. It allows the clinician to focus on the information that is most relevant for that person while disregarding legitimate findings that may be less relevant.

To organize the report using an individualized personal model requires some creativeness and talent on the part of the clinician, and the task of writing the report becomes more time consuming and harder to accomplish. Clinicians wanting to follow this model may draw some guidance from fiction writers and noticing how they describe their characters.

One organizational scheme that is frequently used in literature starts with the description of the protagonist's personality. An event or a life situation is then portrayed in a way that allows us to understand the interaction between the individual's personality and the particular event or life situation. The rest of the story then follows naturally from the portrayal of this interaction.

Take, for instance, *A Beautiful Mind*, the fictionalized story of Nobel Prize winner John Nash by Sylvia Nasar, made into a popular film with Russell Crowe and Jennifer Connelly and directed by Ron Howard. The main character, John Nash, is portrayed at the beginning as an eccentric individual, a person who is very awkward in social situations and likes to write out his mathematical equations with a wax pencil on windowpanes. Although he is aware of social conventions, he intentionally behaves in a way that bluntly disregards such conventions. His approach to dating, for instance, is to propose to the lady that the two of them not waste time with social niceties and proceed immediately to have sex. He is a loner by design: He states that he does not like people and that people do not like him. An intellectually brilliant student at Princeton University, he aspires to be someone who would have a lasting historical impact on humanity. In clinical terms, he can be described as a schizotypal narcissistic personality.

These aspects of Nash's personality conspired so that he was very dissatisfied with his life when he became a university professor. The successes that would make the rest of humanity envious, such as being a distinguished professor at one of the best universities of the world, were too mundane and unexciting for Nash; the delusional system that developed as a defensive escape to a fantasy life was more interesting and exciting. In that fantasy life he can use his talents to save the United States from the annihilation that would result from a nuclear attack. It is only when he understands that this fantasy life, as enticing as it was, was leading to a much less rewarding life than his real life that he could fight the addiction to that fantasy life and resign himself to the life of a college professor.

If the clinician uses that story to generate a model that could be used to write a psychological testing report, the sequence would start with a description of the examinee's personality, continue with a characterization of the situation the examinee has to face, detail the problems and challenges of that situation, and describe what evolves out of the interaction of the particular personality with the environment. Those elements, resulting from the interaction between the individual's personality and the environmental press, in turn have an effect on both the individual and environment, an effect that can be the subject of further discussion. Exhibit 12.1 offers an example of a case written using the personality scheme.

Another scheme that is often used in literature and that can be borrowed for our purposes is the "coming of age" scheme. A good example in contemporary literature can be found in *Dead Poets Society* (Kleinbaum, 1986). The novel details the coming of age of adolescent pupils at an exclusive conservative boys' prep school. One of the students, Neil Perry, wants to be an actor, a plan that is much opposed by his authoritative father. Encouraged by a charismatic professor, John Keating, Perry signs up for a lead role in a play. When his father discovers what is happening, he pulls Perry out of the school. The story ends tragically, with Perry killing himself with his father's gun and the charismatic professor being fired.

Using this scheme, a psychologist can review the struggles that the examinee is having at a particular stage in life and in his or her pursuit of goals and aspirations. The environmental requirements or restrictions can then be reviewed to explain how the examinee is reacting to the situation. The term *coming of age* could be generalized into a *developmental* scheme so that it applies to stages of life other than the adolescent stage. In the case of children, this developmental scheme can apply to earlier developmental issues in the school or family. Similarly, the scheme can even be applied to issues of older adults facing retirement, loss of function, medical problems, the need for an assisted living facility, or a nursing home. The examiner can follow Erikson's (1950) or Levinson's (1978, 1996) stages of life to communicate an understanding the developmental issues the examinee is facing. Exhibit 12.2 offers an example of a case written using the development scheme.

Another scheme that is often used in literature and elsewhere is the *overcoming obstacles* scheme. In the 1988 film *Stand and Deliver*, we meet Jaime Escalante (Edward James Olmos), a mathematician who left a lucrative job at a private enterprise to pursue his dream of teaching in an inner city school. Against all odds, including the defeatist attitude of his colleagues, Escalante convinces a group of students to use math as their window to the land of opportunity. He harps on the occupational choice of flipping hamburgers at a fast-food restaurant or having the more exciting and better paying jobs that a good education can procure. To have a chance to be admitted and funded at a reasonable university, however, the group has to accomplish the impossible task of doing well on the Advanced Placement SAT. The plot thickens when the grueling semester of hard work and the excellent performances on the test are discounted on the suspicion that the group has cheated. Success is eventually achieved when the students are able to repeat their feat and do well again on a second taking of the test.

This theme of working hard to achieve a goal is one that can be used productively with some of our examinees. Typically we see examinees only when the goal was not achieved or when the goal has been achieved but some turn of fate has robbed them of the benefits they expected to reap. A flip side of the *overcoming obstacles* scheme is the *downward spiral* scheme where the person fails, time after time, to make the appropriate effort to master the needed skills and, as a result, becomes gradually less and less functional. These schemes give a clinician a chance to document a coherent view of what is happening with the individual, allowing an orderly presentation of tested data. Exhibit 12.3 offers an example of a report written in this manner.

The *differential diagnosis* scheme, also seen often enough in literature, forces a choice between alternative views or courses of action and documents the reasons for the choices that are made. A good example is Andre Dubus's short story "Killing," which was made into a movie (*In the Bedroom*) in 2001. Dr. Matt Fowler (portrayed by Tom Wilkinson in the movie), a physician in a little fishing town in Maine, has a choice to make. He can remain in town, even though he and his wife are constantly running into Richard Strout (played by William Mapother), the violent man who killed their son. He could leave town and forsake their long established history there. Or he could take justice into his own hands, presumably correcting the injustice that was made when Richard was able to get off on a technicality. The advantages and disadvantages of each of these choices can be examined and weighed. In a similar manner, a clinician can explore how the psychological testing of a particular person may support one diagnosis over another (e.g., major depressive episode over bipolar affective disorder, schizoaffective disorder over schizophrenia). Exhibit 12.4 offers an example of a test report written in this manner.

The schemes described in this chapter represent only a few of the possible ideas for organizing the discussion section. Many other ideas may be derived from literary models or may be created with a specific individual in mind. Moreover, a discussion may be organized using elements of more than one scheme.

Conclusion

My mother was a psychologist. She was in graduate school when I was a child. My small contribution to her graduate work was to serve as examinee for whatever instrument she was studying. Although I was usually intrigued by any test she gave me, the Rorschach was by far the most exciting. Part of this excitement came from the fact that I could (and did) create my own set of inkblot plates using watercolors. I hope my enthusiasm for this instrument, as well as my awareness of the instrument's limitations, came through in the pages of this book.

Some of the ideas discussed throughout the book, especially in this chapter, reflect my own development as a Rorschach clinician. I tried to portray the ways in which I have assimilated the literature and systematized my work. Although Rorschach clinicians may have a great deal in common, every one of us develops, in due time, a unique way of administering the test and interpreting the protocols. I hope that my work can help in the struggle that clinicians must go through in order to develop their own Rorschach skills and style.

EXHIBIT 12.1

Personality Report That Uses a Personality Scheme to Organize Content

---

REPORT OF PSYCHOLOGICAL EVALUATION

REPORT IN BRIEF: Case 12.1 is a 20-year-old White single woman who was admitted into the psychiatric ward after an episode of emotional dyscontrol in which she threatened to kill herself. Most of the symptomatology seen appeared to be fueled by the patient's histrionic-borderline personality. The report discusses her attentional problems and describes the personality issues in detail.

PRESENTING COMPLAINTS: Case 12.1 became "hysterical" prior to her hospitalization, acting in a very emotional manner and talking about killing herself by throwing herself downstairs. According to the chart, the patient's mother explained that Case 12.1 "loves drama" and has episodes in which she starts "screaming, pacing, rocking, and shaking." The patient acknowledged that she was very impulsive and likely to have "jerk reactions" in which she has no control of her emotions. Case 12.1 believes she has been depressed "on and off" for the last two years, mostly because she sees her peers moving ahead in life whereas she is "stuck" in her present life situation. She believes she has trouble keeping relationships because she "pushes people away."

Case 12.1 was concerned that she had an attention deficit disorder. She noted that she is "easily distracted" and has "trouble focusing."

There was also a concern about a possible bipolar affective disorder, mostly because of the lability of her emotions. For brief periods of time her speech may become pressured and she may appear overenergized. She denied ever feeling grandiose or showing any other signs of manic behavior.

According to the chart, Case 12.1's mother complained that the patient lies often and is inclined to take objects that do not belong to her. The patient explained that her parents are too "strict" and that she has been forced to lie in order to live the normal life of a 20 year old. The objects she has taken have been mostly clothes that she borrowed from her sister, with the intention of returning the apparel after she wore it.

PSYCHOSOCIAL STRESS: Case 12.1 broke up with her boyfriend a week prior to her hospitalization and was feeling very guilty about it.

PSYCHIATRIC HISTORY: For the last 6 months Case 12.1 had been attending family sessions with her parents and a psychologist. This therapist had actually recommended testing but the work was never done. For a period of time Case 12.1 was also medicated with Adderall for her possible attention deficit disorder. The patient stated that this medication had allowed her to be "more focused" in class and allowed her "head to calm down," so that she stopped experiencing her usual racing thoughts. Case 12.1 denied ever having any problems with substance abuse.

The incidence of psychiatric disorders in the family was remarkable only for alcoholism in the case of her great grandfather.

MEDICAL HISTORY: The patient suffers from allergy-induced asthma. She is medicated with Advair twice a day and takes Maxair when needed.

SOCIAL HISTORY: The oldest of three siblings, Case 12.1 was born and raised in the Chicago-land area. Her 46-year-old mother is a college graduate and works for a construction firm. She tends to be the disciplinarian in the family, and the patient has trouble getting along with her. The father is 48 years old. A union electrician, now he is employed as a supervisor. He is "softer" than the patient's mother, and Case 12.1 has a better relationship with him.

(continued)

EXHIBIT 12.1 (Continued)

Case 12.1 is followed by a brother and a sister. The brother, Mitch (17), is a junior in high school. He is a good athlete and has been doing well. Although Mitch is very "opinionated," he tends to keep to himself. Alyssa (15) is a high school sophomore. She was characterized as a very bold and self-assured adolescent who "knows what she wants in life."

It seems that, in spite of the family sessions, the relationship between Case 12.1 and her parents became "too toxic," according to the patient. Last January, as a result, she moved in with her maternal aunt and the aunt's family. Besides the aunt and uncle the family includes four children ranging in age from 1 to 7 years old. Although Case 12.1 has been able to get along better in that environment, she complained that she does not have any time for herself when she is home.

Case 12.1 had been with her 22-year-old boyfriend for over 2 years. The relationship had always been very conflictual. Case 12.1 explained that she "pushed him over the edge" by telling mutual friends that she was about to "dump him." What happened instead was the boyfriend was the one to call off the relationship on the patient's birthday. The boyfriend has three jobs so that part of the problem was that he did not have enough time for her.

EDUCATIONAL HISTORY: Case 12.1 has been taking college courses. She plans to reapply for admission to another university where she would like to study.

OCCUPATIONAL HISTORY: For the last year the patient has been employed at an accessories store at a mall, a store that sells earrings and the like.

MENTAL STATUS EXAMINATION: At the time of the examination the patient was alert, oriented, verbal, and coherent. The speech and language functions were intact. Other intellectual functions were formally assessed and are discussed below. The thought process was orderly and effective. The thought content was unremarkable. The affective response was appropriate to the content of the conversation. The mood was within normal limits and demonstrated a good range of emotions. No suicidal or homicidal ideation was verbalized. The psychomotor activity and anxiety levels were within the normal range. The patient was cooperative.

TEST RESULTS:

Shipley – Second Edition

Subtest	Raw Score	Standard Score	Percentile Rank
Vocabulary	22	86	18
Abstractions	13	83	32
Blocks	13	93	32
Composite A	179	89	23
Composite B	179	88	21

EXHIBIT 12.1 *(Continued)*

Wechsler Adult Intelligence Scale - Fourth Edition
Composite Score Summary

Scale	Sum of Scaled Scores	Composite Score	Percentile Rank	95% Confidence Interval	Qualitative Description
Working Memory	17	WMI 92	30	86-99	Average
Processing Speed	19	PSI 97	42	89-106	Average

Confidence Intervals are based on the Overall Average SEMs. Values reported in the SEM column are based on the examinee's age.

Index Level Discrepancy Comparisons

Comparison	Score 1	Score 2	Difference	Critical Value .05	Significant Difference Y / N	Base Rate Overall Sample
WMI - PSI	92	97	−5	12.46	N	39.5

Base rate by overall sample.
Statistical significance (critical value) at the .05 level.

Working Memory Subtests Summary

Subtest	Raw Score	Scaled Score	Percentile Rank	Reference Group Scaled Score	SEM
Digit Span	22	7	16	7	0.9
Arithmetic	14	10	50	10	1.2
(Letter-Number Seq.)	17	8	25	8	1.16

Processing Speed Subtests Summary

Subtest	Raw Score	Scaled Score	Percentile Rank	Reference Group Scaled Score	SEM
Symbol Search	30	9	37	9	1.31
Coding	72	10	50	10	1.16

Subtest Level Discrepancy Comparisons

Subtest Comparison	Score 1	Score 2	Difference	Critical Value .05	Significant Difference Y / N	Base Rate
Digit Span–Arithmetic	7	10	−3	2.57	Y	16.9
Symbol Search–Coding	9	10	−1	3.41	N	40.1

Statistical significance (critical value) at the .05 level.

(continued)

EXHIBIT 12.1 (*Continued*)

Wechsler Adult Intelligence Scale - Fourth Edition
Process Level Discrepancy Comparisons

Process Comparison	Score 1	Score 2	Difference	Critical Value .05	Significant Difference Y/N	Base Rate
Digit Span Forward– Digit Span Backward	7	7	0	3.65	N	
Digit Span Forward– Digit Span Sequencing	7	9	–2	3.6	N	31.7
Digit Span Backward– Digit Span Sequencing	7	9	–2	3.56	N	28
Longest DS Forward– Longest DS Backward	6	4	2	—	—	58
Longest DS Forward– Longest DS Sequence	6	6	0	—	—	
Longest DS Backward– Longest DS Sequence	4	6	–2	—	—	36.5

Statistical significance (critical value) at the .05 level.

Barkley Adult ADHD Rating Scale - Fourth Edition

	RS	TS
1. Inattention		
Total Score	19	90
Symptom Count	1	
2. Hyperactivity		
Total Score	12	93
Symptom Count	2	
3. Impulsivity		
Total Score	11	96
Symptom Count	2	
4. Sluggish Cognitive Tempo		
Total Score	20	87
Symptom Count	3	
Total Scores		
ADHD Score	42	94
Inattention Symptom Count	1	86
Hyperactivity and Impulsivity Symptom Count	4	95
ADHD Symptom Count	5	91
Sluggish Cognitive Tempo Symptom Count	3	88

The Millon Clinical Multiaxial Inventory—III

Personality Style Scales:	Raw Score	Base Rate
1–Introversive (Schizoid)	7	61
2A–Inhibited (Avoidant)	5	41
3–Cooperative (Dependent)	15	85**

EXHIBIT 12.1 (*Continued*)

4–Dramatic (Histrionic)	20	80 *
5–Confident (Narcissistic)	16	70
6A–Competitive (Antisocial)	15	83 *
7–Disciplined (Compulsive)	3	11
8A–Negativistic (Passive Aggressive/Explosive).	16	80 *
Severe Personality Scales:		
2B–Depressive	14	80 *
6B–Aggressive/Sadistic	11	67
8B–Self-Defeating	9	81 *
S–Schizotypal	5	59
C–Borderline	19	93 **
P–Paraphrenic	6	62
Clinical Symptom Scales:		
A–Anxiety	10	81 *
H–Somatic Preoccupations	11	71
N–Hypomania	15	94 **
D–Dysthymia	12	74
B–Alcohol Abuse	6	63
T–Drug Abuse	6	64
R–Post Traumatic Stress Disorder	5	49
SS–Psychotic Thinking	13	68
CC–Psychotic Depression	10	65
PP–Psychotic Delusion	1	24
Modifier Indices:		
X–Disclosure	126	76 *
Y–Desirability	13	59
Z–Debasement	20	77 *
V–Validity	0	

Rorschach Inkblot Test
The results of this test will be incorporated into the discussion section below.

Thematic Apperception Test (TAT)
The results of this test will be incorporated into the discussion section below.

INTELLECTUAL ASSESSMENT: The mental status examination gave no indications of cognitive deficits. The score from the Shipley showed Case 12.1 functioning at the top of the low average range, and at about the 20th percentile. This level of functioning was consistent with her educational history.

As shown by the Barkley Adult ADHD Rating Scale, Case 12.1 believed she had an attention deficit disorder. In fact, her perception was that her attention deficit involved all aspects of this disorder: inattention, hyperactivity, impulsivity, and a sluggish cognitive tempo. The test data, however, argued against that perception.

When attention was measured by means of the Working Memory Index of the Wechsler Adult Intelligence Scale, the score obtained was consistent with her more general abilities

(*continued*)

EXHIBIT 12.1 (*Continued*)

shown by the Shipley. The Working Memory Index (92) placed her in the average range and the 30th percentile of people of her age. The patient was not hyperactive during the testing and was not overly productive with the projective tests (she only had 16 responses on the Rorschach). She was not particularly impulsive in that she often took her time to do her tasks. Finally, the findings demonstrated a good mental tempo as measured by the Processing Speed Index of the Wechsler Adult Intelligence Scale. The Processing Speed Index (97) also placed her in the average range and at the 42nd percentile of the population.

In spite of these findings, it was clear that Case 12.1 had trouble focusing at times. The problem she had was most clearly seen during the administration of the Arithmetic subtest of the Wechsler Adult Intelligence Scale. She started this subtest by telling the examiner that she had never been able to do math and was going to perform very poorly (she did not). At times when different items were presented, the patient became a bit emotional, asserted that she could not do the problem "in (her) head," that she needed to have "paper and pencil," and became a bit derailed with these concerns. Surprisingly, when she was encouraged to "do (her) best" by the examiner, it turned out that she remembered all of the pieces of data from the first reading of the math problem and that she was often able to give the right answer. Unfortunately, for several of these items the patient had taken too long with her derailment and could not be given the point she would have earned otherwise. Nevertheless, the feat of having taken in all the information, and being able to retain the information through the period of time when she was focusing on something else, showed that there was nothing wrong with her attention span.

EMOTIONAL ASSESSMENT: People can be inattentive and function poorly for a variety of reasons, and some of these reasons have nothing to do with the traditionally defined attention deficit disorder. Case 12.1's inattentiveness had to do with her histrionic nature and her difficulty maintaining her focus. It involved the intrusion of emotionally laden material into the task. Case 12.1 was perhaps too young to be diagnosed with a personality disorder, but the behaviors that get her into trouble, including the events that led to the present hospitalization, are of a histrionic-borderline nature.

Histrionics are colorful and emotional individuals. In a manner that may be almost pathognomonic of histrionics, Case 12.1 took the time to come up with an actual name for every one of the protagonists in the stories she gave to the Thematic Apperception Test. Histrionics seek stimulation, excitement, and attention. They react very readily to situations around them, often becoming very involved in them, but typically the involvement does not last. This pattern of getting involved and ending up bored is repeated one time after another. The histrionic person is very good at making positive first impressions. Their ability to react to unexpected situations, their alertness, and their search for attention make them colorful and charming socialites in parties or other social gatherings. Often, however, they can be too loud and dramatic. They can be demanding and uncontrollable, especially in occasions when they are emotionally involved. They may have intense emotional friendships, but these friendships may be short-lived and replaced when boredom sets in. They are dependent on others but their dependency has a very different flavor from the dependency of inadequate individuals in that they need the attention of others rather than actual help in getting things done. As a result, they may be much less submissive than other types of dependent individuals.

Case 12.1's personality produces a pervasive instability of moods, interpersonal relationships, and self-image. The test scores indicated that she typically reacts in an impulsive and over-emotional way. Her affective response tends to be labile, at times demonstrating an excessive emotional intensity or involvement. Potentially self-damaging acts are likely to be part of the history, including recurrent suicidal behavior. Sadness, hopelessness, and aimlessness are often underlying the more obvious emotional response. Similar individuals have

EXHIBIT 12.1 (*Continued*)

significant problems with authority and resent any controls placed on them. They can be aggressive or angry. They are typically plagued by destructive ideas, which may be directed toward themselves or toward others. Their anger may be temporarily displaced by bothersome feelings of guilt or remorse. This individual's self-image is also problematic, as she is likely to feel worthless and be encumbered by self-doubt while, at the same time, feel used by others. Chronic feelings of emptiness, frantic efforts to avoid abandonment, and transient paranoid ideation or dissociative symptoms may be present.

Case 12.1's histrionic-borderline personality reportedly led to a "toxic" environment at the home of her parents. She was then farmed out to the home of an aunt and uncle who apparently had more tolerance for her histrionic behaviors. The event that led to the patient being hospitalized was the break-up with her boyfriend. It seemed that, in a histrionic-borderline fashion, she told mutual friends that she was about to break up with the boyfriend. Perhaps tired of the emotional roller coaster, the boyfriend apparently jumped the gun and terminated with her before she had time to end it with him. Instead of feeling relief, her melodramatic reaction was totally consistent with her personality, an inappropriate cry for attention in front of the aunt's home. If the patient were to continue with this personality into adulthood she would be considered to have a personality disorder.

On the positive side, the indications for a true affective disorder were not impressive. Case 12.1 may very well experience anxiety and depression, but these symptoms are likely to be part of the affective instability of the borderline and to be of short duration. Similarly, the patient appeared to be in good contact with reality.

DIAGNOSTIC IMPRESSIONS:
I.   Adjustment disorder with mixed disturbance of emotions and conduct – 309.4
II. Histrionic borderline personality
III. Allergy induced asthma
IV. External Stress: Breakup with boyfriend
V.   Level of Functioning: Serious symptoms present (GAF = 50)

RECOMMENDATIONS: Continued evaluation for the use of psychotropic medications in reducing the symptomatology was indicated. However, to whatever extent the problems are of a characterological nature, as suggested above, the medications may not be very helpful.

Case 12.1 may be helped with therapy or counseling. Given the personality style that Case 12.1 demonstrated in the testing, some recommendations can be made about the kind of therapeutic relationship that she would find most comfortable. For instance, an emphasis on formalities such as being on time for the session or keeping an interpersonal distance during the session is likely to feel unfriendly and dissatisfying to her. The therapist may need to be tolerant of emotionality on the part of the patient and even a certain amount of conflict. The type of relationship that would feel egosyntonic to Case 12.1 would be one where she is very much the center of attention and one where demonstrations of affection and support flow readily, especially from the therapist to the patient.

The goals of Case 12.1's treatment may include (a) to increase her awareness of her own emotions, the deeper reasons for her anger, disappointment, or any other feeling she may be experiencing, (b) to help her look at self-defeating behaviors that will eventually bring her significant problems, and (c) to moderate her reactions to interactions with others so that she does not "split" the good and the bad, and is able to relate in a more stable manner.

Personality Report That Uses a Developmental Scheme to Organize Content

REPORT OF PSYCHOLOGICAL EVALUATION

REPORT IN BRIEF: Case 12.2 is a 36-year-old single mother who was admitted into the psychiatric ward after a suicidal gesture. The patient became too upset after her request for discharge was rejected to continue with the testing. The plan to return the following day had to be abandoned because she continued to be upset. She was then discharged so that the testing was never completed.

The results that were obtained showed mostly characterological problems in the form of a borderline personality disorder with histrionic elements. Intertwined with the personality disorder have been an anxiety disorder and substance abuse tendencies. The evidence for an affective disorder, on the other hand, was not very impressive.

PRESENTING COMPLAINTS: Case 12.2 was admitted into the hospital after an incident in which she threw herself off a second story balcony in a suicidal gesture. The incident took place after the patient had taken 10 Xanax throughout the day in an attempt to "calm herself" down. When talking to the examiner, the patient stated that she had jumped off the balcony in order to get "attention" from her boyfriend and that she had no intention of killing herself. The patient's 9-year-old daughter witnessed the balcony episode and the Department of Children and Family Services was informed by the hospital of this occurrence.

The patient was obviously sad during the interview and had several crying spells. She claimed that she was only feeling sad because she was "missing" her daughters and that sadness was typically not a problem for her.

Case 12.2 saw her problem as being one of anxiety and panic attacks. The panic attacks may last for an hour and tend to occur once every other week, typically in response to a controversy with her boyfriend. During the attacks she feels like "jumping out of her skin" and hyperventilates. The patient's anxiety also causes her to have stomach upsets, which she relieves through self-induced vomiting.

Case 12.2 acknowledged having significant anger problems. When she becomes angry, she "has to hit something," and she has been known to hit her boyfriend on occasion.

Substance abuse in the recent past has seemingly included anxiolytic medications. She apparently obtains prescriptions for this type of medication from different physicians. Case 12.2 also abuses caffeine, drinking as much as four cups of coffee, five Cokes, and several energy drinks a day.

Case 12.2 spoke of being "manicky" and was concerned with the possibility that she suffered from a bipolar affective disorder. The bipolar episodes she recalled where mostly marked by anger and her tendency to make "mountains out of molehills." At such times she becomes "panicky" and needs to "take deep breaths." The patient, however, has had a "low self-esteem" her entire life and denied ever feeling grandiose. She also denied ever overspending her budget, being promiscuous, or experiencing other manic behaviors.

PSYCHOSOCIAL STRESS: The precipitant for the episode that led to the patient's hospitalization was her fight with her boyfriend.

PSYCHIATRIC HISTORY: This is the first psychiatric admission for Case 12.2 but has been treated for years for her emotional problems. She has been under the care of Dr. —. The patient was treated with Zoloft recently; other medications have included Xanax and Pristiq. At the time of the testing she was on Depakote and Klonopin.

EXHIBIT 12.2 (*Continued*)

Case 12.2 has a history of an eating disorder. She recalled how she was obese as a child and was picked on by other children as a result. She was binging and purging during her teenage years. Although she has self-induced vomiting in the recent past, she claimed that it was no longer because of an eating disorder but because of her stomach being upset as a result of her anxiety level. However, to this day she has trouble seeing herself as a "thin person."

The patient denied having any difficulties with substance abuse, but some issues were presented above with her use of the Xanax. The incidence for psychiatric problems in the family is remarkable for a bipolar disorder in the case of both her mother and brother.

MEDICAL HISTORY: Case 12.2 has never had any significant medical problems. She was reportedly in good physical health at the time of the testing.

SOCIAL HISTORY: The younger of two siblings, Case 12.2 was born and raised in the Chicago-land area. Both of her parents are 57 years old. She characterized her mother as a "manipulator" who is difficult to get along with. The mother is being treated for a bipolar affective disorder. She is employed in the housekeeping department of a hotel. The patient's father has "anger management problems." He is a truck driver. Case 12.2 has a 37-year-old brother who also has anger management problems. The brother is in his second marriage and has five children, three from his previous marriage. He worked in construction but was recently laid off.

Case 12.2 has never been married. At the age of 18 she moved in with a boyfriend, but this relationship only lasted a few months and ended when the patient attached herself to another boyfriend. For the 8 years that followed she was with this man, a person who is 13 years her senior. This second boyfriend is the father of both of the patient's children. He is reportedly a very controlling individual, and the two of them broke up and got back together on several occasions.

For the last three years Case 12.2 has been living with her current boyfriend. The boyfriend is 11 years older than the patient. A recovering heroin abuser, the boyfriend has been on Methadone maintenance and has been heroin-free for the last 3 months. They have a conflictual relationship and the boyfriend was said to be verbally abusive. He was unemployed at the time of the evaluation and lives on Social Security disability.

Case 12.2 has two daughters. — (9) is a fourth grader. — (7) is in second grade. Both of her daughters are said to be in good health and have presented no problems.

EDUCATIONAL HISTORY: Case 12.2 has an associate degree from — Community College. She recalled being a good student during her high school years.

OCCUPATIONAL HISTORY: For the last 11 years the patient has worked as an orthodontist assistant. She enjoys the work and has not had any occupational problems.

DISCUSSION: Case 12.2 was apparently the product of a dysfunctional home. Her mother has been treated for a bipolar affective disorder and was characterized as interpersonally manipulative. Her father had "anger problems" and was reportedly abusive when the patient was growing up. The patient has an older brother who has also had difficulties with his temper. To this day the patient does not get along with her family.

Partly because of the family dysfunction, Case 12.2 was seemingly not able to accomplish the tasks of the early stages of development, such as the ability to form enduring attachments

(continued)

EXHIBIT 12.2 *(Continued)*

while developing an individuated identity. She demonstrated identity and self-esteem problems early in life, struggling with bulimia through her adolescent years. Later on, the usual conflicts of adolescence could not be handled in an optimal manner, and the patient escaped from the parental home prematurely, at the age of 18. The means of escape were provided by a boyfriend she had at the time, a person that the parents disapproved of. By the time she left the home of her parents she seemed to have had a flawed personality disorder, a personality consisting of a borderline core with histrionic elements.

Describing this personality in more detail, the test results suggested a pervasive instability of moods, interpersonal relationships, and self-image. The scores would indicate that Case 12.2 typically reacts in an impulsive and overemotional way. The affective response tends to be labile, at times showing apathy and numbness while, at other times, demonstrating an excessive emotional intensity or involvement. Potentially self-damaging acts have been part of the history, including her suicidal gesture. Sadness, hopelessness, and aimlessness are often underlying the more obvious emotional response.

Similar individuals have significant problems with authority and resent any controls placed on them. They can be aggressive or angry. They are typically plagued by destructive ideas, which may be directed toward themselves or toward others. Their anger may be temporarily displaced by bothersome feelings of guilt or remorse. Similar people take offense over seemingly minor issues. In some cases they appear to be always looking for injustices and are likely to confront the other person with whatever objections they may have. Additionally, they typically have an explosive temper, likely to erupt in an angry outburst at a moment's notice. These are difficult people at best: Excitable and irritable, they often have a history of treating others in a rough or mean manner and of angrily "flying off the handle" whenever they are confronted or opposed. The history she has with her present boyfriend, with domestic quarrels that have brought the police over on five different occasions, obviously highlights this aspect of her personality. The anger management problem is coded diagnostically as an intermittent explosive disorder.

Case 12.2's self-image is also problematic, as she is likely to feel worthless and be encumbered by self-doubt while, at the same time, feel used by others. Chronic feelings of emptiness, frantic efforts to avoid abandonment, and transient paranoid ideation or dissociative symptoms have been present.

The patient seemed psychologically fragile. The Rorschach was very guarded. This was in dire contrast to the clinical presentation of an overemotional and not well-controlled individual. The few responses obtained were given with a certain amount of apprehension, with expressed concerns about how the responses would be interpreted. Case 12.2 minimized the substance abuse problems she has had and tried to explain away the episode that led to her hospitalization. The use of denial and projection were repeatedly seen in the testing.

Case 12.2's adult history was also consistent with the personality diagnosis. After a short relationship with her first boyfriend, she had an unstable eight-year relationship with a man who was 13 years her senior. For the last 3 years Case 12.2 has been with her current boyfriend, another man who is older than she. (The attraction to older men could be possibly conceived as an attempt to find a nurturing parental figure.) The current boyfriend, however, is a substance–abusing unemployed man and appeared to be even more dysfunctional than the previous boyfriend. The kind of unstable and conflictual relationships the patient has been able to establish are consistent with the interpersonal instability that is part of the borderline personality.

EXHIBIT 12.2 (*Continued*)

In addition to the patient's characterological problems, the indications were that Case 12.2 suffers from anxiety and a panic disorder. She had been abusing caffeinated beverages and anxiolytic medications.

On the positive side, the testing showed good contact with reality. When she is not in one of her emotional roller coasters she may be able to function fairly well. For the last 11 years, for example, the patient has been working as an orthodontist assistant and apparently has done well on this job. Although she is a high-energy individual, there were no signs of over-productivity in the testing and Case 12.2's history did not show the usual signs of a bipolar disorder (e.g., grandiosity, overspending, promiscuity).

DIAGNOSTIC IMPRESSIONS:

I-   Panic disorder without agoraphobia – 300.01
     Intermittent explosive disorder – 312.34
     Anxiolytic abuse – 305.40
     Caffeine-related disorder not otherwise specified – 292.9
     Bulimia nervosa in partial remission – 307.51
     Partner relational problem–V61.10
II- Borderline personality disorder with histrionic elements – 301.83
III- No known medical problems contributing
IV- External Stress: Relational problems
V-   Level of Functioning: Serious symptoms present (GAF = 45)

RECOMMENDATIONS: Continued evaluation for the use of psychotropic medications in reducing the symptomatology was indicated.

Since the patient appeared to be moderately hyper-energized by nature, she should be strongly encouraged to stop drinking caffeinated beverages.

Case 12.2 needs to make a firm commitment to stop using improperly prescribed anxiolytic drugs. (She should be under the care of one psychiatrist and should not seek prescriptions from other professionals.) In order to maintain abstinence it will probably be necessary for her to actively participate in an outpatient program including a self-help group.

Case 12.2 would also benefit from a continuation of her psychotherapy. The goals of this treatment may include (a) to increase her awareness of her own emotions, the deeper reasons for her anger, disappointment, or any other feeling she may be experiencing, (b) to help her look at self-defeating behaviors that will eventually bring her significant problems, and (c) to moderate her reactions to interactions with others so that she does not "split" the good and the bad and is able to relate in a more stable manner.

EXHIBIT 12.3

Personality Report That Uses an Overcoming Obstacles Scheme to Organize Content

REPORT OF PSYCHOLOGICAL EVALUATION

REPORT IN BRIEF: Case 12.3 is a 54-year-old white gentleman who was admitted into the psychiatric ward because of suicidal ideation. He was intoxicated at the time of admission. The testing showed depression and mild signs of hypomania. A significant problem with alcohol abuse was also seen.

PRESENTING COMPLAINTS: The patient had been feeling despondent for the last eight months. He had also felt helpless and hopeless about his life situation. He believed that his life had been "spiraling downward." He had been spending a large amount in bed and had lost his motivation. Finally, Case 12.3 was bothered by suicidal thoughts and the thought that his life was not worth living. The day prior to hospitalization he reportedly took a mild overdose of medication (Seroquel).

The patient had been drinking quite excessively, and was intoxicated at the time of his admission into the hospital.

Case 12.3 was also mildly hypomanic. He experienced "racing thoughts" all of the time and was mildly over-energized.

PSYCHOSOCIAL STRESS: The patient's income had been reduced because of a downturn of the real estate business. His wife was diagnosed and treated for breast cancer two years ago. The patient has the responsibility for the care of four elderly relatives.

PSYCHIATRIC HISTORY: Case 12.3 has a long history of alcohol abuse and dependence. He has experienced shakes, blackouts and withdrawal symptoms as a result of his alcohol intake. He has had car accidents and has been charged with driving under the influence. The patient has been treated on multiple occasions for his alcoholism (at — Hospital in 1988, 1991 and 1993, and at — Hospital in 1984). He has been an active member of Alcoholics Anonymous and achieved a three-year period of sobriety starting in 1988. More recently he maintained sobriety for 18 months.

The patient also has a long history of treatment for bipolar mood fluctuations. He reportedly had manic episodes during the 80's and was admitted in the manic state to — Hospital in 1988. During those episodes the patient recalled that he did not need to sleep more than two hours per night, was drinking excessively, was spending large amounts of money, and was grandiose. For the last two decades the episodes have been less severe, better characterized as hypomania. In 1992 he received six electroshock treatments at —; these treatments were effective in relieving the depression at first but the patient relapsed rapidly after the treatments stopped. He has been under Dr. —'s care for many years. Case 12.3 has been tried on a variety of medications including Valium, Xanax, lithium carbonate, Tegretol, nortriptyline, Seroquel, Depakote, Effexor, and Lexapro. Often he has been non-compliant with the treatment. Several suicidal attempts have taken place.

Case 12.3 has not abused other drugs besides alcohol. The incidence of psychiatric disorders in the family has been remarkable for alcoholism in the case of his father, paternal grandfather, a paternal aunt, and two maternal aunts. His father reportedly also suffers from a bipolar disorder. The mother was a victim of Alzheimer's disease.

MEDICAL HISTORY: The patient has a history of hypothyroidism, which is treated with Synthroid.

EXHIBIT 12.3 *(Continued)*

SOCIAL HISTORY: The older of two siblings Case 12.3 was born and raised in —. The mother is 73 years old and suffers from Alzheimer's disease. She has also had a stroke. The mother lives in an assisted living facility. She was an outgoing person in her younger years and worked as a secretary at a law firm. The patient's father is 75 years old. Besides being an alcoholic, the patient also believes the father suffered from bipolar effective disorder. The father is actively drinking and lives with the patient. In his younger years the father was employed as train operator. Case 12.3's 49-year-old sister is married and has three children. She has apparently been doing well.

The patient married his present wife 30 years ago. This was the first marriage for both of them. The 53-year-old wife is recovering from the treatment for breast cancer. With her illness she lost the secretarial job at a school that she had held for 24 years. The wife is now working as a secretary at a doctor's office.

Case 12.3 has a daughter who is 29 years old. The daughter is married but has no children. She works for an advertising agency.

EDUCATIONAL HISTORY: Case 12.3 recalled being an excellent student though high school. He has a Master's in Business Administration from —- University.

OCCUPATIONAL HISTORY: The patient worked most of his life as a real estate broker. He has been with his current office for the last 25 years. In the recent past he has not done well financially due to the downturn of the real estate business.

MENTAL STATUS EXAMINATION: At the time of the examination the patient was alert, oriented, verbal and coherent. There were no indications of cognitive deficits. The thought process was orderly and effective. The thought content was unremarkable. The affective response was appropriate to the content of the conversation. The mood was mildly despondent and had some range of emotions. Suicidal ideation had been present on admission. The psychomotor activity was mildly accelerated, with the patient working at a fast pace and speaking rapidly. The anxiety level was within the normal range. The patient was very cooperative.

TEST RESULTS:
Shipley – Second Edition

Subtest	Raw Score	Standard Score	Percentile Rank
Vocabulary	35	110	75
Abstractions	9	81	10
Blocks	12	98	45
Composite A (Voc and Abs)	191	94	34
Composite B (Voc and Blocks)	208	103	58

Alcohol Use Inventory (AUI)
Benefits
1. Drinks to improve sociability, percentile rank = 25
2. Drinks to improve mental functioning = 26
3. Drinks to manage mood = 99 ↑↑↑
4. Drinks to deal with marital problems = 68

(continued)

EXHIBIT 12.3 (*Continued*)

Styles
5. Gregarious	= 52
6. Compulsive	= 29
7. Sustained drinking	= 06↓↓

Consequences
8. Loss of control	= 25
9. Social role maladaptation	= 15↓
10. Perceptual withdrawal symptoms	= 34
11. Somatic withdrawal symptoms	= 08↓↓
12. Marital problems	= 58

Concerns and Acknowledgments
13. Quantity of alcohol	= 57
14. Guilt and worry	= 99 ↑↑↑
15. Prior attempts to deal with drinking	= 97↑↑↑
16. Receptivity for help	= 31
17. Awareness of drinking problems	= 51

Factor-analytically Derived Second-level Factors
18. (A) Drinks to enhance functioning	= 33
19. (B) Obsessive sustained drinking	= 12↓↓
20. (C) Directly-expressed uncontrolled life disruption	= 25
21. (D) Indirectly-expressed uncontrolled life disruption	= 78↑
22. (E) Anxious concern about drinking	= 99↑↑↑
23. (F) Acknowledgment of drinking problems	= 52

Factor-analytically Derived Third-level Factor
24. (G) Involvement with alcohol	= 28

Beck Depression Inventory
Raw score = 42 (Severe depression)

The Millon Clinical Multiaxial Inventory – II and III

Personality Style Scales:	Scores=>	Raw	Base Rate
1 - Introversive (Schizoid)	=	15	80*
2 - Inhibited (Avoidant)	=	13	72
3 - Cooperative (Dependent)	=	8	65
4 - Dramatic (Histrionic)	=	14	41
5 - Confident (Narcissistic)	=	15	54
6A - Competitive (Antisocial)	=	10	67
7 - Disciplined (Compulsive)	=	17	48
8A - Negativistic (Passive-Aggressive/Explosive)	=	9	61
Personality Aberration Scales:			
2B - Depressive	=	22	100***
6B - Aggressive/Sadistic	=	5	38
8B - Self-Defeating	=	12	67*

EXHIBIT 12.3 *(Continued)*

Personality Style Scales:	Scores=>	Raw	Base Rate
S - Schizotypal	=	10	63
C - Borderline	=	11	59
P - Paraphrenic	=	9	63
Clinical Symptom Scales:			
A - Anxiety	=	16	102***
H - Somatic Preoccupations	=	7	62
N - Hypomania	=	6	59
D - Dysthymia	=	18	100***
B - Alcohol Abuse	=	13	85**
T - Drug Abuse	=	11	69
R - Post Traumatic Stress Disorder	=	12	52
SS - Psychotic Thinking	=	14	71
CC – Major Depression	=	23	112***
PP - Psychotic Delusion	=	4	62
Modifier Indices:			
X - Disclosure	=	135	79*
Y - Desirability	=	11	51
Z - Debasement	=	25	85
V - Validity	=	0	

Rorschach Inkblot Test
The results of this test will be incorporated into the discussion section below.

Thematic Apperception Test (TAT)
The results of this test will be incorporated into the discussion section below.

INTELLECTUAL ASSESSMENT: The mental status examination gave no indications of cognitive or memory deficits. The score from the Shipley suggested that Case 12.3 has average intellectual abilities.

EMOTIONAL ASSESSMENT: Case 12.3 exemplifies the type of person who has had a difficult life as a result of psychiatric problems, and who may have done the best he could under the circumstances. Perhaps influenced by both genetic and life experiences, the patient has suffered from a bipolar affective disorder and alcoholism his entire life. He arguably could have done better with his affective instability if he would have been more compliant with treatment, but part of that disorder is an affinity for not liking the medications and getting off the prescribed scheduled. Similarly, he could be faulted for his alcohol relapses but, especially when the alcoholism is seen co-morbidly with a bipolar affective disorder, the drinking is often fueled by the mood instability. Bipolar patients often drink excessively during manic or depressive episodes, even if they are not alcoholics. In any event, the rest of this section will describe the findings in more detail.

In the recent past Case 12.3 has been sad, and has demonstrated a dysphoric or melancholic mood. People with similar test profiles show diminished interest in their daily activities,

(continued)

EXHIBIT 12.3 (Continued)

and do not derive much pleasure from their current involvements. Life may become a burden, an unwanted task that has little personal meaning. Making decisions, even about minor matters, may be difficult, with the individual encumbered by indecisiveness. At times the patient may have crying spells. Much morbid thinking about death was predominantly present in the stories he gave to the Thematic Apperception Test. Most concerning, suicide ideation has been present. Low self-esteem and feelings of worthlessness may be accompanied by guilt about past actions. Similar individuals typically experience vegetative symptoms, such as a loss of appetite, sleep difficulties, fatigability, or a low energy level. They may move at a slow pace, or become anxious and agitated.

Although Case 12.3 was not in a manic state at the time of the examination, hypomanic symptoms were seen, and the test profile was consistent with a bipolar affective disorder. Judging from the Rorschach, for instance, the patient tended to be over-productive. His mode of operation included a great deal of movement, emotion and excitement. Individuals with similar test scores can be expected to have an elevated mood and some tendency toward grandiosity. They experience a decreased need for sleep. They are typically over-energized and overly talkative, sometimes speaking fast in a pressured sort of way. They may demonstrate a flight of ideas, going from one topic to the next in a disorganized manner. At times they become overly invested in a project, or in pleasurable activities, and can no longer follow a reasonable daily schedule. No longer able to moderate their activities, they become too driven by their goals to conduct their business effectively.

Case 12.3 has obviously shown a maladaptive pattern of alcohol consumption. Similar individuals exhibit a significant impairment of their performance and behavior in association to the substance abuse. They may spend an inordinate amount of time obtaining alcohol, and may behave in an unacceptable social manner as a result of their chemical consumption. They typically continue to use alcohol after being aware that their chemical consumption has persistent and deleterious effects on their lives. The Alcohol Use Inventory suggested that part of Case 12.3's motivation for drinking might have been as a way of managing his moods. The association between moods and drinking was clearly seen in the following story that the patient gave to card 3BM of the Thematic Apperception Test:

> This is a very depressed person, curled up in the corner not able to show her head, very desperate. She looks like she is very out of it because of some event in her life. A death of a loved one, or drinking and using drugs

The testing suggested the presence of a borderline personality disorder. The problem is that most of the borderline signs that the patient acknowledged (e.g., irresponsible behaviors, sexual promiscuity, lack of clear direction in life, mood instability) are common symptoms of an alcohol-abusing bipolar affective disorder individual. Predicating against the personality disorder was the fact that the patient functioned relatively well when his mood and alcohol were under control. Moreover, his history showed the kind of marital and occupational stability that would be uncommon for a person with a borderline personality disorder.

On the positive side, Case 12.3's Rorschach showed good contact with reality and a balanced approach to the world in terms of seeing both the overall picture and the finer details. He is a sociable individual with good social skills.

DIAGNOSTIC IMPRESSIONS:

I- Bipolar affective disorder, mixed – 296.63
    Alcohol intoxication in remission – 303.00
    Alcohol dependence in remission – 303.90
    Alcohol abuse – 305.00

EXHIBIT 12.3 (*Continued*)

II- No personality disorder
III- Hypothyroidism
IV- External Stress: Financial problems, wife's cancer, caretaking responsibilities
V- Level of Functioning: Serious symptoms (GAF=45)

RECOMMENDATIONS: Continued evaluation for the use of psychotropic medications in reducing the symptomatology was indicated. The patient would also be helped by a period of supportive psychotherapy. It would be especially beneficial if he can explore the problems he has had as a result of his treatment non-compliance and the importance of following religiously the treatment plan.

Case 12.3 needs to make a firm commitment to stop drinking. In order to maintain abstinence it will probably be necessary for him to actively participate in an outpatient program including a self-help group.

EXHIBIT 12.4

Personality Report That Uses A Differential Diagnosis Scheme to Organize Content

REPORT OF PSYCHOLOGICAL EVALUATION

REPORT IN BRIEF: Case 12.4 is a 20-year-old woman who was admitted into the psychiatric ward for the treatment of a depression. The Rorschach and the Thematic Apperception Test revealed a profound level of disorganization and a very remarkable sexual preoccupation. The level of dysfunction seen was too severe to represent psychotic features of an affective disorder. In fact, she was too disorganized to be able to do any of the self-report inventories. The testing raised the concern about a disorder in the schizophrenic spectrum.

PRESENTING COMPLAINTS: Case 12.4 was hospitalized for the treatment of depression. In the recent past she had been feeling sad and had lost her motivation, so that it is "not fun to do anything" anymore. The hospital chart noted that she had been moody and irritable, inclined to blame others for real or imagined mistreatments. Case 12.4 explained that she "hated the world, believing that it was not a happy place." Her affect had been flat and she demonstrated psychomotor retardation.

There were also indications that Case 12.4 was psychotic. At times she admitted hearing conversations that were "mean," or voices telling her that people were lying. She spoke of having to "fulfill a prophecy," of the belief that she had been "predetermined" to be "unhappy," but could not explain these ideas any further. The patient voiced concern about revealing too much personal information and worried what would happen if the examiner learned "everything" there was to know about her.

PSYCHOSOCIAL STRESS: A senior in high school, Case 12.4 was worried about her future, and whether or not she should attend college.

PSYCHIATRIC HISTORY: After becoming depressed a year ago the patient was admitted into — where she was treated for two weeks with Wellbutrin and Abilify. She continued her treatment at the — Clinic. In the more distant past, the patient acknowledged that she had "behavioral problems."

MEDICAL HISTORY: Case 12.4 denied having any significant medical problems or injuries.

EXHIBIT 12.4 (*Continued*)

SOCIAL HISTORY: Case 12.4's adoptive mother is a single parent. She is 57 years old and a real estate broker. Case 12.4 noted that they have not been getting along well. The patient has felt that her mother did not "love" her anymore: The mother was no longer "nice and warm" and had "disconnected" from the patient. Case 12.4 complained that her mother needs to be in control, and was resentful that her mother brought her to the hospital.

Case 12.4 has one good girlfriend. She is concerned about getting too close to her friend, fearing that people might think she is lesbian. When asked about romantic relationships, it appeared that she did not have any such experiences because she doesn't "like men either." The question of whether she is a loner has been a bit of an issue for her.

EDUCATIONAL HISTORY: Case 12.4 is a sophomore at — College. When speaking of her schooling, Case 12.4 noted that the school was a Catholic school and that she was not too sure she was Catholic.

OCCUPATIONAL HISTORY: In the recent past Case 12.4 quit a part time job she had at a pizza restaurant.

MENTAL STATUS EXAMINATION: At the time of the examination this right-handed patient was alert, oriented, verbal and coherent. The thought process was quite disorganized. The thought content was confused and delusional; it appeared that the patient has been having auditory hallucinations. The affective response was appropriate to the content of the conversation. The mood was extremely dysphoric and had practically no range of emotions (very occasionally she was able to show a faint smile). Suicidal ideation has been present. The psychomotor activity was quite slow. The anxiety level was within the normal range. The patient was cooperative.

DISCUSSION: There was no doubt that Case 12.4 was depressed. This was the reason for her hospitalization and the main presenting complaint prompting the request for the present evaluation. She had been feeling sad, had lost her motivation, and spoke of the world as an unhappy place. Judging from the Rorschach she was de-energized and was bothered by morbid thoughts.

The presence of psychotic symptoms was also obvious prior to the evaluation, but these symptoms were seen as psychotic features of her affective disorder. In fact, some of the psychotic thinking was even mood congruent, as the patient talked about mistreatment, the mean voices she heard, and her being predetermined to be unhappy. The diagnostic issue then becomes how disturbed the thinking process has to be before that issue is seen as a primary problem, rather than one that would disappear when the affective disorder episode abates.

Case 12.4 was too dysfunctional to do much of the testing. She became too confused and unfocused when attempting to complete the Shipley or a self-report inventory (the Millon Clinical Multiaxial Inventory). The instruments that could be successfully completed were the Rorschach and the Thematic Apperception Test, due to the fact that these instruments are much more interactive.

The Rorschach protocol had only 16 responses. This test revealed a very fearful and fragile individual with the many "scary" animals or "fearful monsters" that were included among the patient's associations. When she was able to associate to a human being, it was in the context of a threatening situation involving "blood." Her sexual preoccupation was shown by the fact that seven of her 16 responses involved a man's "private parts."

Both the scary and the sexual responses, of course, spoke to the issues that were preoccupying her mind. In most cases the shape of the section of the inkblot she was focusing on did not look at all like the response she was offering, indicating a substantial loss of contact with reality. In other words, her associations were determined by her own obsessions rather than by the out-

EXHIBIT 12.4 (*Continued*)

side stimulus of the figures presented to her. The patient had similar problems on the Thematic Apperception Test where many of her stories were disjointed and odd. In real life she would be expected to be too preoccupied with her fears and sexual obsessions to be able to carry a regular conversation in a logical and sequential manner. Similar people are so preoccupied with their own issues that they do not have a real interest in the world around them.

Case 12.4's responses were typically so disorganized as to be quite dysfunctional. She often began with some assertion that did not make too much sense (e.g., "something I saw with my cousin"). That assertion, upon further inquiry, would turn out to be one of her obsessions (e.g., "his private part"). She could never support her reasoning appropriately by pointing to parts of the inkblot that resembled the shape of the associated response (e.g., in this case she ended up by stating that "none" of the inkblot actually reminded her of the cousin or his penis, but that the inkblot "just" made her think of it). This is the kind of primary thought process that is too idiosyncratic and immature to be effective. Similar people are odd and are too much into their own world to be able to transact business in a reasonable way in society.

The fact that Case 12.4's thinking was so disorganized and dysfunctional posed a differential diagnostic dilemma. Technically, as long as the psychotic thinking accompanied symptoms of an affective disorder, the affective disorder takes precedence, and the psychosis is seen as a feature of that disorder. This view can be easily understood in a case where the poor thinking is a minor element of the clinical picture. In the present case, however, her thinking was so disorganized and dysfunctional that it begged to be seen as a major problem in its own behalf.

Because of Case 12.4's young age, and the fact that this was the first major episode of the disorder, it was too early to discern what the course of the disorder would be. She appeared to be too dysfunctional to be seen as simply the case of a major depression with psychotic features, but the determination needed to be made as to whether the thought disorder would disappear when the depression abated. If so, in spite of the severity of the thought disorder, the thinking problems would be seen as an element of the affective disorder.

Given the severity of the thought disorder, however, the two other alternatives that must be considered are the schizoaffective disorder and schizophrenia. Of these two differential diagnostic alternatives, the schizoaffective disorder appeared the most likely, due to the fact that the patient was very depressed. What would be expected in that case is that some of the schizophrenic-like symptomatology would persist, even after the patient has recovered from her depression.

DIAGNOSTIC IMPRESSIONS:
I-   Schizophreniform disorder – 295.40
       Major depressive episode, recurrent – 296.34
II-   Personality evaluation deferred
III- No known medical problems contributing
IV-   External Stress: Family issues
V-   Level of Functioning: Serious impairment (GAF=25)

RECOMMENDATIONS: Continued evaluation for the use of psychotropic medications in reducing the symptomatology was indicated.

A clear diagnosis could not be reached at the time of the present evaluation for the reasons explained above. The possibility of updating this evaluation in six months or after the patient has recovered should be considered.

Appendix
Psychiatric Norms

n the area of personality assessment, different instruments have used different reference groups. The Minnesota Multiphasic Personality Inventory (MMPI; Hathaway & McKinley, 1943) and the current revision of this test (MMPI-2; Butcher, Dahlstrom, Graham, Tellegen, & Kaemmer, 1989), for example, were standardized with a nonclinical population, and psychiatric patients were excluded from the norms. In contrast, the Millon Clinical Multiaxial Inventory (MCMI; Millon, 1977) and the two later editions of this test (MCMI-II; Millon, 1987; MCMI-III, Millon, 1994) were standardized with psychiatric patients. Each of these approaches has advantages and disadvantages. When we discover differences between an examinee and a nonclinical sample, the findings can be used to determine that the individual has emotional problems. However, these differences could be simply due to the person's being a psychiatric patient.

The prevalent modern norms for the Rorschach (Exner, 2003; Meyers, 2007) have used nonclinical samples. In contrast, the norms presented in this Appendix are psychiatric norms. An argument for the use of psychiatric norms is that, when testing an individual who has been having emotional problems, the clinician would want to compare that person to other people who also had emotional problems. Such a comparison would allow the clinician to see how the individual is unique in the group of psychiatric patients, rather than how he or she differs from a group of people who have never had those problems. In other words, if what the clinician wanted to discover is whether the person had emotional problems, then the nonpsychiatric norms would provide the right comparison group. In that case any differences between the individual and those norms would be indicative of an attribute that was not in line with the emotionally healthy population. In most cases, however, the clinician already knows that the individual being tested has emotional problems, and that fact is not something in need of discovery. What the clinician wants to know is what unique attributes the person has within the psychiatric group that may be related to their particular disturbance. Psychiatric norms also allow the clinician to investigate how the examinee resembles patients with certain disturbances (Weiner, 2001).

Method

The sample was collected from psychiatric patients consecutively referred for a psychological evaluation over a period of 30 years, from 1980 to 2010. The patients were tested following Comprehensive System procedures (see Chapter 2 for departures), and records that had less than 14 responses were excluded. The protocols were scored in accordance to Comprehensive System rules.

The original sample consisted of 1,670 psychiatric patients. The sample size was reduced to 930 after children (younger than 16) and patient protocols with missing data were removed. The examinees were tested at one of three urban hospitals or at a private office. The responses and scores were entered into the Hermann computer program (Choca & Garside, 1992). The sample population was 44% men and 56% women. The mean age of participants was 34.6 years, with a standard deviation of 16.1 years. The ages ranged from 16 to 90 years.

Figure A.1 shows the discharge diagnoses of a randomly chosen subsample. Comorbidity of diagnoses was shown by 33 or 58.9% of the patients in this sub-sample, with the average patient having 1.73 diagnoses. The norms collected in this manner are shown in Table A.1.

Discussion

The means for this psychiatric sample were similar to those of Exner's (2003) nonclinical sample in many ways. There were practically no differences, for instance, in the average number of responses. The

FIGURE A.1

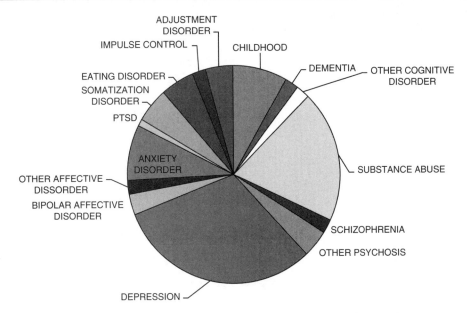

Diagnostic percentiles of a randomly chosen sub-sample of 56 patients.

location, form quality, and content scores were also very similar. On the other hand, notable differences were also found. For example, the mean F%, or responses that were based only on the form features on the inkblot, were more than one standard deviation higher in the psychiatric population than in Exner's nonpatient sample. Considered together, these data suggested that a psychiatric population may be more constricted and less creative or productive than nonclinical individuals.

In the psychiatric population, movement responses, both active and passive, occurred less frequently than in Exner's nonpatient sample. Because a higher frequency of movement responses are thought to indicate an ability to reason, use one's imagination, and think abstractly (Exner, 2003), a lower frequency in the psychiatric population suggested a decreased ability to reason and engage in higher forms of conceptualization.

TABLE A.1

Psychiatric Norms for the Roschach Inkblot Test

Variable	M	SD
No. of responses (R)	21.46	8.37
Whole response (W)	9.25	4.33
Detail response (D)	9.67	6.00
Unusual detail response (Dd)	2.04	3.70
White space response (S)	1.66	1.83
Rotations	1.01	2.85
Movement response (M)	2.79	2.33
Animal movement response (FM)	2.57	2.08
Inanimate movement (m)	1.04	1.37
FM+m	4.00	3.00
Form-Color (FC)	1.13	1.37
Color-Form (CF)	1.56	1.73
Color (C)	0.21	0.64
Color Naming (Cn)	0.04	0.27
Weighted Color Sum (WSumC)	2.40	2.00
Sum of Achromatic Color Responses (SumC')	0.84	1.37
Sum of Texture Responses (SumT)	0.44	0.86
Sum of Vista Responses (SumV)	0.72	2.11
Sum of Shading Responses (SumY)	0.33	0.82
Color shade blend	0.23	0.31
Form dimension (FD)	0.28	0.67
F	10.89	5.97
F%	37.00	25.00
Lambda	1.25	1.98
Active movement (a)	3.99	2.89
Passive movement (p)	1.63	1.74
Intellect	0.61	1.61
Blends	1.54	1.89
Affective ratio (Afr)	0.49	0.19
Populars	4.41	1.66
XA%	0.57	0.39
Isolate/R	0.12	0.14
Pure Human Response (H)	2.08	1.85
Fictional Human Response (H)	0.78	1.34
Part Human Response (Hd)	1.38	2.31
Fictional Part Human Response (Hd)	0.29	0.70
Human Experience (Hx)	0.07	0.41
All Human Content	3.59	4.03
Pure Animal Response (A)	7.68	3.30
Fictional Animal Response (A)	0.65	1.05
Part Animal Response (Ad)	1.34	1.71
Fictional Part Animal Response (Ad)	0.10	0.36
Somatization Response (An)	0.82	1.26
Art	0.48	0.93
Ay	0.08	0.30

TABLE A.1 (*Continued*)

Variable	M	SD
Bl	0.25	0.62
Bt	1.08	1.35
Clothing (Cg)	0.91	1.28
Cl	0.24	0.57
Ex	0.16	0.47
Fi	0.30	0.61
Food	0.29	0.68
Ge	0.12	0.60
Hh	1.62	2.01
Ls	0.50	0.98
Na	0.49	0.87
Sc	0.18	0.51
Sx	0.44	1.34
Somatization Response (Xy)	0.08	0.36
Idio	0.01	0.15
Fictional	1.42	2.26
Fictional humans	0.83	1.58
Fictional animals	0.58	1.09
Whole sum	8.76	5.92
Part sum	2.42	3.62
Isolation Index	0.12	0.14
Somatization	0.71	1.26
Deviant Verbalizations Level 1 (DV1)	0.13	0.56
Incongruous Combinations Level 1 (INC1)	0.15	0.48
Deviant Responses Level 1 (DR1)	0.05	0.33
Fabulized Combinations Level 1 (FAB1)	0.07	0.30
Deviant Verbalizations Level 2 (DV2)	0.13	1.01
INC2	0.08	0.37
Deviant Responses Level 2 (DR2)	0.01	0.17
Fabulized Combinations Level 2 (FAB2)	0.04	0.26
Inappropriate Logic (ALOG)	0.08	0.33
Contamination (CON)	0.17	0.59
Abstract Content (AB)	0.23	0.76
Aggressive Responses (AG)	0.31	0.87
Cooperative Movement (COP)	0.31	0.71
Color Projection Responses (CP)	0.01	0.09
Morbid Content (MOR)	0.50	1.20
Personal Responses (PER)	0.45	1.18
Perseveration (PSV)	0.47	1.20
Special Score Sum	2.33	3.68
Sum 6 Sp Sc	0.72	1.79
Lvl 2 Sp Sc	0.21	1.07
WSum6	2.68	7.05

References

Abramowitz, J. S., & Deacon, B. J. (2005). Obsessive-compulsive disorder: Essential phenomenology and overlap with other anxiety disorders. In J. S. Abramowitz & A. C. Houts (Eds.), *Concepts and controversies in obsessive-compulsive disorder* (pp. 119–135). New York, NY: Springer. doi:10.1007/0-387-23370-9_6

Acklin, M. W. (1992). Psychodiagnosis of personality structure I: Psychotic personality organization. *Journal of Personality Assessment, 58,* 454–463. doi:10.1207/s15327752jpa5803_2

Acklin, M. W. (1993). Psychodiagnosis of personality structure II: Borderline personality organization I. *Journal of Personality Assessment, 61,* 329–341. doi:10.1207/s15327752jpa6102_13

Acklin, M. W. (1995). Integrative Rorschach interpretation. *Journal of Personality Assessment, 64,* 235–238. doi:10.1207/s15327752jpa6402_3

Acklin, M. W. (1997a). Psychodiagnosis of personality structure: Borderline personality organization. In In J. R. Meloy, M. W. Acklin, C. B. Gacono, J. F. Murray, and & C. A. Peterson (Eds.), *Contemporary Rorschach interpretation* (pp. 109–121). Mahwah, NJ: Erlbaum Associates.

Acklin, M. W. (1997b). Psychodiagnosis of personality structure: Psychotic personality organization. In J. R. Meloy, M. W. Acklin, C. B. Gacono, J. F. Murray, & C. A. Peterson

(Eds.), *Contemporary Rorschach interpretation* (pp. 11–20). Mahwah, NJ: Erlbaum Associates.

Acklin, M. W., & Fechner-Bates, S. (1989). Rorschach developmental quality and intellectual factors. *Journal of Personality Assessment, 53,* 537–545. doi:10.1207/s15327752jpa5303_10

Alexander, S. E. (1995). The relationship of projective test indices to prosocial behaviors, altruism, and loneliness. *Dissertation Abstracts International, 56B,* 0513.

Allport, G. W. (1937). *Personality: A psychological interpretation.* New York, NY: Holt.

Allport, G. W. (1961). *Pattern and growth in personality.* New York, NY: Holt.

American Psychiatric Association. (1948). *Diagnostic and statistical manual of mental disorders.* Washington, DC: Author.

American Psychiatric Association. (1968). *Diagnostic and statistical manual of mental disorders* (2nd ed.). Washington, DC: Author.

American Psychiatric Association. (1980). *Diagnostic and statistical manual of mental disorders* (3rd ed.). Washington, DC: Author.

American Psychiatric Association. (1994). *Diagnostic and statistical manual of mental disorders* (4th ed.). Washington, DC: Author.

American Psychiatric Association. (2012). *Diagnostic and statistical manual of mental disorders* (5th ed.). Washington, DC: Author.

Ames, L. B., Learned, J., Metraux, R. W., & Walker, R. N. (1952). *Child Rorschach responses.* New York, NY: Harper & Row.

Ames, L. B., Metraux, R. W., & Walker, R. N. (1971). *Adolescent Rorschach responses.* New York, NY: Brunner/Mazel.

Archer, R. P., & Krishnamurthy, R. (1993). Combining the Rorschach and the MMPI in the assessment of adolescents. *Journal of Personality Assessment, 60,* 132–140.

Aronow, E., Reznikoff, M., & Moreland, K. (1994). *The Rorschach technique.* Boston, MA: Allyn and Bacon.

Aronow, E., Reznikoff, M., & Moreland, K. (1995). The Rorschach: Projective technique or psychometric test? *Journal of Personality Assessment, 64,* 213–228. doi:10.1207/s15327752jpa6402_1

Aronow, E., Weiss, K. A., & Reznikoff, M. (2001). *A practical guide to the Thematic Apperception Test.* Philadelphia, PA: Brunner Routledge/Taylor & Francis.

Baity, M. R., & Hilsenroth, M. J. (2002). Rorschach Aggressive Content (AgC) variable: A study of criterion validity. *Journal of Personality Assessment, 78,* 275–287. doi:10.1207/S15327752JPA7802_04

Baldessarini, R. J., Finklestein, S., & Arana, G. W. (1983). The predictive power of diagnostic tests and the effect of prevalence of illness. *Archives of General Psychiatry, 40,* 569–573. doi:10.1001/archpsyc.1983.01790050095011

Balottin, U., Rossi, M., Rossi, G., Viganò, L., Nanti, M., Salini, S., . . . Termine, C. (2009). The Rorschach test and Gilles de la Tourette's syndrome: A pilot case-control study. *Brain & Development, 31,* 657–665. doi:10.1016/j.braindev.2008.10.003

Barley, W. D., Dorr, D., & Reid, V. (1985). The Rorschach Comprehensive System Egocentricity Index in psychiatric patients. *Journal of Personality Assessment, 49,* 137–140. doi:10.1207/s15327752jpa4902_5

Bartell, S. S., & Solanto, M. V. (1995). Usefulness of Rorschach Inkblot Test in assessment of attention deficit hyperactivity disorder. *Perceptual and Motor Skills, 80,* 531–541. doi:10.2466/pms.1995.80.2.531

Bechran, M. A. (1998). Latinos' perceptions of Rorschach inkblots: An examination of the popular response. *Dissertation Abstracts International, 59-B,* 0863.

Beck, S. J. (1950). *Rorschach's Test, basic processes.* New York, NY: Grune & Stratton.

Beizmann, C. (1957). Fragmentary perception of content in Rorschach. *Psychologie Française, 2*(8), 85–91.

Bellak, L., & Abrams, D. (1993). *The Thematic Apperception Test, the Children's Apperception Test, and the Senior Apperception Technique in clinical use* (5th ed.). Needham Heights, MA: Allyn & Bacon.

Belter, R. W., Lipovsky, J. A., & Finch, A. J. (1989). Rorschach Egocentricity Index and self-concept in children and adolescents. *Journal of Personality Assessment, 53,* 783–789. doi:10.1207/s15327752jpa5304_14

Bhargava, M., & Saxena, A. (1995). Rorschach differentials of deprived adolescents. *Indian Journal of Clinical Psychology, 22,* 24–29.

Bird Strike: Airplane crash-lands into Hudson River; all aboard reported safe. (2009, January 15). *CNN.* Retrieved from http://articles.cnn.com

Black, E. M. (2003). The use of the Rorschach Inkblot Technique in the detection and diagnosis of child sexual abuse. *Dissertation Abstracts International, 63B,* 4889.

Blackall, G. F. (1995). A descriptive study of the personality structure of pediatric leukemia survivors. *Dissertation Abstracts International, 56B,* 2315.

Blais, M. A., Hilsenroth, M. J., & Fowler, J. C. (1998). Rorschach correlates of the DSM–IV histrionic personality disorder. *Journal of Personality Assessment, 70,* 355–364. doi:10.1207/s15327752jpa7002_12

Blanck, G., & Blanck, R. (1975). *Ego psychology: Theory and practice.* New York, NY: Columbia University Press.

Blatt, S. J., Brenneis, C. B., Schimek, J., & Glick, M. (1976). Normal development and the psychological impairment of the concept of the object in the Rorschach. *Journal of Abnormal Psychology, 85,* 264–273.

Blatt, S. J., & Lerner, P. (1983). The psychological assessment of object representations. *Journal of Personality Assessment, 47,* 7–28. doi:10.1207/s15327752jpa4701_2

Bonieskie, L. M. (2000). An examination of personality characteristics of child custody litigants on the Rorschach. *Dissertation Abstracts International, 61B,* 3271.

Brainard, R. B. (2005). A comparison of learning-disabled children and non-learning-disabled children on the Rorschach: An information processing perspective. *Dissertation Abstracts International, 65B,* 6643.

Brand, B. L., Armstrong, J. G., Loewenstein, R. J., & McNary, S. W. (2009). Personality differences on the Rorschach of dissociative identity disorder, borderline personality disorder, and psychotic inpatients. *Psychological Trauma: Theory, Research, Practice, and Policy, 1,* 188–205. doi:10.1037/a0016561

Brecher, S. (1956). The Rorschach reaction patterns of maternally over-protected and maternally rejected schizophrenics. *Journal of Nervous and Mental Disease, 123,* 41–52. doi:10.1097/00005053-195601000-00006

Brenman, M., & Reichard, S. (1943). Use of the Rorschach in predicting hypnotizability. *Bulletin of the Menninger Clinic, 7,* 183–187.

Broeking, N. M. (2007). Childhood abuse history, attachment patterns, and selected Rorschach response variables. *Dissertation Abstracts International, 68B,* 6291.

Budney, S. E. (1996). The Rorschach color response in the offspring of schizophrenics. *Dissertation Abstracts International, 56-B,* 5161.

Butcher, J. N. (2009). Clinical personality assessment: History, evolution, contemporary models, and practical applications. In J. N. Butcher (Ed.), *Oxford handbook of personality assessment* (pp. 5–21). New York, NY: Oxford University Press.

Butcher, J. N., Dahlstrom, W. G., Graham, J. R., Tellegen, A., & Kaemmer, B. (1989). *MMPI–2: Minnesota Multiphasic Personality Inventory – 2: Manual for administration and scoring.* Minneapolis: University of Minnesota Press.

Cai, C.-H., & Shen, H.-Y. (2007). Self-concept reflected by Rorschach test in private and public college students. *Chinese Mental Health Journal, 21,* 539–543.

Campo, V. (2000). The SCZI Index and the normative sample of Barcelona. In A. Andronikof-Sanglade (Ed.), *Rorschachiana: Yearbook of the International Rorschach Society* (pp. 28–38). Ashland, OH: Hogrefe & Huber Publishers.

Campos, R. C. (2009). Dependency, narcissism and Rorschach: A discussion based on the results of an empirical study. *Journal of Projective Psychology & Mental Health, 16,* 3–7.

Caplan, R., Guthrie, D., Tang, B., Neuchgterlein, K. H., & Asarnow, R. F. (2001). Thought disorder in attention-deficit hyperactivity disorder. *Journal of the American Academy of Child & Adolescent Psychiatry, 40,* 965–972. doi:10.1097/00004583-200108000-00019

Caracena, P. F. (2010). *ROR-Scan* [Computer program]. Edmond, OK: ROR-Scan.

Cassella, M. J. (1999). The Rorschach texture response: A conceptual validation study. *Dissertation Abstracts International, 60B,* 2405.

Chen, T. (1999). A control study of the responses to Rorschach's technique in comparison of normal and schizophrenic children. *Chinese Journal of Clinical Psychology, 7,* 86–88, 104.

Chiva, M. (1973). Statistical analysis of Rorschach responses. *Psychologie Française, 18,* 195–212.

Choca, J. P. (2004). *Interpretative guide to the Millon Clinical Multiaxial Inventory* (3rd ed.). Washington, DC: American Psychological Association.

Choca, J., & Garside, D. (1992). *Hermann: A Rorschach administrator and scoring assistant* (3rd ed.) [Computer program]. Toronto, Ontario, Canada: Multi-Health Systems.

Choca, J., Van Denburg, E., & Mouton, A. (1994, March). *Time for a new look at an old Rorschach marker: Reaction times collected with the Hermann computer program.* Paper presented at the annual meeting of the Society for Personality Assessment, Chicago, IL.

Clausel, J. (1988). Exner's Egocentricity Index from the Rorschach, phenomenal self-esteem, and the perceived availability of narcissistic supplies. *Dissertation Abstracts International, 49,* 2372.

Cocking, R. R., Dana, J. M., & Dana, R. H. (1969). Six constructs to define Rorschach M: A response. *Journal of Projective Techniques & Personality Assessment, 33,* 322–323. doi:10.1080/0091651X.1969.10380155

Cohan, R. (1998). A comparison of sex offenders against minors and rapists of adults on selected Rorschach variables. *Dissertation Abstracts International, 59B,* 2471.

Cohen, L., de Ruiter, C., Ringelberg, H., & Cohen-Kettenis, P. T. (1997). Psychological functioning of adolescent transsexuals: Personality and psychopathology. *Journal of Clinical Psychology, 53,* 187–196. doi:10.1002/(SICI)1097-4679(199702)53:2<187::AID-JCLP12>3.0.CO;2-G

Colligan, S. (1997). The neuropsychology of the Rorschach: An M.D. with M.B.D. In J. R. Meloy, M. W. Acklin, C. B. Gacono, J. F. Murray, & C. A. Peterson (Eds.), *Contemporary Rorschach interpretation* (pp. 535–555). Mahwah, NJ: Erlbaum Associates.

Conti, R. P. (2007). The concealment of psychopathology on the Rorschach in criminal forensic evaluations. *Dissertation Abstracts International, 68B,* 4125.

Cooper, S. H., & Arnow, D. (1986). An object relations view of the borderline defenses: A Rorschach analysis. In M. Kissen (Ed.), *Assessing object relations phenomena* (pp. 143–174). New York, NY: International Universities Press.

Cooper, S. H., Perry, J. C., & Arnow, D. (1988). An empirical approach to the study of defense mechanisms: I. Reliability and preliminary validity of the Rorschach Defense Scales. *Journal of Personality Assessment, 52,* 187–203. doi:10.1207/s15327752jpa5202_1

Cooper, S. H., Perry, J. C., & O'Connell, M. (1991). The Rorschach Defense Scales: II. Longitudinal perspectives. *Journal of Personality Assessment, 56,* 191–201. doi:10.1207/s15327752jpa5602_1

Cotte, S. (1958). Statistical study on the zoomorphic answers (and year) in the Rorschach test of children 12 to 16 years. *Bulletin du Groupement Francais du Rorschach, 10,* 27–32.

Cragnolino, A. (2001). A confirmatory and exploratory investigation of the ideation and cognitive mediation clusters of the Rorschach Comprehensive System. *Dissertation Abstracts International, 62B,* 2051.

Cramer, P. (1996). *Storytelling, narrative, and the Thematic Apperception Test.* New York, NY: Guilford Press.

Cronbach, L. J. (1949). Statistical methods applied to Rorschach scores: A review. *Psychological Bulletin, 46,* 393–429. doi:10.1037/h0059467

Crumpton, E. (1956). The influence of color on the Rorschach test. *Journal of Projective Techniques, 20,* 150–158.

Csercsevits, M. E. (2000). A comparative study of juvenile sex offenders, juvenile delinquents, and juvenile dependents using the Rorschach Inkblot Test. *Dissertation Abstracts International, 61A,* 1288.

Csikszentmihalyi, M. (2008). *Flow: The psychology of optimal experience.* New York, NY: Harper.

Cyrulnik, J. (2000). Aggressive responses in Rorschach protocols of women accused of physical child abuse and neglect. *Dissertation Abstracts International, 61B,* 2812.

Dadario, B. M. (2002). The impact of nonverbal learning disability upon cognitive triad variables of Exner's comprehensive scoring system of the Rorschach Inkblot Technique. *Dissertation Abstracts International, 62-B,* 5367.

Dåderman, A. M., & Jonson, C. (2008). Lack of psychopathic character (Rorschach) in forensic psychiatric rapists. *Nordic Journal of Psychiatry, 62,* 176–185. doi:10.1080/08039480801957327

Dean, K. L., Viglione, D. J., Perry, W., & Meyer, G. J. (2007). A method to optimize the response range while maintaining Rorschach Comprehensive System validity. *Journal of Personality Assessment, 89,* 149–161. doi:10.1080/00223890701468543

De Carolis, A., & Ferracuti, S. (2005). Correlation between the Rorschach test coded and interpreted according to the Comprehensive Exner System and the Eysenck Personality Inventory. *Rorschachiana, 27,* 63–79. doi:10.1027/1192-5604.27.1.63

Demma, A., Cargnel, L., Nicolini, C., & Sedona, P. (2007). Silent words and marks on the skin. Psychologic survey on psoriasic patients, using the Rorschach model. *Medicina Psicosomatica, 52,* 149–153.

de Ruiter, C., & Cohen, L. (1992). Personality in panic disorder with agoraphobia: Rorschach study. *Journal of Personality Assessment, 59,* 304–316. doi:10.1207/s15327752jpa5902_7

de Ruiter, C., & Smid, W. (2007). Rorschach Comprehensive System data for a sample of 108 normative subjects from the Netherlands. *Journal of Personality Assessment, 89,* S113–S118. doi:10.1080/0022 3890701583002

Desbiens, J., Bossé, M., & Côté, G. (2000). Psychopathy and the presence of achromatic colors to Rorschach. *European Review of Applied Psychology/Revue Européenne de Psychologie Appliquée, 50,* 51–57.

Dettmer, T. P. (2009). The effects of family dysfunction on Rorschach protocols of incarcerated juveniles. *Dissertation Abstracts International, 69-B,* 4415.

Donahue, P. J., & Tuber, S. B. (1993). Rorschach adaptive fantasy images and coping in children under severe environmental stress. *Journal of Personality Assessment, 60,* 421–434. doi:10.1207/s15327752jpa6003_1

Draguns, J. G., Haley, E. M., & Phillips, L. (1967). Studies of Rorschach content: A review of the research literature, traditional content categories. *Journal of Projective Techniques & Personality Assessment, 31,* 3–32. doi:10.1080/0091651X.1967.10120338

Duberstein, P. R., & Talbot, N. L. (1993). Rorschach oral imagery, attachment style, and interpersonal relatedness. *Journal of Personality Assessment, 61,* 294–310. doi:10.1207/s15327752jpa6102_10

Dumitrascu, N. (2007). Rorschach Comprehensive System data for a sample of 111 adult nonpatients from Romania. *Journal of Personality Assessment, 89,* S142–S148. doi:10.1080/00223890701583648

Duricko, A. J., Norcross, J. C., & Buskirk, R. D. (1989). Correlates of the Egocentricity Index in children and adolescent outpatients. *Journal of Personality Assessment, 53,* 184–187. doi:10.1207/s15327752 jpa5301_20

Eells, G. T., & Boswell, D. L. (1994). Validity of Rorschach inanimate movement and diffuse shading responses as measures of frustration and anxiety. *Perceptual and Motor Skills, 78,* 1299–1302. doi:10.2466/ pms.1994.78.3c.1299

Egozi-Profeta, V. L. (1999). A comparison of the Roemer and the Rorschach tests as tools for distinguishing characteristics of psychopathy. *Dissertation Abstracts International, 60B,* 1345.

Elfhag, K., Barkeling, B., Carlsson, A. M., Lindgren, T., & Rössner, S. (2004). Food intake with an antiobesity drug (sibutramine) versus placebo and Rorschach data: A crossover within-subjects study. *Journal of Personality Assessment, 82,* 158–168. doi:10.1207/s15327752jpa8202_4

Elfhag, K., Rössner, S., Lindgren, T., Andersson, I., & Carlsson, A. M. (2004). Rorschach personality predictors of weight loss with behavior modification in obesity treatment. *Journal of Personality Assessment, 83,* 293–305. doi:10.1207/s15327752jpa8303_11

Elisens, M. M. (1998). The cognitive and emotional correlates of neglect in school aged children. *Dissertation Abstracts International, 58,* 3920.

Elizur, A. (1949). Content analysis of the Rorschach with regards to anxiety and hostility. *Rorschach Research Exchange and Journal of Projective Techniques, 13,* 247–284.

Ellenberger, H. (1958). Life and work of Hermann Rorschach. *Revista de Psicología General y Aplicada, 13,* 561–613.

Epstein, M. (1998). Traumatic brain injury and self-perception as measured by the Rorschach using Exner's Comprehensive System. *Dissertation Abstracts International, 59,* 0870.

Erard, R. E. (2010, September/October). Introducing the Rorschach Performance Assessment System (R-PAS). *The National Psychologist, 14.*

Erikson, E. (1950). *Childhood and society.* New York, NY: Norton.

Esmail, J. J. (1997). Treatment needs of non-abused siblings of child sexual abuse victims in the PACT (Project Aimed at Coordinated Treatment) program. *Dissertation Abstracts International, 57B,* 5323.

Exner, J. E. (1962). The effect of color on productivity in Cards VIII, IX, X of the Rorschach. *Journal of Projective Techniques, 26,* 30–33. doi:10.1080/08853126.1962.10381074

Exner, J. E. (1974). *The Rorschach: A comprehensive system: Vol. 1. Basic foundations.* New York, NY: Wiley.

Exner, J. E. (1981). Obituary: Samuel J. Beck. *American Psychologist, 36,* 986–987. doi:10.1037/0003-066X.36.9.986

Exner, J. E. (2001). A comment on "The misperception of psychopathology: Problems with norms of the Comprehensive System for the Rorschach." *Clinical Psychology: Science and Practice, 8,* 386–388. doi:10.1093/clipsy/8.3.386

Exner, J. E. (2003). *The Rorschach: A comprehensive system: Vol. 1. Basic foundations and principles of interpretation* (4th ed.). Hoboken, NJ: Wiley.

Exner, J. E., Armbruster, G. L., & Viglione, D. (1978). The temporal stability of some Rorschach features. *Journal of Personality Assessment, 42,* 474–482. doi:10.1207/s15327752jpa4205_6

Exner, J. E., Boll, T. J., Colligan, S. C., Stischer, B., & Hillman, L. (1996). Rorschach findings concerning closed head injury patients. *Assessment, 3,* 317–326. doi:10.1177/1073191196003003011

Exner, J. E., McGuire, H., & Cohen, J. (1990). *Rorschach Interpretation Assistance Program (RIAP)* [Computer program]. Odessa, FL: Psychological Assessment Resources.

Exner, J. E., & Murillo, L. G. (1975). Early prediction of posthospitalization relapse. *Journal of Psychiatric Research, 12,* 231–237. doi:10.1016/0022-3956(75)90002-3

Exner, J. E., Thomas, E. A., & Mason, B. (1985). Children's Rorschachs: Description and prediction. *Journal of Personality Assessment, 49,* 13–20. doi:10.1207/s15327752jpa4901_3

Exner, J. E., & Weiner, I. B. (1982). *The Rorschach: A comprehensive system: Vol. 3. Assessment of children and adolescents.* New York, NY: Wiley.

Exner, J. E., & Wylie, J. R. (1977). Some Rorschach data concerning suicide. *Journal of Personality Assessment, 41,* 339–348. doi:10.1207/s15327752jpa4104_1

Felger, T. E. (1996). Allocation of attentional resources and thought disorder in schizophrenia patients. *Dissertation Abstracts International, 56B,* 6386.

Ferracuti, S., Cannoni, E., Burla, F., & Lazzari, R. (1999). Correlations for the Rorschach with the Torrance tests of creative thinking. *Perceptual and Motor Skills, 89,* 863–870.

Finney, B. C. (1955). Rorschach test correlates of assaultive behavior. *Journal of Projective Techniques, 19,* 6–16. doi:10.1080/08853126.1955.10380601

Fischer, C. T. (2006). Phenomenology, Bruno Klopfer and individualized/collaborative assessment. *Journal of Personality Assessment, 87,* 229–233. doi:10.1207/s15327752jpa8703_03

Fiske, D. W., & Baughman, E. E. (1953). Relations between the Rorschach scoring categories and the total number of responses. *Journal of Abnormal and Social Psychology, 48,* 25–32. doi:10.1037/h0059193

Fowler, J. C., Brunnschweiler, B., Swales, S., & Brock, J. (2005). Assessment of Rorschach dependency measures in female inpatients diagnosed with borderline disorder. *Journal of Personality Assessment, 85,* 146–153. doi:10.1207/s15327752jpa8502_07

Frank, G. (1993). On the validity of hypotheses derived from the Rorschach: The relationship between shading and anxiety, update 1992. *Psychological Reports, 72,* 519–522. doi:10.2466/pr0.1993.72.2.519

Frank, L. K. (1948). *Projective methods.* Springfield, IL: Charles C Thomas.

Franks, K. W., Sreenivasan, S., Spray, B. J., & Kirkish, P. (2009). The mangled butterfly: Rorschach results from 45 violent psychopaths. *Behavioral Sciences & the Law, 27,* 491–506. doi:10.1002/bsl.866

Freud, A. (1965). *Normality and psychopathology in childhood.* New York, NY: International Universities Press.

Gacono, C. B., Bannatyne-Gacono, L. A., Meloy, J. R., & Baity, M. R. (2005). The Rorschach extended aggression scores. *Rorschachiana, 27,* 164–190. doi:10.1027/1192-5604.27.1.164

Gacono, C. B., & Meloy, J. R. (1991). A Rorschach investigation of attachment and anxiety in antisocial personality disorder. *Journal of Nervous and Mental Disease, 179,* 546–552. doi:10.1097/00005053-199109000-00005

Gacono, C. B., & Meloy, J. R. (1992). The Rorschach and the DSM–III–R antisocial personality: A tribute to Robert Lindner. *Journal of Clinical Psychology, 48,* 393–406. doi:10.1002/1097-4679(199205)48:3<393::AID-JCLP2270480319>3.0.CO;2-Z

Gacono, C. B., & Meloy, J. R. (1994). *The Rorschach assessment of aggressive and psychopathic personalities.* Hillsdale, NJ: Erlbaum Associates.

Gacono, C. B., & Meloy, J. R. (2009). Assessing antisocial and psychopathic personalities. In J. N. Butcher (Ed.), *Oxford handbook of personality assessment* (pp. 567–581). New York, NY: Oxford University Press.

Gacono, C. B., Meloy, J. R., & Bridges, M. R. (2000). A Rorschach comparison of psychopaths, sexual homicide perpetrators, and nonviolent pedophiles. *Journal of Clinical Psychology, 56,* 757–777. doi:10.1002/(SICI)1097-4679(200006)56:6<757::AID-JCLP6>3.0.CO;2-I

Gacono, C. B., Meloy, J. R., & Heaven, T. R. (1990). A Rorschach investigation of narcissism and hysteria in antisocial personality. *Journal of Personality Assessment, 55*, 270–279.

Gacono, L. A., & Gacono, C. B. (2008). Some considerations for the Rorschach assessment of forensic psychiatric outpatients. In C. B. Gacono & E. F. Barton (Eds.), *The handbook of forensic Rorschach assessment* (pp. 421–444). New York, NY: Routledge.

Gardner, R. W. (1951). Impulsivity as indicated by Rorschach test factors. *Journal of Consulting Psychology, 15*, 464–468. doi:10.1037/h0061368

Gartner, J., Hurt, S., & Gartner, A. (1989). Psychological test signs of borderline personality disorder: A review of the empirical literature. *Journal of Personality Assessment, 53*, 423–441. doi:10.1207/s15327752jpa5303_1

Gear, K. M. (1996). Rorschach variables as a function of Piagetian level of development in young children. *Dissertation Abstracts International, 57B*, 4084.

Gerard-Sharp, S. (2000). A Rorschach study of interpersonal disturbance in priest same-sex ephebophiles. *Dissertation Abstracts International, 61B*, 2199.

Goldman, G. N. (2001). Rorschach variables as indicators of depression in an inpatient adolescent population. *Dissertation Abstracts International, 62B*, 2483.

Goldman, R. (1960). Changes in Rorschach performance and clinical improvements in schizophrenia. *Journal of Consulting Psychology, 24*, 403–407. doi:10.1037/h0046091

Gordon, M., & Tegtmeyer, P. F. (1982). The Egocentricity Index and self-esteem in children. *Perceptual and Motor Skills, 55*, 335–337.

Gray, J. L. (2006). An exploration of posttraumatic stress disorder in Persian Gulf War veterans through the eyes of the Rorschach. *Dissertation Abstracts International, 66B*, 6272.

Greenwald, D. F. (1990). An external construct validity study of Rorschach personality variables. *Journal of Personality Assessment, 55*, 768–780.

Greenwald, D. F. (1991). Personality dimensions reflected by the Rorschach and the 16PF. *Journal of Clinical Psychology, 47*, 708–715. doi:10.1002/1097-4679(199109)47:5<708::AID-JCLP2270470513>3.0.CO;2-Q

Greenwald, D. F. (1999). Relationships between the Rorschach and the NEO-Five Factor Inventory. *Psychological Reports, 85*, 519–527.

Halpern, F. (1940). Rorschach interpretation of the personality structure of schizophrenics who benefit from insulin therapy. *Psychiatric Quarterly, 14*, 826–833. doi:10.1007/BF01566801

Hamel, M. D. (2000). A normative study of cooperative movement responses among preadolescent Rorschach protocols. *Dissertation Abstracts International, 60B*, 5829.

Handler, L. (1994). Bruno Klopfer, a measure of the man and his work. *Journal of Personality Assessment, 62,* 562–577. doi:10.1207/s15327752jpa6203_16

Handler, L. (2008). A Rorschach journey with Bruno Klopfer: Clinical application and teaching. *Journal of Personality Assessment, 90,* 528–535. doi:10.1080/00223890802388301

Hare, R. D. (1991). *The Hare Psychopathy Checklist—Revised.* Toronto, Canada: Multi-Health Systems.

Hare, R. D. (2003). *The Hare Psychopathy Checklist—Revised (PCL–R) manual* (2nd ed.). Toronto, Ontario, Canada: Multi-Health Systems.

Harper, G., & Scott, R. (1990). Learning disabilities: An appraisal of *Rorschach* response patterns. *Psychological Reports, 67,* 691–696.

Hartmann, E., & Vanem, P. (2003). Rorschach administration: A comparison of the effect of two instructions given to an inpatient sample of drug addicts. *Scandinavian Journal of Psychology, 44,* 133–139. doi:10.1111/1467-9450.00331

Hertz, M. R. (1940). *Percentage charts for use in computing Rorschach scores.* Cleveland, OH: Western Reserve University, Brush Foundation.

Hickey, T. P. (1995). An archival study of Rorschach indicators of sexual abuse in hospitalized adolescent females. *Dissertation Abstracts International, 55-B,* 5071.

Hilsenroth, M. J., Fowler, J. C., Padawar, J. R., & Handler, L. (1997). Narcissism in the Rorschach revisited: Some reflections on empirical data. *Psychological Assessment, 9,* 113–121. doi:10.1037/1040-3590.9.2.113

Himelstein, P. D. (1984). Construct validity of two measures of narcissism. *Dissertation Abstracts International, 44,* 3528.

Holaday, M. (1998). Rorschach protocols of children and adolescents with severe burns: A follow-up study. *Journal of Personality Assessment, 71,* 306–321. doi:10.1207/s15327752jpa7103_2

Holaday, M., Armsworth, M. W., Swank, P. R., & Vincent, K. R. (1992). Rorschach responding in traumatized children and adolescents. *Journal of Traumatic Stress, 5,* 119–129. doi:10.1002/jts.2490050113

Holaday, M. (1998). Rorschach protocols of children and adolescents with severe burns: A follow-up study. *Journal of Personality Assessment, 71,* 306–321.

Holaday, M., Moak, J., & Shipley, M. A. (2001). Rorschach protocols from children and adolescents with Asperger's disorder. *Journal of Personality Assessment, 76,* 482–495. doi:10.1207/S15327752 JPA7603_09

Holt, R. (1977). A method for assessing primary process manifestations and their control in Rorschach responses. In M. A. Rickers-Ovsiankina (Ed.), *Rorschach psychology* (pp. 375–420). New York, NY: Krieger.

Holtzman, W. H., Thorpe, J. S., Swartz, J. D., & Herron, E. W. (1961). *Inkblot perception and personality.* Austin: University of Texas Press.

Horn, S. L., Meyer, G. J., & Mihura, J. L. (2009). Impact of card rotation on the frequency of Rorschach reflection responses. *Journal of Personality Assessment, 91,* 346–356. doi:10.1080/00223890902936090

Hunsley, J., & Bailey, J. M. (1999). The clinical utility of the Rorschach: Unfulfilled promises and an uncertain future. *Psychological Assessment, 11,* 266–277. doi:10.1037/1040-3590.11.3.266

Hunsley, J., & Bailey, J. M. (2001). Whither the Rorschach? An analysis of the evidence. *Psychological Assessment, 13,* 472–485. doi:10.1037/1040-3590.13.4.472

Hutt, M. L., & Shor, J. (1946). Rationale for routine Rorschach "Testing the Limits." *Rorschach Research Exchange, 10,* 70–76. doi:10.1080/08934037.1946.10381180

Ihanus, J., Keinonen, M., & Vanhamäki, S. (1992). Rorschach movement responses and the TAT Transcendence Index in physically handicapped children. *Perceptual and Motor Skills, 74,* 1115–1119.

Ivanouw, J. (2007). Rorschach Comprehensive System data for a sample of 141 adults nonpatients from Denmark. *Journal of Personality Assessment, 89,* S42–S51. doi:10.1080/00223890701583671

Jacobs, A. M. (2008). Concurrent validity of selected Rorschach variables for the assessment of externalizing tendencies in children and adolescents. *Dissertation Abstracts International, 68,* 6310.

Joffe, C. H. (Producer), Allen, W. (Director). (1969). *Take the money and run* (Motion Picture). USA: 20th Century Fox.

Johnson, G. S. (2008). Rorschach variables in opiate and other drug addicted patients with and without PTSD: A community outpatient treatment facility based study. *Dissertation Abstracts International, 69B,* 1957.

Jones, M. (2004). Social competence of adults referred for ADHD or learning disability evaluations: A Rorschach study. *Dissertation Abstracts International, 64B,* 5220.

Kahn, K. J. (2000). Measures of narcissism in the Rorschach: A systematic replication of reflection responses and idealization scores using a college sample. *Dissertation Abstracts International, 60,* 4286.

Kamphuis, J. H., Turn, N., Timmermans, M., & Punamäki, R. L. (2008). Extending the Rorschach Trauma Content index and aggression indexes to dream narratives of children exposed to enduring violence: An exploratory study. *Journal of Personality Assessment, 90,* 578–584. doi:10.1080/00223890802388558

Kennelly, J. J. (2002). Rorschach responding and response sets in child custody evaluations. *Dissertation Abstracts International, 63B,* 3034.

Kernberg, O. (1980). Neurosis, psychosis and the borderline states. In A. M. Freeman, H. I. Kaplan, & B. J. Sadock (Eds.), *Comprehensive textbook of psychiatry* (Vol. III, pp. 1079–1092). Baltimore, MD: Williams & Wilkins.

Kernberg, O. (1984). *Severe personality disorders: Psychotherapeutic strategies*. New Haven, CT: Yale University Press.

Kinder, B. N. (1992). The problems of R in clinical settings and in research: Suggestions for the future. *Journal of Personality Assessment, 58,* 252–259. doi:10.1207/s15327752jpa5802_4

King, D. B., Viney, W., & Woody, W. D. (2009). *A history of psychology: Ideas and context*. Boston, MA: Allyn and Bacon.

Kleiger, J. (1999). *Disordered thinking and the Rorschach: Theory, research and differential diagnosis*. Hillsdale, NJ: Analytic Press.

Kleiger, J. H. (1997). Rorschach's shading responses: From a printer's error to an integrated psychoanalytic paradigm. *Journal of Personality Assessment, 69,* 342–364.

Kleinbaum, N. H. (1986). *Dead poet's society*. New York, NY: Bantam.

Klopfer, B., Ainsworth, M. D., Klopfer, W., & Holt, R. R. (1954). *Developments in the Rorschach Technique* (Vol. I). New York, NY: Harcourt.

Kobler, F. J. (1983). The Rorschach test in clinical practice. *Interdisciplinaria Revista de Psicología y Ciencias Afines, 4,* 131–139.

Kochinski, S., Smith, S. R., Baity, M. R., & Hilsenroth, M. J. (2008). Rorschach correlates of adolescent self-mutilation. *Bulletin of the Menninger Clinic, 72,* 54–77. doi:10.1521/bumc.2008.72.1.54

Konishi, H. (2003). The Lambda in the Rorschach comprehensive system. *Shinrigaku kenkyu Japanese Journal of Psyychology, 73,* 502–505.

Kopplin, K. R. (1999). An exploration of the relationship between Carl Jung's personality typology and selected variables from the Rorschach Inkblot Technique. *Dissertation Abstracts International, 59B,* 5092.

Kottenhoff, H. (1964). Reliability and validity of the animal percentage in Rorschachs. *Acta Psychologica, Amsterdam, 22,* 387–406. doi:10.1016/0001-6918(64)90028-9

Kwawer, J. S. (1980). Primitive interpersonal modes, borderline phenomena, and Rorschach content. In J. Kwawer, H. Lerner, P. Lerner, & A. Sugarman (Eds.), *Borderline phenomena and the Rorschach test* (pp. 89–105). New York, NY: International Universities Press.

Kwawer, J. S., Lerner, H. D., Lerner, P. M., & Sugarman, A. (Eds.). (1980). *Borderline phenomena and the Rorschach test*. New York, NY: International Universities Press.

Lachar, D. (1974). *The MMPI: Clinical assessment and automated interpretations*. Los Angeles, CA: Western Psychological Services.

Lamounier, R., & de Villemor-Amaral, A. E. (2006). Evidence of validity for the Rorschach in the context of traffic psychology. *Revista Interamericana de Psicología, 40,* 167–176.

Lee, H. J., Kim, Z. S., & Kwon, S. M. (2005). Thought disorder in patients with obsessive-compulsive disorder. *Journal of Clinical Psychology, 61,* 401–413. doi:10.1002/jclp.20115

Lelé, A. J. (2006). Perception of reality and norm: Study of the popular responses to Rorschach's psychodiagnostics in Brazil. *Rorschachiana, 28,* 81–99. doi:10.1027/1192-5604.28.1.81

Lerner, P. (1988). Rorschach measures of depression, the false self, and projective identification in patients with narcissistic personality disorder. In H. Lerner and P. Lerner (Eds.), *Primitive mental states and the Rorschach* (pp. 71–93). New York, NY: International University Press.

Lerner, P. M. (1991a). The analysis of content revisited. *Journal of Personality Assessment, 56,* 145–157.

Lerner, P. (1991b). *Psychoanalytic theory and the Rorschach.* Hillsdale, NJ: The Analytic Press.

Lerner, P. M. (1992). Toward an experiential psychoanalytic approach to the Rorschach. *Bulletin of the Menninger Clinic, 56,* 451–464.

Lerner, P. M. (2004). Further thoughts on an experiential psychoanalytic approach to the Rorschach. *Bulletin of the Menninger Clinic, 68,* 152–163. doi:10.1521/bumc.68.2.152.35949

Lerner, P. M. (2007). On preserving a legacy: Psychoanalysis and psychological testing. *Psychoanalytic Psychology, 24,* 208–230. doi:10.1037/0736-9735.24.2.208

Lerner, P. M., & Lerner, H. (1980). Rorschach assessment of primitive defenses in borderline personality structure. In J. S. Kwawer, H. D. Lerner, P. M. Lerner, & A. Sugarman (Eds.), *Borderline phenomena and the Rorschach test* (pp. 257–274). New York, NY: International Universities Press.

Levinson, D. (1978). *The seasons of a man's life.* New York, NY: Knopf.

Levinson, D. (1996). *The seasons of a woman's life.* New York, NY: Knopf.

Liaboe, G. P., & Guy, J. D. (1985). The Rorschach "father" and "mother" cards: An evaluation of the research. *Journal of Personality Assessment, 49,* 2–5. doi:10.1207/s15327752jpa4901_1

Linton, H. B. (1954). Rorschach correlates of response to suggestion. *Journal of Abnormal and Social Psychology, 49,* 75–83. doi:10.1037/h0058273

Liu, A. C. (2002). Differentiating types of aggression utilizing Rorschach profiles of a child and adolescent inpatient sample with Exner's comprehensive system. *Dissertation Abstracts International, 63B,* 534.

Locke, S. R. (1999). Adult attention deficit disorder: Its impact on Rorschach scores. *Dissertation Abstracts International, 60B,* 0850.

Loevinger, J. (1976). *Ego development: Conceptions and theories.* San Francisco, CA: Jossey-Bass.

Loftis, R. (1997). A comparison of delinquents and nondelinquents on Rorschach measures of object relations and attachments: Implications for conduct disorder, antisocial personality disorder and psychopathy. *Dissertation Abstracts International, 58-B,* 2720.

Lorentz, R. P. (1995). Back pain and mental distress worker's compensation claimants: A Rorschach and MMPI study of emotional regulation. *Dissertation Abstracts International, 56-B*, 1113.

Lottenberg Semer, N., & Yazigi, L. (2009). The Rorschach and the body: The study of self-esteem in enuretic children through the Rorschach method. *Rorschachiana, 30*, 3–25. doi:10.1027/1192-5604.30.1.3

Loving, J. L., & Russell, W. F. (2000). Selected Rorschach variables of psychopathic juvenile offenders. *Journal of Personality Assessment, 75*, 126–142. doi:10.1207/S15327752JPA7501_9

Malone, J. A. (1996). Rorschach correlates of childhood incest history in adult women in psychotherapy. *Dissertation Abstracts International, 56B*, 5176.

Martin, J. D., MaKinster, J. G., & Pfaadt, N. K. (1983). Intercorrelations among white space responses on Rorschach, ego strength, conformity and self-esteem. *Perceptual and Motor Skills, 57*, 743–748. doi:10.2466/pms.1983.57.3.743

Mayman, M. (1967). Object representation and object relations in Rorschach responses. *Journal of Projective Techniques & Personality Assessment, 31*, 17–24. doi:10.1080/0091651X.1967.10120387

Mayman, M. (1977). A multidimensional view of the Rorschach movement response. In M. Rickers-Ovsiankina (Ed.), *Rorschach psychology* (pp. 229–250). Huntington, NY: Krieger.

McCarroll, B. R. (1998). Caregiving disruptions and attachment in psychiatric inpatient adolescents. *Dissertation Abstracts International, 59B*, 2457.

Meloy, J. R., Acklin, M. W., Gacono, C. B., Murray, J. F., & Peterson, C. A. (1997). *Contemporary Rorschach interpretation.* Mahwah, NJ: Erlbaum Associates.

Mesirow, T. R. (1999). Self-mutilation: Analysis of a psychiatric forensic population. *Dissertation Abstracts International, 60B*, 2354.

Meyer, G. J., (1992). Response frequency problems in the Rorschach: Clinical and research implications with suggestions for the future. *Journal of Personality Assessment, 58*, 231–244.

Meyer, G. J. (1999a). The convergent validity of the MMPI and Rorschach scales: An extension using profile scores to define response and character styles on both methods and a reexamination of simple Rorschach response frequency. *Journal of Personality Assessment, 72*, 1–35. doi:10.1207/s15327752jpa7201_1

Meyer, G. J. (1999b). Introduction to the special series on the utility of the Rorschach in clinical assessment. *Psychological Assessment, 11*, 235–239. doi:10.1037/1040-3590.11.3.235

Meyer, G. J. (2001). Evidence to correct misperceptions about Rorschach norms. *Clinical Psychology: Science and Practice, 8*, 389–396. doi:10.1093/clipsy.8.3.389

Meyer, G. J., & Archer, R. (2001). The hard science of Rorschach research: What do we know and where do we go? *Psychological Assessment, 13,* 486–502. doi:10.1037/1040-3590.13.4.486

Meyer, G. J., Erdberg, P., & Schaffer, T. W. (2007). Toward international normative reference data for the Comprehensive System. *Journal of Personality Assessment, 89*(Suppl. 1), S201–S216. doi:10.1080/00223890701629342

Meyer, G. J., & Kurtz, J. E. (2006). Advancing personality assessment terminology: Time to retire "objective" and "projective" as personality test descriptors. *Journal of Personality Assessment, 87,* 223–225. doi:10.1207/s15327752jpa8703_01

Meyer, G. J., Riethmiller, R. J., Brooks, R. D., Benoit, W. A., & Handler, L. (2000). A replication of Rorschach and MMPI–2 convergent validity. *Journal of Personality Assessment, 74,* 175–215. doi:10.1207/S15327752JPA7402_3

Meyer, G. J., Viglione, D. J., Mihura, J. L., & Erard, R. E. (2011, March). *Rorschach Performance Assessment System (R-PAS): Overview and case illustration.* Workshop presented at the annual meeting of the Society for Personality Assessment, Boston, MA.

Meyer, G. J., Viglione, D. J., Mihura, J. L., Erard, R. E., & Erdberg, P. (2011). *Rorschach Performance Assessment System.* Toledo, OH: Rorschach Performance Assessment System, LLC.

Mihura, J. L., Nathan-Montano, E., & Alperin, R. J. (2003). Rorschach measures of aggressive drive derivatives: A college student sample. *Journal of Personality Assessment, 80,* 41–49. doi:10.1207/S15327752JPA8001_12

Miller, T. A. (1999). Rorschach assessment of object relations and affect control in domestic violent and non-violent couples. *Dissertation Abstracts International, 59,* 4069.

Millon, T. A. (1983). *Millon Clinical Multiaxial Inventory manual* (3rd ed.). Minneapolis, MN: Pearson Assessments.

Millon, T. A. (1990). *Toward a new personology: An evolutionary model.* New York, NY: Wiley.

Millon, T. A. (1994). *Manual for the MCMI-III.* Minneapolis, MN: National Computer Systems.

Millon, T. A. (2011). *Disorders of personality: Introducing a DSM/ICD spectrum from normal to abnormal* (3rd ed.). New York, NY: Wiley.

Mishra, D., Kumar, R., & Prakash, J. (2009). Rorschach thought disorders in various psychiatric conditions. *Journal of Projective Psychology & Mental Health, 16,* 8–12.

Mishra, S., & Gupta, M. P. (2008). Rorschach profile of neurotic patients. *Journal of Projective Psychology & Mental Health, 15,* 134–144.

Moise, F., Yinon, Y., & Rabinowitz, A. (1988–1989). Rorschach inkblot movement responses as a function of motor activity or inhibition. *Imagination, Cognition and Personality, 8,* 39–48.

Moreland, K., & Reznikoff, M. (1995). Integrating Rorschach interpretation by carefully placing more of your eggs in the content basket. *Journal of Personality Assessment, 64,* 239–242. doi:10.1207/s15327752jpa6402_4

Morris, W. W. (1943). Prognostic possibilities of the Rorschach method in metrazol therapy. *The American Journal of Psychiatry, 100,* 222–230.

Mulder, J. L. (1997). Assessment of emotionally disturbed adolescents using the Rorschach: An analysis of the EA/es relationship. *Dissertation Abstracts International, 58A,* 1200.

Murray, H. A. (1943). *The Thematic Apperception Test.* Cambridge, MA: Harvard University Press.

Murray, J. F. (1992). Toward a synthetic approach to the Rorschach: The case of a psychotic child. *Journal of Personality Assessment, 58,* 494–505. doi:10.1207/s15327752jpa5803_5

Murray, J. F. (1993). The Rorschach search for the borderline holy grail: An examination of personality structure, personality style and situation. *Journal of Personality Assessment, 61,* 342–357. doi:10.1207/s15327752jpa6102_14

Murray, J. F. (1997). Toward a synthetic approach to the Rorschach: The case of a psychotic child. In J. R. Meloy, M. W. Acklin, C. B. Gacono, J. F. Murray, & C. A. Peterson (Eds.), *Contemporary Rorschach interpretation* (pp. 53–64). Mahwah, NJ: Erlbaum Associates.

Musewicz, J. D. (2010). Current assessment practice, personality measurement, and Rorschach usage by psychologists. *Dissertation Abstracts International, 71,* 2736.

Nesser, J. A. (2000). Inanimate movement and diffuse shading responses as indices of uncontrollable stress and the role of attributional style: A Rorschach validation study. *Dissertation Abstracts International, 61B,* 2266.

Neville, J. W. (1995). Validating the Rorschach measures of perceptual accuracy. *Dissertation Abstracts International, 55B,* 4128.

Nezworski, M. T., & Wood, J. M. (1995). Narcissism in the comprehensive system for the Rorschach. *Clinical Psychology: Science and Practice, 2,* 179–199. doi:10.1111/j.1468-2850.1995.tb00038.x

O'Connell, M. (1986). Thought disorder, borderline psychopathology, and the psychological test situation. *Dissertation Abstracts International, 46B,* 4023–4024.

Ornduff, S. R., Centeno, L., & Kelsey, R. M. (1999). Rorschach assessment of malevolence in sexually abused girls. *Journal of Personality Assessment, 73,* 100–109. doi:10.1207/S15327752JPA730107

Osher, Y., & Bersudsky, Y. (2007). Thought disorder in euthymic bipolar patients: A possible endophenotype of bipolar affective disorder? *Journal of Nervous and Mental Disease, 195,* 857–860. doi:10.1097/NMD.0b013e318156832d

Pantle, M. L., Ebner, D. L., Hynan, L. S. (1994). *The Rorschach and the assessment of impulsivity.* Journal of Clinical Psychology, 50, 633–638.

Paul, A. M. (2004). *The cult of personality testing*. New York, NY: Free Press.

Perry, W., Geyer, M. A., & Braff, D. L. (1999). Sensorimotor gating and thought disturbance measured in close temporal proximity in schizophrenic patients. *Archives of General Psychiatry, 56*, 277–281. doi:10.1001/archpsyc.56.3.277

Perry, W., & Potterat, E. (1997). Beyond personality assessment: The use of the Rorschach as a neuropsychological instrument in patients with amnestic disorders. In J. R. Meloy, M. W. Acklin, C. B. Gacono, J. F. Murray, & C. A. Peterson (Eds.), *Contemporary Rorschach interpretation* (pp. 557–575). Mahwah, NJ: Erlbaum Associates.

Perry, W., Potterat, E., Auslander, L., Kaplan, E., & Jeste, D. (1996). A neuropsychological approach to the Rorschach in patients with dementia of the Alzheimer type. *Assessment, 3*, 351–363. doi:10.1177/1073191196003003014

Peters, J. E., & Nunno, V. J. (1996). Measuring the effect of the Rorschach Color Cards (VIII–X) on perceptual accuracy and special scores in differentiating borderline from schizophrenic protocols. *Journal of Clinical Psychology, 52*, 581–588. doi:10.1002/(SICI)1097-4679(199609)52:5<581::AID-JCLP14>3.0.CO;2-A

Peterson, C. A. (1997). A borderline policeman: AKA, a cop with no COP. In J. R. Meloy, M. W. Acklin, C. B. Gacono, J. F. Murray, & C. A. Peterson (Eds.), *Contemporary Rorschach interpretation* (pp. 157–176). Mahwah, NJ: Erlbaum Associates.

Peterson, C. A., & Horowitz, M. (1990). Perceptual robustness of the nonrelationship between psychopathology and popular responses on the Hand Test and the Rorschach. *Journal of Personality Assessment, 54*, 415–418. doi:10.1207/s15327752jpa5401&2_38

Petot, D. (2005). Suicidal ideation among children aged six: Their reality and their expression in Rorschach. *Revue Européenne de Psychologie Appliquée, 55*, 267–276.

Petot, J.-M. (2005). Are the relationships between NEO PI-R and Rorschach markers of openness to experience dependent on the patient's test-taking attitude? *Rorschachiana, 27*, 30–50.

Petrosky, E. M. (2005). The relationship between the morbid response of the Rorschach Inkblot Test and self-reported depressive symptomatology. *Journal of Projective Psychology & Mental Health, 12*, 87–98.

Petrosky, E. M. (2006). The relationship between early memories and the Rorschach Inkblot Test. *Journal of Projective Psychology & Mental Health, 13*, 37–54.

Phillips, L., & Smith, J. G. (1953). *Rorschach interpretative advanced technique*. New York, NY: Grune & Stratton.

Pichot, P. (1984). Centenary of the birth of Hermann Rorschach. *Journal of Personality Assessment, 48*, 591–596. doi:10.1207/s15327752jpa4806_3

Pinheiro, R. T., Da Silva, M., Wagner, A. V. Pinheiro, K. A. Da Silva, R. A., Souza, L. D. M. (2008). Psychopathology of cocaine-dependent patients in a therapeutic community. *Adicciones, 20,* 73–80.

Pinto, A. F. (1999). A Rorschach study of object representations and attachment in male adolescents with disruptive behaviors. *Dissertation Abstracts International, 59B,* 5105.

Piotrowski, Z. A., & Bricklin, B. (1961). A second validation of a long-term Rorschach prognostic index for schizophrenic patients. *Journal of Consulting Psychology, 25,* 123–128. doi:10.1037/h0043807

Pires, A. A. (2000). National norms for the Rorschach normative study in Portugal. In R. H. Dana (Ed.), *Handbook of cross-cultural and multicultural personality assessment* (pp. 367–392). Mahwah, NJ: Erlbaum Associates.

Prandoni, J. R., Jensen, D. E., Matranga, J. T., & Waison, M. O. (1973). Selected Rorschach response characteristics of sex offenders. *Journal of Personality Assessment, 37,* 334–336. doi:10.1080/00223891.1973. 10119880

Presley, G., Smith, C., Hilsenroth, M., & Exner, J. E. (2001). Clinical utility of the Rorschach with African Americans. *Journal of Personality Assessment, 77,* 491–507. doi:10.1207/S15327752JPA7703_09

Priyamvada, R., Kumari, S., Ranjan, R., Prakash, J., Singh, A., & Chaudhury, S. (2009). Rorschach profile of schizophrenia and depression. *Journal of Projective Psychology & Mental Health, 16,* 37–40.

Ramachandra, S. (1994). Rorschach and the creative artists. *Journal of Projective Psychology & Mental Health, 1,* 39–50.

Rapaport, D., Gill, M., & Schafer, R. (1946). *Diagnostic psychological testing (Vol. 2).* Chicago, IL: Yearbook Publishers.

Rapaport, D., Gill, M., & Schafer, R. (1968). In R. Holt (Ed.), *Diagnostic psychological testing* (pp. 268–463). New York, NY: International University Press.

Ray, A. B. (1963). Juvenile delinquency by Rorschach inkblots. *Psychologia, 6,* 190–192.

Reilly, R. C. (2002). Rorschach indications of violent potential in male conduct-disordered adolescents. *Dissertation Abstracts International, 63B,* 583.

Richardson, H. (1963). Rorschach of adolescent approved school girls, compared to Ames normal adolescents. *Rorschach Newsletter (London), 8,* 3–8.

Ridley, S. E. (1987). The high score approach to scoring two Rorschach measures of cognitive development. *Journal of Clinical Psychology, 43,* 390–394. doi:10.1002/1097-4679(198705)43:3<390::AID-JCLP2270 430313>3.0.CO;2-G

Rissi, J. (1998). Roemer symbol test distinctions between DSM–IV antisocial personality disordered moderate and severe PCL–R psychopaths. *Dissertation Abstracts International, 59B,* 0885.

Robinson, D. (1995). *An intellectual history of psychology*. Madison: University of Wisconsin Press.

Rorschach, H. (1921). *Psychodiagnostik*. Bern, Switzerland: Bitcher.

Rosso, S. J. (2004). Manifestations of aggression: Examining the relationship between the Rorschach, teacher report, and therapeutic change. *Dissertation Abstracts International, 64B*, 4633.

Ryan, G. P., Baerwald, J. P., & McGlone, G. (2008). Cognitive mediational deficits and the role of coping styles in pedophile and ephebophile Roman Catholic clergy. *Journal of Clinical Psychology, 64*, 1–16. doi:10.1002/jclp.20428

Sacco, L. C. (1990). Correlates of Exner's Egocentricity Index in an adolescent psychiatric population. *Dissertation Abstracts International, 50*, 5893.

Sah, A. P. (1989). Personality characteristics of accident free and accident involved Indian railway drivers. *Journal of Personality and Clinical Studies, 5*, 203–206.

Sakuragi, A. (2006). The applicability of Exner's Comprehensive System of the Rorschach to a Japanese population. *Dissertation Abstracts International, 66–8*, 6330.

Sangro, F. M. (1997). Location tables, form quality and popular responses in a Spanish sample of 470 subjects. In I. Weiner (Ed.), *Rorschachiana XXII: Yearbook of the International Rorschach Society* (pp. 38–66). Ashland, OH: Hogrefe & Huber.

Schachtel, E. (1966). *Experiential foundations of Rorschach's test*. New York, NY: Basic Books.

Schafer, R. (1948). *Clinical applications of psychological tests*. New York, NY: International Universities Press.

Schafer, R. (1954). *Psychoanalytic interpretation in Rorschach testing*. New York, NY: Grune and Stratton.

Scherpenisse, E. D. (2006). The other-directed adolescent: Associated personality processes as measured by the Rorschach. *Dissertation Abstracts International, 67*, 1194.

Schneider, R. B., Huprich, S. K., & Fuller, K. M. (2008). The Rorschach and the Inventory of Interpersonal Problems. *Rorschachiana, 29*, 3–24. doi:10.1027/1192-5604.29.1.3

Schultheiss, O. C. (2007). A memory-systems approach to the classification of personality tests: Comment on Meyer and Kurtz (2006). *Journal of Personality Assessment, 89*, 197–201. doi:10.1080/00223890701357431

Sciara, A. D., & Ritzler, B. A. (2006). *The Little Book on Administration for the Rorschach Comprehensive System*. Asheville, NC: Grove Clinic.

Seligman, M. E. P. (2011). *Flourish: A visionary new understanding of happiness and well-being*. New York, NY: Free Press.

Seligman, M. E. P., & Csikszentmihalyi, M. (2000). Positive psychology: An introduction. *American Psychologist, 55*, 5–14. doi:10.1037/0003-066X.55.1.5

Serper, M. R. (1993). Visual controlled information processing resources and formal thought disorder in schizophrenia and mania. *Schizophrenia Research, 9,* 59–66. doi:10.1016/0920-9964(93)90010-G

Sherman, M. H. (1952). A comparison of formal and content factors in the diagnostic testing of schizophrenia. *Genetic Psychology Monographs, 46,* 183–234.

Shimonaka, Y., & Nakasato, K. (1991). Aging and terminal changes in Rorschach responses among the Japanese elderly. *Journal of Personality Assessment, 57,* 10–18. doi:10.1207/s15327752jpa5701_2

Shontz, F. C., & Green, P. (1992). Trends in research on the Rorschach: Review and recommendations. *Applied & Preventive Psychology, 1,* 149–156. doi:10.1016/S0962-1849(05)80136-2

Siegal, R. S., & Rosen, I. C. (1962). Character style and anxiety tolerance: A study in intrapsychic change. In H. Strupp & L. Luborsky (Eds.), *Research in psychotherapy* (pp. 206–217). Washington, DC: American Psychological Association.

Siemsen, R. A. (1999). Relationships of Rorschach and MMPI-2 variables to the Hare Psychopathy Checklist-Revised among mentally ill incarcerated felons. *Dissertation Abstracts International, 60B,* 2367.

Silberg, J. L., & Armstrong, J. G. (1992). The *Rorschach* test for predicting suicide among depressed adolescent inpatients. *Journal of Personality Assessment, 59,* 290–303. doi:10.1207/s15327752jpa5902_6

Silva, D. (2001). The effect of color on the productivity of Card X of the Rorschach. *Rorschachiana, 25,* 123–138.

Silverstein, M. (1999). *Self psychology and diagnostic assessment.* Mahwah, NJ: Erlbaum Associates.

Simon, M. J. (1985). The Egocentricity Index and self-esteem in court-ordered psychiatric evaluations. *Journal of Personality Assessment, 49,* 437–439. doi:10.1207/s15327752jpa4904_13

Simon, M. J. (1989). Comparison of the Rorschach comprehensive system's Isolation Index and MMPI Social Introversion score. *Psychological Reports, 65,* 499–502. doi:10.2466/pr0.1989.65.2.499

Singer, M. T. (1977). The borderline diagnosis and psychological tests: Review and research. In P. Hartocollis (Ed.), *Borderline personality disorders* (pp. 193–212). New York, NY: International Universities Press.

Singh, O. P. (2001). Developmental quality analysis of the whole responses (W) among the Rorschach protocols of institutionalized children. *Journal of Personality and Clinical Studies, 17,* 45–49.

Skadeland, D. R. (1986). Bruno Klopfer: A Rorschach pioneer. *Journal of Personality Assessment, 50,* 358–361. doi:10.1207/s15327752jpa 5003_4

Small, A., Teagno, L., Madero, J., Gross, H., & Ebert, M. (1982). A comparison of anorexics and schizophrenics on psychodiagnostic measures. *The International Journal of Eating Disorders, 1,* 49–56. doi:10.1002/1098-108X(198221)1:3<49::AID-EAT2260010306>3.0.CO;2-O

Smith, B. L. (1997). White bird: Flight from the terror of empty space. In J. R. Meloy, M. W. Acklin, C. B. Gacono, J. F. Murray, & C. A. Peterson (Eds.), *Contemporary Rorschach interpretation* (pp. 191–215). Mahwah, NJ: Erlbaum Associates.

Smith, J. E., Hillard, M. C., Walsh, R. A., & Kubacki, S. R. (1991). Rorschach assessment of purging and nonpurging bulimics. *Journal of Personality Assessment, 56*, 277–288. doi:10.1207/s15327752jpa5602_8

Smith, S. R., Bistis, K., Zahka, N. E., & Blais, M. A. (2007). Perceptual-organizational characteristics of the Rorschach task. *The Clinical Neuropsychologist, 21*, 789–799. doi:10.1080/13854040600800995

Soares, C. J. (2002). Cooperative movement in Rorschach responses among inpatient and nonpatient samples. *Dissertation Abstracts International, 63B*, 1084.

Sommer, R. (1957). Rorschach animal responses and intelligence. *Journal of Consulting Psychology, 21*, 358. doi:10.1037/h0042634

Sommer, R., & Sommer, D. T. (1958). Assaultiveness and two types of Rorschach color responses. *Journal of Consulting Psychology, 22*, 57–62. doi:10.1037/h0048621

Steisel, I. M. (1952). The Rorschach test and suggestibility. *Journal of Abnormal and Social Psychology, 47*, 607–614. doi:10.1037/h0061051

Stephenson, M. B. (1996). A validation study of the Rorschach food response. *Dissertation Abstracts International, 56B*, 4594.

Stern, D. N. (1985). *Interpersonal world of the infant: A view from psychoanalysis and developmental psychology.* New York, NY: Basic Books.

Storment, C. T., & Finney, B. C. (1953). Projection and behavior: A Rorschach study of assaultive mental hospital patients. *Journal of Projective Techniques, 17*, 349–360. doi:10.1080/08853126.1953.10380498

Stotsky, B. A. (1952). A comparison of remitting and nonremitting schizophrenics on psychological tests. *Journal of Abnormal and Social Psychology, 47*, 489–496. doi:10.1037/h0060270

Strickland, V. L. (2006). A descriptive study of boys with AD/HD referred for special education evaluation. *Dissertation Abstracts International, 67*(2-B), 170.

Sultan, S., Andronikof, A., Fouques, D., Lemmel, G., Mormont, C., Réveillère, C., & Saïas, T. (2004). French standards for the Rorschach Comprehensive System: First results on a sample of 146 adults. *Psychologie Française, 49*, 7–24. doi:10.1016/j.psfr.2003.11.002

Sultan, S., & Meyer, G. J. (2009). Does productivity impact the stability of Rorschach scores? *Journal of Personality Assessment, 91*, 480–493. doi:10.1080/00223890903088693

Tai, S., Haddock, G., & Bental, R. (2004). The effects of emotional salience on thought disorder in patients with bipolar affective disorder. *Psychological Medicine: A Journal of Research in Psychiatry and the Allied Sciences, 34*, 803–809.

Teglasi, H. (2010). *Essentials of TAT and other storytelling techniques assessment* (2nd ed.). New York, NY: John Wiley & Sons.

Tegtmeyer, P. F., & Gordon, M. (1983). Interpretation of white space responses in children's Rorschach protocols. *Perceptual and Motor Skills, 57,* 611–616. doi:10.2466/pms.1983.57.2.611

Tibon, S. (2000). Personality traits and peace negotiations: Integrative complexity and attitudes toward the Middle East peace process. *Group Decision and Negotiation, 9,* 1–15. doi:10.1023/A:1008779305643

Townsend, J. K. (1967). The relation between Rorschach signs of aggression and behavioral aggression in emotionally disturbed boys. *Journal of Projective Techniques & Personality Assessment, 31,* 13–21. doi:10.1080/0091651X.1967.10120427

Traenkle, K. A. (2002). An empirical evaluation of Rorschach white space scoring. *Dissertation Abstracts International, 62 (8B),* 3839.

Trenerry, M. R., & Pantle, M. L. (1990). MAPI code types in an inpatient crisis unit sample. *Journal of Personality Assessment, 55,* 683–691.

Ulloa, R. E., Birmaher, B., Axelson, D., Williamson, D. E., Brent, D. A., Ryan, N. D., . . . Baugher, M. (2000). Psychosis in a pediatric mood and anxiety disorders clinic: Phenomenology and correlates. *Journal of the American Academy of Child & Adolescent Psychiatry, 39,* 337–345. doi:10.1097/00004583-200003000-00016

van der Gaag, R. J., Caplan, R., van Envgeland, H., Loman, F., & Buitelaar, J. K. (2005). A controlled study of formal thought disorder in children with autism and multiple complex developmental disorders. *Journal of Child and Adolescent Psychopharmacology, 15,* 465–476. doi:10.1089/cap.2005.15.465

Vanem, P. C., Krog, D., & Hartman, E. (2008). Assessment of substance abusers on the MCMI-III and the Rorschach. *Scandinavian Journal of Psychology, 49,* 83–91. doi:10.1111/j.1467-9450.2007.00608.x

Van Patten, K., Shaffer, T. W., Erdberg, P., & Canfield, M. (2007). Rorschach Comprehensive System data for a sample of 37 non-patient/non-delinquent adolescents from the United States. *Journal of Personality Assessment, 89,* S188–S192. doi:10.1080/00223890701583507

Vermeylen, N., Bauwens, F., Lefevre, A., & Linkowski, P. (2005). Le test de Rorschach et la pensée opératoire dans l'approche théorique du transsexualisme. *Annales Médico-Psychologiques, 163,* 387–393. doi:10.1016/j.amp.2005.04.001

Viglione, D. J. (1995). Basic considerations regarding data analysis. In J. E. Exner (Ed.), *Issues and methods in Rorschach research* (pp. 195–226). Hillsdale, NJ: Lawrence Earlbaum.

Viglione, D. J. (1999). A review of recent research addressing the utility of the Rorschach. *Psychological Assessment, 11,* 251–265. doi:10.1037/1040-3590.11.3.251

Viglione, D. J., & Hilsenroth, M. J. (2001). The Rorschach: Facts, fictions, and future. *Psychological Assessment, 13,* 452–471. doi:10.1037/1040-3590.13.4.452

Vijayakumaran, K. P., Ravindran, A., & Sahasranam, K. V. (1994). Rorschach indices of primary and secondary anxiety in the Exner comprehensive system. *Journal of Psychological Researches, 38,* 14–18.

Vinson, D. B. (1960). Responses to the Rorschach test that identify thinking, feelings, and behavior. *Journal of Clinical and Experimental Psychopathology, 21,* 34–40.

Wagreich, M. (2008). Neuropsychological and behavioral correlates of prenatal cocaine exposure in boys with severe psychopathology. *Dissertation Abstracts International, 68B,* 6986.

Walters, R. H. (1953). A preliminary analysis of the Rorschach records of fifty prison inmates. *Journal of Projective Techniques, 17,* 437–446. doi:10.1080/08853126.1953.10380509

Wasyliw, O. E., Benn, A. F., Grossman, L. S., & Haywood, T. W. (1998). Detection of minimization of psychopathology on the Rorschach in cleric and noncleric alleged sex offenders. *Assessment, 5,* 389–397. doi:10.1177/107319119800500408

Watson, R. A., & Pantle, M. L. (1993). Reflections on the Rorschach and the Millon Adolescent Personality Inventory. *Perceptual and Motor Skills, 77*(3, Pt 2, 1138. doi:10.2466/pms.1993.77.3f.1138

Weber, C. A., Meloy, J. R., & Gacono, C. B. (1992). A Rorschach study of attachment and anxiety in inpatient conduct-disordered and dysthymic adolescents. *Journal of Personality Assessment, 58,* 16–26. doi:10.1207/s15327752jpa5801_2

Weiner, I. B. (1994). The Rorschach Inkblot Method (RIM) is not a test: Implications for theory and practice. *Journal of Personality Assessment, 62,* 498–504. doi:10.1207/s15327752jpa6203_9

Weiner, I. B. (2001). Considerations in collecting Rorschach reference data. *Journal of Personality Assessment, 77,* 122–127. doi:10.1207/S15327752JPA7701_08

Weiner, I. B. (2003). *Principles of Rorschach interpretation.* Mahwah, NJ: Erlbaum Associates.

Werner, H. (1957). *Comparative psychology of mental development.* New York, NY: International Universities Press.

Wideman, B. G. (1998). Rorschach responses in gifted and nongifted children: A comparison study. *Dissertation Abstracts International, 59B,* 0905.

Widiger, T. A., Sanderson, C., & Warner, L. (1986). The MMPI, prototypal typology, and borderline personality disorder. *Journal of Personality Assessment, 50,* 540–553. doi:10.1207/s15327752jpa5004_2

Wilson, A. (1988). Levels of depression and clinical assessment. In H. Lerner and P. Lerner (Eds.), *Primitive mental states and the Rorschach* (pp. 441–462). New York, NY: International University Press.

Winnicott, D. W. (1961). Ego distortion in terms of true and false self. In *The maturational process and the facilitating environment* (pp. 140–152). New York, NY: International Univesity Press.

Winnicott, D. W. (1963). The development for the capacity for concern. *Bulletin of the Menninger Clinic, 27,* 167–176.

Wood, J. M., Lilienfeld, S. O., Nezworski, M. T., Garb, H. N., Allen, K. H., & Wildermuth, J. L. (2010). Validity of Rorschach Inkblot scores for discriminating psychopaths from non-psychopaths in forensic populations: A meta-analysis. *Psychological Assessment, 22,* 336–349. doi:10.1037/a0018998

Wood, J. M., Nezworski, M. T., Garb, H. N., & Lilienfeld, S. O. (2001). The misperception of psychopathology: Problems with norms of the Comprehensive System for the Rorschach. *Clinical Psychology: Science and Practice, 8,* 350–373. doi:10.1093/clipsy.8.3.350

Wood, J. M., Nezworski, M. T., Lilienfeld, S. O., & Garb, H. N. (2003). *What's wrong with the Rorschach?* San Francisco, CA: Jossey-Bass.

Wood, J. M., Nezworski, M. T., & Stejkal, W. J. (1996). The comprehensive system for the Rorschach: A critical examination. *Psychological Science, 7,* 3–10. doi:10.1111/j.1467-9280.1996.tb00658.x

Wood, W. (2000). Rorschach validity in a fake-good set: Ability of non-patients to conceal weaknesses. *Dissertation Abstracts International, 60B,* 5824.

Young, M. H., Justice, J., & Erdberg, P. (1999). Risk factors for violent behavior among incarcerated male psychiatric patients: A multimethod approach. *Assessment, 6,* 243–258. doi:10.1177/107319119900600305

Zaccario, M. L. (2001). A confirmatory and exploratory investigation of the information processing and cognitive mediation clusters of the Rorschach comprehensive system. *Dissertation Abstracts International, 61B,* 3868.

Zetzel, E. R. (1949). Anxiety and the capacity to bear it. *International Journal of Psychoanalysis, 20,* 1–12.

Zhong, S., Jing, J., Wang, L., & Yin, Q. (2007). Analysis on Rorschach Inkblot Test in children with attention deficit hyperactivity disorder. *Chinese Journal of Clinical Psychology, 15,* 545–547.

Index

Abstract Content (ABS) score, 96–97
Achromatic cards
    and Affective Ratio, 38
    and differential Reaction Time, 48
    responses to chromatic cards vs., 125–126
Achromatic color responses, 70
Achromatic color sum (Sum C′) composite, 70
Acklin, M. W., 10, 29
Active movement (a) responses, 60–61
Adjusted Difference (Adj D) score, 7–8, 111–112
Administration interpretatives
    in case example, 142–143
    characteristics of, 131–132
Administration of test, 17–25
    card rotation, 24–25
    and clinician–examinee relationship, 18
    Free Association Phase, 18–19
    Inquiry Phase, 20
    interpretation during, 131–132, 142–143
    mechanical, 119, 132
    reaction time, 24
    Testing the Limits method, 20–24
Adolescents
    Aggressive responses by, 97
    developmental scheme for, 214–215
    Egocentricity Index for, 115
    Experience Balance for, 109
    Suicide Constellation for, 117
(Ad) responses (fictional part animal
        responses), 80–81
Ad (part animal) responses, 79

Affectional needs, 62–63
Affective Ratio (Afr), 37–38
African Americans, Cooperative Movement
        score of, 95
AG. See Aggressive response scoring
AGC (Aggressive Content) score, 97
Age, examinee
    and animal responses, 78
    and Egocentricity Index, 115
    and form responses, 55
    and movement responses, 57
    and Whole versus Parts ratio, 81
Aggression, explosion responses and, 83
Aggressive Content (AGC) score, 97
Aggressive Movement (AGM) score, 97
Aggressive response scoring (AG), 97–98
    and Cooperative Movement score, 95
    and Morbid content, 102
AGM (Aggressive Movement) score, 97
Alcoholic individuals, weighted Sum6 of, 105
Alliance, therapeutic, 150, 153
Allport, G. W., 5–6
ALOG (Inappropriate Logic) score, 101, 104
Ambiguity, 126
    and response sequence, 124–125
    willingness to deal with, 54–55. See also
        Lambda
Ambitensive style, 109
A% measure, 78
Amended responses, 154
Anatomy (An) responses, 86

Animal movement (FM) responses, 59
  and control, 57
  core assumptions about, 14
  examinee age and prevalence of, 57
Animal responses, 78–81
  distinctions in, 74
  fictional, 79
  fictional part, 80–81
  part, 79
  pure, 78–79
An (anatomy) responses, 86
Anthropological (Ay) associations, 82
Anxiety, 63, 65
A (pure animal) response, 78–79
(A) responses (fictional animal responses), 79
a (active movement) responses, 60–61
Arnow, D., 29
Aronow, E., 15
Art, perception of, 81–82
Aspirational Index, 108, 112
Attachment, texture responses and, 62
Average range, Rorschach score, 31
Ay (anthropological) associations, 82

Background research, for psychological test report, 210–211
Bailey, J. M., 11
A Beautiful Mind (Sylvia Nasar), 214
Beck, S. J., 45
Beck, Samuel, 6–7
Behavioral observations, 132
Bipolar affective disorder, 88–89
Bl (perception of blood), 82–83
Black, as color, 70
Blended determinants, 70–72, 113
Blood, perception of (Bl), 82–83
Borderline personality disorder
  Form Quality of patients with, 90
  Rorschach test and diagnosis of, 10, 155
Borderline personality organization, 28–29
Boundary problems
  in daily functioning, 89
  and overinclusiveness, 123
  in Thought Disordered profile, 155
Bulimia, 97

Card I
  popular responses to, 43
  white space responses to, 42
  whole responses to, 39
Card II
  theme of, 126
  white space responses to, 42
  whole responses to, 39
Card III
  Cooperative Movement score and responses to, 95
  popular responses to, 43

  theme of, 126
  whole responses to, 39
Card IV
  in response sequence, 124–125
  structure of, 126
  theme of, 126
  whole responses to, 39
Card V
  detail responses to, 40
  popular responses to, 43
  in response sequence, 125
  structure of, 126
  whole responses to, 39
Card VI
  response time for, 127
  theme of, 126
  whole responses to, 39
Card VII
  theme of, 126
  whole responses to, 39
Card VIII
  popular responses to, 43
  structure of, 126
  whole responses to, 39
Card IX
  structure of, 126
  whole responses to, 39
Card X
  structure of, 126
  whole responses to, 39
Card rotation
  in Rebellious Antagonism profile, 153
  and reflection responses, 44
  scores for, 47–48
  and test administration, 24–25
Card structure, 125–126
Card themes, 126–127
CDI (Coping Deficit Index), 113–114
CF (color form) responses, 66–67
Cg (clothing) responses, 85
Challenging situations, responses to, 126
Character disorders, 67
Children
  animal responses by, 78
  Cooperative Movement scores for, 95
  developmental scheme for, 214–215
  Egocentricity Index for, 115
  Experience Balance for, 109
  Form Quality of, 90
  form responses by, 55
  human responses by, 75
  Personal responses by, 103
Choca, J., 48
Chromatic (color) cards
  and Affective Ratio, 38
  and differential Reaction Time, 48
  and response sequence, 124
  responses to achromatic vs., 125–126

Chromatic color responses, 65–70
  and achromatic color responses, 70
  and achromatic color sum composite, 70
  blended, 72
  color form, 66–67
  color naming, 67–68
  color ratio for, 68–69
  and control, 53
  form-color, 65–66
  in Impulsive Over-Emotional profile, 154
  lack of, 128–129
  location on psychogram, 52–53
  pure, 67
  in Rebellious Antagonism profile, 153
  Sum Color composite for, 68
  in Thought Disordered profile, 155
  weighted color sum composite for, 69
CI (Complexity Index), 113
Circumstantial responses, 100
Clarification, seeking, 23–24
Clarification Phase (R-PAS), 20
Clinicians
  engagement of, 119–120, 132
  examinee–clinician relationship, 18
  observations by, 132–133, 212
  use of profiles by, 149
  use of Rorschach Inkblot Test by, 8–11
Clothing (Cg) responses, 85
Cn (color naming) responses, 67–68
Cognitive Codes, 94–95
Cognitive development, human responses and, 75
Cognitively Impaired profile
  case example, 164–169
  characteristics of, 150–152
Cognitive triad, 28
Cohan, Richard, 14
Color cards. *See* Chromatic cards
Color form (CF) responses, 66–67
Color naming (Cn) responses, 67–68
Color Projection (CP) responses, 98
Color ratio, 68–69
Color responses. *See* Chromatic color responses
Color-shading blends, 72
"Color shock," 124
"Coming of age" scheme, 214–215
Comments, examinee, 132
Complementary information, in psychological test
    report, 212
Complexity Index (CI), 113
Complexity of response, response time and, 127
Complex markers, 107–108
Compliant task approach, 120
Composites, 108–112
  achromatic color sum, 70
  Adjusted D, 111–112
  Difference score, 111
  Experience Actual, 108
  Experience Balance Pervasive, 110

Experienced Stimulation, 110
  fictional part human, 77
  Fictional Sum, 80
  Interpersonal Interest Sum, 77
  Level 2 Special Scores, 105
  part human, 76
  somatization, 86
  Sum Color, 68
  weighted color sum, 69
Computer programs, checking norms with, 31
Confidence levels, reporting, 209–210
Conflicting information, in psychological test
    report, 212
Confusion, in Cognitively Impaired profile, 151
CON (Contamination) score, 98–99, 104
Consensus Rorschach, 15
Constellation, Suicide, 117
Constriction ratio, 112
Contamination (CON) score, 98–99, 104
Content of associations, 73–86
  animal responses, 78–81
  anthropological, 82
  art, perception of, 81–82
  blood, perception of, 82–83
  clothing responses, 85
  explosion responses, 83
  fire, perception of, 83–84
  food responses, 84–85
  human responses, 75–78
  Isolation Index for, 85–86
  in Morbid-Dysphoria profile, 156, 157
  and movement responses, 57
  in popular responses, 43
  response-level interpretations of, 128
  and response time, 127
  role of, 73–75
  sex responses, 84
  somatization areas, 86
  Structural Summary interpretatives from, 144
Control
  and attention to form of inkblot, 53–54
  and color-form responses, 66
  and color ratio, 68
  and inanimate movement responses, 60
  Lambda as measure of, 55
  and movement responses, 57
  and pure color responses, 67
  and weighted color sum, 69
Controlling task approach, 120–121
Conventionality
  and popular responses, 42–44
  and Unusual Form Quality, 91
Cooper, S. H., 29
Cooperative Movement (COP) score, 95–96
Coping Deficit Index (CDI), 113–114
Core assumptions, research on, 14
Couples therapy, Consensus Rorschach in, 15
CP (Color projection) responses, 98

Crumpton, E., 65
Culture
    and Cooperative Movement score, 95
    and popular responses, 43
Cutoff level, Rorschach score, 31–32

Data, in psychological test reports, 209
Dd (unusual details) score, 41
Dead Poets Society (N. H. Kleinbaum), 214–215
Declarative personality tests, 27
Defenses, profile-level interpretation of, 29
Delusional thinking, 87–89
Dependency, 84–85
Dependency Index, 114
Depression, pure color responses and, 67
Depression Index (DEPI), 11, 114–115
Depressive affect, Morbid content and, 102
Detail responses (D score), 40–41
    and Over-Controlled Micro-View profile, 152
    and overinclusiveness, 122
    profile-level interpretation of, 147–148
    Testing the Limits method for, 22
Determinants (psychogram)
    blended, 70–72, 113
    overview of, 51–54
Developmental Quality (DQ), 46–47
Developmental scheme, 214–215, 224–227
Deviant Responses (DRs), 100, 104, 105
Deviant Verbalizations (DVs), 99, 104, 105
Diagnostic and Statistical Manual of Mental Disorders, 148
Diagnostic and Statistical Manual of Mental Disorders,
    3rd ed. *(DSM-III)*, 148
Diagnostic and Statistical Manual of Mental Disorders,
    4th ed. *(DSM-IV)*, 148
Diagnostic and Statistical Manual of Mental Disorders,
    5th ed. *(DSM-5)*, 10, 148
Diagnostic value of Rorschach, 147–149
    for borderline personality disorder, 10, 155
    for neuropsychological problems, 150
    for personality organization, 29
    and profile-level interpretation, 148
    for psychological classification, 148–149
    for psychopathic personality, 10–11
    Suicide Constellation, 11
Difference (D) score composite, 111–112
Differential diagnosis, of personality organization, 29
Differential diagnosis organizational scheme, 216,
    233–235
Differential Reaction Time (Differential RT), 48, 50
Discomfort
    and blended responses, 71
    and vista responses, 63
Disorganization, 110
Dissociative identity disorder, 105
Distancing behavior, vista responses and, 63
Distress, 60
Distrust, 115–116
Doubles, in responses, 44–45

Downward spiral scheme, 215, 228–233
DQ (Developmental Quality), 46–47
Draguns, J. G., 75
Drive theory, 15
DRs. *See* Deviant Responses
D score. *See* Detail responses
D (Difference) score composite, 111–112
DSM-5 (*Diagnostic and Statistical Manual of Mental
    Disorders*, 5th ed.), 10, 148
DSM-III (*Diagnostic and Statistical Manual of Mental
    Disorders*, 3rd ed.), 148
DSM-IV (*Diagnostic and Statistical Manual of Mental Dis-
    orders*, 4th ed.), 148
Dubas, Andre, 216
DVs. *See* Deviant Verbalizations

EA (Experience Actual) composite, 108
EBPer (Experience Balance Pervasive) composite, 110
EB (Experience Balance) ratio, 107, 109
eb (Experience Base) ratio, 110
Effort, examinee, 45–46, 78
Egocentricity Index, 44–45, 115
Ego theory, 15
Einstein, Albert, 107
Emotion
    and Color Projection responses, 98
    and color responses, 53
    in Hyper-energized Euphoria profile, 157
    inhibition/internalization of, 112
    and Morbid-Dysphoria profile, 156, 157
    and response to color cards, 124, 125
Emotional pain, 63
Emotional reactivity, Affective Ratio and, 37–38
Empathy, 58
Energy, examinee, 36–37
Enuresis, Form Quality and, 90
Erikson, E., 215
Erlebnistypus, 107, 109
es (Experienced Stimulation) composite, 110
Examinee(s)
    clinician–examinee relationship, 18
    comments of, as administrative
        interpretatives, 132
    effort exerted by, 45–46, 78
    energy of, 36–37
    as focus of psychological test report, 209
    profile fit of, 149
    refusal to participate, 19
    unpredictability of responses from, 33
Exner, John, 5, 7, 11, 17, 19, 20, 28, 30, 44, 64, 67,
    75, 148, 213, 238–239
Exner norms, 30. *See also specific scores*
Exner-Weiner system of profile interpretation, 28
Expansiveness of thinking, 71
Experience Actual (EA) composite, 108
Experience Balance Pervasive (EB Pervasive; EBPer)
    composite, 110
Experience Balance (EB) ratio, 107, 109
Experience Base (eb) ratio, 110

Experienced Stimulation (es) composite, 110
Experience with others, view of, 77–78
Explosion responses (Ex), 83
External orientation, 109
Extratensive style, 109

Fabulized Combinations (FAB) score, 100–101,
    104, 105
Faking bad, 95
False negatives, 33
"Father" card, 126
FC (form-color) responses, 65–66
FD (form dimension) score, 64
Fi (perception of fire), 83–84
Fictional animal [(A)] responses, 79
Fictional human [(H)] responses, 76
Fictional part animal [(Ad)] responses, 80–81
Fictional part human [(Hd)] composite, 77
Fictional Ratio, 80–81
Fictional Sum, 80
Findings-based scheme, 212–213
Fire, perception of (Fi), 83–84
FM responses. *See* Animal movement responses
Focused Rorschach, 20
Follow-up inquiries, 21–24
Food responses, 84–85
Form, of Abstract Content responses, 96
Form-color (FC) responses, 65–66
Form dimension (FD) score, 64
Formless ABS responses, 96
Form Quality (FQ) score, 89–93
    in Cognitively Impaired profile, 151
    and Developmental Quality, 46
    for human movement responses, 93
    in Over-Controlled Micro-View profile, 152
    in Thought Disordered profile, 155
Form responses (F score)
    and Lambda, 54–56
    and movement responses, 57
    on psychogram, 51, 52
FQ score. *See* Form Quality score
FQx– (Minus Form Quality), 92
FQx+ (Positive Form Quality), 89–90
FQxo (Ordinary Form Quality), 90–91
FQxu (Unusual Form Quality), 91
Free Association Phase, 18–19
F% responses
    and Lambda, 56
    psychiatric norms for, 239
Frustration tolerance, Difference score and, 111
F score. *See* Form responses
Function scheme, 213

Gender differences, in Reaction Time, 48
Global scores, 35–50
    Affective Ratio, 37–38
    card rotations, 47–48
    Developmental Quality, 46–47
    Egocentricity Index, 44–45

manner of approach, 38–42
    number of responses, 36–37
    organizational activity, 45–46
    popular responses, 42–44
    Reaction Time, 48–50
    Structural Summary interpretatives from,
        143–144
    terminology, 35–36
Good quality responses
    ad hoc questioning about, 23–24
    and response sequence, 124–125
Green, P., 5
Guarded Minimal Compliance profile
    case example, 159–163
    characteristics of, 149–150
    Cognitively Impaired profile vs., 150, 151

Haley, E. M., 75
Hamlet (William Shakespeare), 61
Hare, R. D., 10
(Hd) composite (fictional part human composite), 77
Hd (part human) composite, 76
Health Insurance Portability and Accountability Act
    (HIPAA), 209
Helplessness, shading responses and, 65
Hermann (program), 48, 127
HIPAA (Health Insurance Portability and Account-
    ability Act), 209
History, patient, 210
Histrionic personality style, 33
Holtzman Inkblot Test, 19
(H) responses (fictional human responses), 76
H (pure human) responses, 75–76
Human movement:animal movement ratio, 59
Human movement (M) responses, 58
    and control, 57
    core assumptions about, 14
    Form Quality of, 93
    prevalence with age, 57
    ratio of animal to, 59
Human responses, 75–78
    distinctions in, 74
    fictional, 76
    fictional part human composite, 77
    and Interpersonal Interest ratio, 77–78
    and Interpersonal Interest Sum, 77
    pure, 75–76
    in Thought Disordered profile, 155
Hunsley, J., 11
Hutt, M. L., 21
HVI (Hypervigilance Index), 115–116
Hyper-energized Euphoria profile
    case example, 196–206
    characteristics of, 157–158
Hypervigilance Index (HVI), 115–116

Identity, profile-level interpretations of, 29
Idiographic approach. *See also* Response-level
    interpretations

Idiographic approach *continued*
   defined, 6
   nomothetic vs., 5–8
II (Intellectualization Index), 116
Implausible relationships, 100
Impulsive Over-Emotional profile
   case example, 177–183
   characteristics of, 154–155
Inanimate movement (m) responses, 57, 60
Inappropriate Logic (ALOG) score, 101, 104
Inappropriate phrases, 100
Inattention, response time and, 127
Incongruous Combinations (INC) score, 101–102
   in Level 2 Special Scores composite, 105
   in Six Special Score Sum, 104
Independence, 47
Indices, 112–117
   Aspirational, 108, 112
   Complexity, 113
   Coping Deficit, 113–114
   Dependency, 114
   Depression, 11, 114–115
   Egocentricity, 44–45, 115
   Hypervigilance, 115–116
   Intellectualization, 116
   Isolation, 85–86
   Obsessive Compulsive Style, 116–117
   Perceptual Thinking, 117
Individualized personal schemes, 213. *See also specific types of organizational schemes*
Information (in psychological test reports)
   complementary vs. conflicting, 212
   integration of, 211
   necessary, 208
Inhibition of emotion, 112
Inquiry Phase, 20
   purpose of, 25
   responses given in, 154, 157
Integration, of images, 45–46
Intellectual capacity, blended responses and, 71
Intellectualization, 82
Intellectualization Index (II), 116
Intelligence, animal movement responses and, 59
Interest in others, 77–78
Internalization of emotion, 112
Internal orientation, 58, 109
Internal psychic function, attention to, 51, 52
International Norms, 12, 30–31. *See also specific scores*
Interpersonal Interest ratio, 77–78
Interpersonal Interest Sum, 77
Interpersonal issues
   and Cooperative Movement score, 95
   and overinclusiveness, 124
   profile-level interpretations of, 29
Interpretive methodology, 27–33
   profile-level interpretation, 28–30
   response-level interpretation, 32

score-level interpretation, 30–32
and unpredictability of examinee responses, 33
Interpretative process, 131–146
   administration interpretatives in, 131–132, 142–143
   case example, 133–146
   item interpretatives in, 132–133, 143
   sequence interpretatives in, 133, 145
   Structural Summary interpretatives in, 133, 143–145
In the Bedroom (film), 216
Introspection, 64
Introversive style, 109
Invested task approach, 120
Isolation Index, 85–86
Item interpretatives
   in case example, 143
   characteristics of, 132–133

Journal for Personality Assessment, 6
Jung, Carl, 6

Kernberg, O., 28–29
"Killing" (Andre Dubas), 216
Kinder, B. N., 19
Kleiger, J., 8
Kleinbaum, N. H., 214–215
Klopfer, Bruno, 6–7, 21
Klopfer system, 122
Kobler, Frank, 8, 9, 12, 25
Kottenhoff, H., 78
Kurtz, J. E., 27
Kwawer, J. S., 29

Lambda
   and Affective Ratio, 38
   in Morbid-Dysphoria profile, 156
   in Over-Controlled Micro-View profile, 152
   from psychograms, 54–56
Language, psychological test report, 208
Learning, interest in, 82
Lerner, P., 6, 73
Level 1 prompts, 21
Level 1 Special Scores, 94, 105
Level 2 prompts, 21
Level 2 Special Scores
   composite of, 105
   qualitative and quantitative aspects of, 94
   in weighted Sum6 score, 105
Level 3 prompts, 21
Level of personality organization, 28
Levels of confidence, reporting, 209–210
Levinson, D., 215

MAH (Mutuality of Autonomy—Health), 94
Manic state, profile of examinee in, 196–206
Manner of approach
   detail responses, 40–41

scores for, 38–42
Structural Summary interpretatives from, 144
and Testing the Limits method, 22
unusual details, 41
white space, 42
whole responses, 39–40
MAP (Mutuality of Autonomy—Pathology), 94
Markers. *See also specific markers by name*
    complex, 107–108
    for particular functions, 14
    response time as, 24
    terminology, 13–14
    varied interpretations of, 8
Maturity, 57, 81
Mayman, M., 58, 74
MCMI (Millon Clinical Multiaxial Inventory), 33, 237
MCMI-II (Millon Clinical Multiaxial Inventory), 237
MCMI-III. *See* Millon Clinical Multiaxial Inventory
Mental mismanagement, 100
Mental structure, 28
Meyer, G. J., 27
Millon, T. A., 61
Millon Clinical Multiaxial Inventory (MCMI),
    33, 237
Millon Clinical Multiaxial Inventory (MCMI-II), 237
Millon Clinical Multiaxial Inventory (MCMI-III),
    28, 147, 237
Minnesota Multiphasic Personality Inventory
    (MMPI), 237
Minnesota Multiphasic Personality Inventory
    (MMPI-2)
    average range, 31
    norms of, 237
    profile-level interpretations, 28, 147
Minus Form Quality (FQx-), 92–93
Missing focus, prompts relating to, 21
MMPI (Minnesota Multiphasic Personality
    Inventory), 237
MMPI-2. *See* Minnesota Multiphasic Personality
    Inventory
Morbid (MOR) content, 102–103
Morbid-Dysphoria profile
    case example, 190–195
    characteristics of, 156–157
MOR (Morbid) content, 102–103
"Mother" card, 126
Mouton, A., 48
Movement responses. *See also specific types, e.g.:*
    Human movement (M) responses
    and Cooperative Movement score, 95–96
    in Hyper-energized Euphoria profile, 157
    interpretations of lack of, 128–129
    psychiatric norms for, 239–240
    on psychograms, 51–52, 57–62
    in Rebellious Antagonism profile, 153
    Structural Summary interpretatives from, 144
M responses. *See* Human movement responses
m (inanimate movement) responses, 57, 60

Murray, J. F., 10, 155, 156
Mutuality of Autonomy—Health (MAH), 94
Mutuality of Autonomy—Pathology (MAP), 94

Narcissism, 143
Nasar, Sylvia, 214
Nash, John, 214
Negative controlling approach, 120
Negative elements, in psychological test reports, 208
Negative RT Differential score, interpretations of, 50
Negatives, false, 33
Neologisms, 99
Neurologically impaired individuals, 150–151
Neuropsychological problems, diagnosing, 150
Neurotic personality organization, 28–29
Nezworski, M. T., 44
Nomothetic approach
    defined, 5–6
    idiographic vs., 5–8
Nonclinical samples, norms from, 237–238
Nondeclarative personality tests, 27
Norms for Rorschach scores, 30–32
    Exner, 30
    International, 12, 30–31
    psychiatric, 30, 31, 237–241
Number of responses (R score), 36–37
    in Cognitively Impaired profile, 151
    encouraging greater, 18–19
    in Guarded Minimal Compliance profile,
        149–150
    in Hyper-energized Euphoria profile, 157, 158
    minimum required, 19
    and number of animal responses, 78
    in Over-Controlled Micro-View profile, 152
    from rotated cards, 24
    and unusual details, 41
    variance in, 19
    and whole responses, 40

Object relations theory, 7, 15
Observations
    as administrative interpretatives, 132
    as item interpretatives, 132–133
    in psychological test report, 212
Obsessive Compulsive Style Index (OCS), 116–117
ODL (Oral Dependence Language), 94
Open C (pure color) responses, 67
Openness to Experience Scale, 71
Oppositional attitude, 47
Optimism, 60
Oral Dependence Language (ODL), 94
Ordinary Form Quality (FQxo), 90–91
Organizational activity (Zf), 45–46
Organizational schemes (psychological test report),
    212–235
    "coming of age," 214–215
    developmental, 214–215, 224–227
    differential diagnosis, 216, 233–235

Organizational schemes *continued*
    downward spiral, 215, 228–233
    examples, 217–235
    findings-based, 212–213
    function, 213
    individualized personal, 213
    overcoming obstacles, 215, 228–233
    personality, 213–214, 217–223
    single description, 212–213
Overcoming obstacles scheme, 215, 228–233
Over-Controlled Micro-View profile, 152–153
Overinclusive responses, 122–124
Overstrivers, 112

Paragraph organization, test report, 209
Part animal (Ad) responses, 79
Part human (Hd) composite, 76
Passive-aggressive task approach, 121
Passive movement (p) responses, 60–61
Pathological groups, color responses of, 67
Patient history, in psychological test report, 210
Peculiar Logic (PEC) score, 101
Pedophiles, differentiation of, 14–15
Perceptual Thinking Index (PTI), 117
Performance-based personality tests, 27
PER (Personal) responses, 103–104
Perry, J. C., 29
Perseveration (PSV) score, 103
Personality inventories, 28, 147
Personality organization
    differential diagnosis of, 29
    level of, 28
    personality style vs., 28–29
Personality scheme, 213–214, 217–223
Personality style, 28–29
Personality tests, 27
Personal responses (PER), 103–104
Phillips, L., 74, 75, 128
Poor quality responses
    ad hoc questioning about, 22–23
    by psychotic individuals, 128
    and response sequence, 124–125
Popular responses (P score)
    as global score, 42–44
    in Guarded Minimal Compliance profile, 150
    response-level interpretations of, 121–122
Positive attributes, in psychological test reports, 208
Positive controlling approach, 120
Positive Form Quality (FQx+), 89–90
Positive psychology movement, 208
Positive RT Differential score, interpretations of, 50
Post hoc questioning, 22–24
Posttraumatic stress disorder, 92
p (passive movement) responses, 60–61
Problem-solving style
    and active/passive movement responses, 61–62
    and Rorschach Inkblot Test, 27
    strength of, 110

Productivity, encouraging, 18–19
Profile-level interpretation. *See also* Rorschach
    profiles
    advantages of, 147–148
    and diagnostic criteria, 148
    methodology for, 28–30
Projective tests, 27, 211
Prompts, in test administration, 21
P score. *See* Popular responses
PSV (Perseveration) score, 103
Psychiatric norms. *See also specific scores*
    benefits of, 237–238
    for Rorschach Inkblot Test, 30, 31, 237–241
    for standardized tests, 237
Psychoanalytic profiles, 29–30
Psychoanalytic tradition, 15–16
Psychograms, 51–72
    blended determinants on, 70–72
    chromatic color on, 65–70
    form dimension score on, 64
    Lambda from, 54–56
    movement responses on, 57–62
    overview of determinants, 51–54
    shading responses on, 64–65
    texture responses on, 62–63
    vista responses on, 63
Psychological classification, 148–149
Psychological testing, preparing examinees for, 18
Psychological test report(s), 207–235
    with developmental scheme, 214–215, 224–227
    with differential diagnosis scheme, 216, 233–235
    examples, 217–235
    information in, 208
    for interpretative case example, 145–146
    organizational schemes for, 212–235
    with overcoming obstacles scheme, 215, 228–233
    with personality scheme, 213–214, 217–223
    recommended practices for, 208–210
    writing process for, 210–212
Psychopathic personality, 10–11
Psychopathy, 10
Psychotic individuals
    content of responses by, 128
    delusional thinking by, 87–89
    Murray's definition of, 156
    weighted Sum6 for, 105
Psychotic personality organization, 28–29
PTI (Perceptual Thinking Index), 117
Pure animal (A) response, 78–79
Pure color (pure C; open C) responses, 67
Pure human (H) responses, 75–76

Qualitative approach. *See* Idiographic approach
Quantitative approach. *See* Nomothetic approach

Rapists, differentiation of, 14–15
Ratios
    Affective, 37–38
    color, 68–69

Constriction, 112
Experience Balance, 109
Experience Base, 110
Fictional, 80–81
human movement:animal movement, 59
Interpersonal Interest, 77–78
Whole versus Parts, 81
Reaction Time (RT)
and administration of test, 24
for chromatic vs. achromatic cards, 125–126
in Cognitively Impaired profile, 151
Differential, 48, 50
in Hyper-energized Euphoria profile, 157, 158
in Impulsive Over-Emotional profile, 154
in Morbid-Dysphoria profile, 156, 157
and response-level interpretations, 127
scores for, 48–50
Reactivity, 37–38, 108
Reality, perception of, 87–88
Reality therapy, 87–88
Reasoning, faulty, 94. *See also* Special Scores
Rebellious Antagonism profile
case example, 170–176
characteristics of, 153–154
"Recovery card," 125
Redundancies, 99
Reflection responses, 44–45, 47
Relationships
clinician–examinee, 18
of scores in Structural Summary, 32
Repetitive responses, 150
Research, for psychological test report, 210–211
Response-level interpretations, 119–129
and card structure, 125–126
and card themes, 126–127
of content, 128
methodology for, 32
of response sequence, 124–125
of response time, 127
of task approach, 120–121
of thought processing, 121–124
Response Phase (R-PAS), 18–19
Responses
discussing examinee's vs. popular, 21
number of, 36–37
patterns and sequence of, 125
suggesting, 21
unpredictability of, 33
Response sequence. *See also* Sequence
interpretatives
interpretations of, 124–125
and Reaction Time, 127
Response time. *See* Reaction Time (RT)
RIAP (Rorschach Interpretative Assistance
Program), 31
Ritzler, Barry, 12
Robinson, Daniel, 9
ROR-Scan, 31
Rorschach, Hermann, 9, 150

Rorschach Comprehensive System
content categories, 74
current adherents to, 12
development of, 5
enhancements to test administration, 17–18
idiographic approach of, 7
popular responses in, 43
productivity required for, 19
recent critics of, 11
and response time/card rotation, 24
Rorschach inkblot method, 120
Rorschach Inkblot Test, 3–16
core assumptions of, 14
correlation of MCMI and, 33
criticism of, 11–12
examining thought process with, 4, 88–89
limitations of, 9
as measuring device, 3–4
misuse of, 9–11
nomothetic vs. idiographic approaches to, 5–8
psychiatric norms for, 237–241
psychoanalytic tradition, 15–16
Rorschach Performance Assessment System, 12
scores and markers for, 13–14
Thematic Apperception Test vs., 8
Rorschach Institute, 6
Rorschach Interpretative Assistance Program
(RIAP), 31
Rorschach Performance Assessment System
(R-PAS), 12, 13
Aggressive responses in, 97
Clarification Phase in, 20
Cognitive vs. Thematic Codes of, 94–95
number of responses for, 19
Peculiar Logic in, 101
Response Phase, 18–19
Special Scores added by, 94
Rorschach profiles, 147–206
case examples, 159–206
Cognitively Impaired, 150–152, 164–169
of examinee in manic state, 196–206
of examinee with substance abuse issues,
170–176
Guarded Minimal Compliance, 149–150, 159–163
Hyper-energized Euphoria, 157–158
Impulsive Over-Emotional, 154–155, 177–183
Morbid-Dysphoria, 156–157, 190–195
Over-Controlled Micro-View, 152–153
and psychiatric diagnoses, 147–149
Rebellious Antagonism, 153–154, 170–176
Thought Disordered, 155–156, 184–189
Rorschach protocols
Cognitively Impaired case example, 164–167
for examinee in manic state, 196–203
for examinee with substance abuse issues,
170–173
Hyper-energized Euphoric case example, 196–203
Impulsive Over-Emotional case example,
177–180

Rorschach protocols *continued*
    interpretative case example, 134–138
    Minimally Compliant case example, 159–161
    Morbid-Dysphoric case example, 190–192
    Rebellious Antagonistic case example, 170–173
    Thought-Disordered case example, 184–187
Rorschach Research Exchange, 6
Rorschach Training Center, 12
R-PAS. *See* Rorschach Performance Assessment System
R-PAS Optimized Norms, 12
R score. *See* Number of responses
RT. *See* Reaction Time

Schachtel, E., 7, 132
Schafer, R., 33
Schizophrenia
    and Form Quality, 90, 92
    and pure color responses, 67
    and weighted Sum6, 105
Sciara, Anthony, 12
S-CON (Suicide Constellation), 11, 117
Score-level interpretation, 30–32
Scores
    norms for, 30–32
    and response-level interpretations, 32
    terminology, 13–14
    validity of, 25
Score sequence
    Cognitively Impaired case example, 167
    for examinee in manic state, 204
    for examinee with substance abuse issues, 174
    Hyper-energized Euphoric case example, 204
    Impulsive Over-Emotional case example, 181
    interpretative case example, 139
    Minimally Compliant case example, 161
    Morbid-Dysphoric case example, 193
    Rebellious Antagonistic case example, 174
    Thought-Disordered case example, 187
Self-concept, 75
Self-esteem, 44
Self psychology, 15
Sequence interpretatives, 133, 145
Sex (Sx) responses, 84
Sexual predators, 14–15, 127
S-% Form Quality variable, 92–93
Shading (Y) responses
    color-shading responses, 72
    on psychograms, 51–52, 64–65
Shakespeare, William, 61
Shontz, F. C., 5
Shor, J., 21
Singer, 1977, 155
Single description scheme, 212–213
Six Special Score Sum (Sum6), 104–106
Slippage, thought process, 104
Smith, B. L., 8, 15–16
Smith, J. G., 74, 128
Soares, C. J., 95

Social Introversion Scale, 86
Social norms, control and, 53, 54
Social relationships, potential for, 75
Society for Personality Assessment, 6
Somatization areas, 86
Special Scores, 94–106
    Abstract Content score, 96–97
    Aggressive responses, 97–98
    in Cognitively Impaired profile, 151
    Color Projection responses, 98
    Contamination score, 98–99
    Cooperative Movement score, 95–96
    Deviant Responses, 100
    Deviant Verbalizations score, 99
    Fabulized Combinations score, 100–101
    in Guarded Minimal Compliance profile, 149
    Inappropriate Logic score, 101
    Incongruous Combinations score, 101–102
    as item interpretative, 133
    Level 2, 105
    Morbid content, 102–103
    from overinclusive responses, 123–124
    Perseveration score, 103
    Personal responses, 103–104
    Six Special Score Sum, 104
    in Thought Disordered profile, 155
    weighted Sum6, 105–106
S score. *See* White space responses
Stand and Deliver (film), 215
Stress, Difference score and, 111
Structural Summary
    Cognitively Impaired case example, 168–169
    color naming responses in, 68
    correlation of scores in, 32
    for examinee in manic state, 205–206
    for examinee with substance abuse issues, 175–176
    and focused Rorschach, 20
    Hyper-energized Euphoric case example, 205–206
    Impulsive Over-Emotional case example, 182–183
    interpretative case example, 140–141
    Minimally Compliant case example, 162–163
    Morbid-Dysphoric case example, 194–195
    Rebellious Antagonistic case example, 175–176
    score interpretation from, 30
    Thought-Disordered case example, 188–189
Structural Summary interpretatives. *See also specific types, e.g.:* Global scores
    in case example, 143–145
    characteristics of, 133
Structured cards, responses to, 126
Substance abuse
    and Form Quality, 90, 92
    profile of examinee with substance abuse issues, 170–176
Suicide Constellation (S-CON), 11, 117
Sullenberger, Chelsey, 53
Sum6 (Six Special Score Sum), 104–106
Sum C' (achromatic color sum) composite, 70

Sum Color (SumC) composite, 68
Superficiality, 81–82, 85
Sx (sex) responses, 84

Take the Money and Run (film), 73
Task approach
    as administration interpretative, 132
    and response-level interpretations, 120–121
TAT (Thematic Apperception Test), 8, 211
Tense, for psychological test reports, 210
Testing the Limits method, 20–25
    manner of approach from, 22
    post hoc questioning in, 22–24
    prompts vs., 21
    response-level interpretations from, 128–129
Test reports. *See* Psychological test report(s)
Texture (T) responses, 51–52, 62–63
Thematic Apperception Test (TAT), 8, 211
Thematic Codes, 94–95
Therapeutic alliance, 150, 153
Thought Disordered profile
    case example, 184–189
    characteristics of, 155–156
Thought disturbance, 117
Thought process, 87–106
    of Cognitively Impaired individual, 151–152
    complexity of, 71, 113
    and delusions, 87–88
    Form Quality score for examining, 89–93
    response-level interpretation of, 121–124
    Rorschach test for examining, 4, 88–89
    Special Scores for examining, 94–106
    Structural Summary interpretatives for, 144–145
Thought process disturbances, 88–89
Titchener, Edward, 53
Training, control and, 53
Transparencies, 100
Treatment response, human responses and, 75
T (texture) responses, 51–52, 62–63
Type II errors, 33

Uncontrolled responses, 54
Understrivers, 112
Uniqueness, of Rorschach protocol, 33
Unpredictability, of examinee responses, 33
Unstructured cards, responses to, 126
Unusual details (Dd) score, 41
Unusual Form Quality (FQxu), 91

Van Denburg, E., 48
Vista (V) responses, 51–52, 63

Watchfulness, 115–116
Weighted color sum (WSumC) composite, 69
Weighted Six Special Score Sum (weighted Sum6), 105–106
Weiner, I. B., 8, 28
White Americans, Cooperative Movement score of, 95
White space responses (S score), 42
    and Form Quality, 90, 92–93
    in Hyper-energized Euphoria profile, 158
    in Rebellious Antagonism profile, 153
    and unusual details, 41
Whole responses (W score), 39–40
    and Aspirational Index, 108
    in Hyper-energized Euphoria profile, 158
    and overinclusiveness, 123
Whole versus Parts Ratio, 81
Williams, Ted, 87
Wood, J. M., 10–11, 14, 44
Writing process, psychological test report, 210–212
W score. *See* Whole responses
WSumC (weighted color sum) composite, 69
Wundt, Wilhelm, 53

X+% Form Quality score, 90
Xray (Xy) responses, 86

Y responses. *See* Shading responses

Zf (organizational activity), 45–46

About the Author

James P. Choca, PhD, is the chair of the Psychology Department and a full professor at Roosevelt University in Chicago. He joined Roosevelt in 1999 to head the doctoral program in clinical psychology. Dr. Choca had been the head of the Psychology Service at the Lakeside Veterans' Administration Medical Center and an associate professor in the psychology program at the Northwestern University Medical School. His work with the Millon Clinical Multiaxial Inventory culminated with the publication of an interpretative guide for this instrument, a popular American Psychological Association book that is currently in its third edition. More recently Dr. Choca has been involved in the creation of computerized tests, such as the Halstead Category Test. A Cuban American, he has done diagnostic and research work with psychological instruments for Spanish-speaking individuals.